Children, Rights and Modernity in China

Studies in Childhood and Youth
Series Editors: Allison James, University of Sheffield, UK, and Adrian James, University of Sheffield, UK.

Titles include:

Kate Bacon
TWINS IN SOCIETY
Parents, Bodies, Space and Talk

David Buckingham, Sara Bragg, Mary Jane Kehily
YOUTH CULTURES IN THE AGE OF GLOBAL MEDIA

David Buckingham and Vebjørg Tingstad (*editors*)
CHILDHOOD AND CONSUMER CULTURE

Tom Cockburn
RETHINKING CHILDREN'S CITIZENSHIP

Sam Frankel
CHILDREN, MORALITY AND SOCIETY

Allison James
SOCIALISING CHILDREN

Allison James, Anne Trine Kjørholt and Vebjørg Tingstad (*editors*)
CHILDREN, FOOD AND IDENTITY IN EVERYDAY LIFE

Nicholas Lee
CHILDHOOD AND BIOPOLITICS
Climate Change, Life Processes and Human Futures

Manfred Liebel, Karl Hanson, Iven Saadi and Wouter Vandenhole (*editors*)
CHILDREN'S RIGHTS FROM BELOW
Cross-Cultural Perspectives

Orna Naftali
CHILDREN, RIGHTS AND MODERNITY IN CHINA
Raising Self-Governing Citizens

Helen Stapleton
SURVIVING TEENAGE MOTHERHOOD
Myths and Realities

Afua Twum-Danso Imoh, Robert Ame
CHILDHOODS AT THE INTERSECTION OF THE LOCAL AND THE GLOBAL

Hanne Warming
PARTICIPATION, CITIZENSHIP AND TRUST IN CHILDREN'S LIVES

Rebekah Willett, Chris Richards, Jackie Marsh, Andrew Burn, Julia C. Bishop
(*editors*)
CHILDREN, MEDIA AND PLAYGROUND CULTURES
Ethnographic Studies of School Playtimes

Studies in Childhood and Youth
Series Standing Order ISBN 978-0-230-21686-0 hardback
(*outside North America only*)

You can receive future titles in this series as they are published by placing a standing order.

Please contact your bookseller or, in case of difficulty, write to us at the address below with your name and address, the title of the series and the ISBN quoted above.
Customer Services Department, Macmillan Distribution Ltd, Houndmills, Basingstoke, Hampshire RG21 6XS, England

Children, Rights and Modernity in China

Raising Self-Governing Citizens

Orna Naftali
The Hebrew University of Jerusalem

First published 2014 by
PALGRAVE MACMILLAN

Palgrave Macmillan in the UK is an imprint of Macmillan Publishers Limited, registered in England, company number 785998, of Houndmills, Basingstoke, Hampshire RG21 6XS.

Palgrave Macmillan in the US is a division of St Martin's Press LLC, 175 Fifth Avenue, New York, NY 10010.

Palgrave Macmillan is the global academic imprint of the above companies and has companies and representatives throughout the world.

Palgrave® and Macmillan® are registered trademarks in the United States, the United Kingdom, Europe and other countries

ISBN: 978-1-137-34658-2

This book is printed on paper suitable for recycling and made from fully managed and sustained forest sources. Logging, pulping and manufacturing processes are expected to conform to the environmental regulations of the country of origin.

A catalogue record for this book is available from the British Library.

A catalog record for this book is available from the Library of Congress.

In memory of my mother, Talia

Contents

Acknowledgements

The research and writing of this book required the help of numerous people and institutions. My field research in Shanghai was made possible by the help and support of Fan GR at East China Normal University. I am also deeply grateful for the invaluable friendship and outstanding help of Yang Junhong; of Xie Ning and her family; of Tao LF and Jillian Zhang; of Alley Ai and Cathy Xu; and of Qiang QM, Zhou Q., and Ye LX in Shanghai. I owe a huge debt, of course, to the kind assistance and generous cooperation of faculty and staff at the schools I have called Whitewater and Affiliated, and to all the Shanghai mothers and grandmothers who have welcomed me into their homes and agreed to share their views and life stories with me.

I am enormously grateful to Mayfair Mei-hui Yang, whose knowledge, insights, and valuable guidance have been a true inspiration throughout the years. I am equally indebted to Francesca Bray, Mary Hancock, and Sabine Frühstück for their valuable advice, acute observations, and persistent words of encouragement.

I am grateful to Philippa Grand, the Head of the Social Sciences Team, and the editors of the Studies in Childhood and Youth Series at Palgrave Macmillan, for encouraging me to submit the manuscript to this series. I would also like to thank the anonymous reviewers who commented on earlier versions of the manuscript.

Additional thanks go to my colleagues in the Department of Asian Studies at the Hebrew University of Jerusalem: Yuri Pines, Gideon Shelach, and Nissim Otmazgin, who have supported me in completing this book.

Finally, I also want to acknowledge the considerable institutional support that made this project feasible. In the United States, a UC Regents Special Fellowship enabled the gathering of field data which forms the basis of the book.

Post-doctoral fellowships from the Lady Davis Fellowship Trust, the Harry S. Truman Research Institute for the Advancement of Peace, and the Louis Frieberg Center for East Asian Studies at the Hebrew University of Jerusalem, and a Hebrew University intramural research fund allowed me to conduct further research for this project and later to revise and edit the book manuscript.

Above all, I am deeply grateful to my husband, Dean, whose tremendous help, outstanding patience, and moral support have made this book a reality.

Introduction

In 1995, an educator and columnist for the *Sichuan Daily* newspaper described a scene that took place in a city in southwest China. A crowd was watching a woman in her thirties half-carrying and half-dragging a small boy from a public playground. The woman was twisting the boy's ear with one hand, hitting him with the other, and shouting that her son "had brought her nothing but shame."

"Raising him has not been easy since his good-for-nothing father left me, but this ungrateful creature doesn't even care!" she yelled at the crowd. "He is failing in math. He is failing in Chinese. All he does is play all day! He just drives me mad!"

In the column, entitled *"Bu yi dangzhong xun zi"* ["Don't admonish children in public"], the author and educator Suying Zhang, describes watching the exchange in silence then sadly walking away.

It is a scene that raises a series of compelling questions about the place of childhood in contemporary urban China; about the way a child's formative years are viewed by adults, including parents, educators, and the general public; and the space in which the child is allowed to develop. Why, for instance, were the spectators of the scene—the narrator included—content merely to observe the interaction between the mother and her son and not to intervene? Is beating a child in public acceptable behavior in contemporary urban China? If so, what compelled the writer to report this story and to strongly admonish readers against employing such "rough and crude (*jiandan cubao*)" disciplinary measures against their own children? And what would the irate mother have made of the author's suggestion that in the future, she "patiently" discuss matters with her child in the "privacy" of her home, so as not to inflict further "damage" on the boy's fragile "sense of self-esteem (*zizun xin*)"? Finally, why was the *Sichuan Daily*, a newspaper published by the Chinese Communist Party (CCP), so willing to report this story and to promote more benign, less brutal ways of treating China's young?

This book addresses these questions by exploring, through an ethnographic study, the emergence of a new type of thinking about children and their rights in contemporary China. It traces the construction of a Chinese discourse on children's rights in post-1989 government, academic, media, and pedagogic publications. It further examines how urban Chinese teachers and caregivers, and indeed children themselves, creatively interpret and appropriate the notion of rights for their own purposes. In the process, Chinese citizens transform the very meaning of childhood, power, and subjectivity in post-socialist urban China.

Children's rights and the distinct form of Chinese modernity

Over the course of the twentieth century, children everywhere have served as symbols of the future, as objects of regulation and development at school, and as the focus of heated debates over cultural and national identities. Nowhere has this been more evident than in China where disputes over the education of the young have been pivotal to processes of nation-building, modernization, and subject formation during the Republican (1911–49) and Maoist (1949–76) periods. Today, when the People's Republic of China (PRC) is undergoing profound social and economic changes and is re-emerging as a leading global power, childhood once again serves as an important locus for discussions of modernity and selfhood, national identity and citizenship. If in the 1950s and 1960s, Chinese children largely represented "little soldiers" in the service of the Party and the revolution, these days they are frequently recast as rights-bearing, autonomous subjects. How did this shift—a movement from, to paraphrase Merle Goldman (2005), "small comrades" to "small subjects"—come about?

This book explores the intricate links between the emergence of a new concept of childhood in contemporary urban China, the country's recent reintegration within the global market economy, and the ensuing social transformations the process has brought about. At the same time, I also examine how changes in conceptualizations of children and in the proper way of treating them reflect changes in the relationships between minors and their caregivers, as well as between the Chinese state and its citizenry in the post-socialist era.

Examining the issue through the lens of children's rights, the larger aim of this study is two-fold: first, I seek to explore how the emergent idea of Chinese children as persons with rights, including the right to express independent views, to protection from violence, and to safeguard their own privacy, is transforming family and school life in contemporary urban China. Second, I examine how this transformation contributes to a broader shift in the strategies through which power and constraint are exercised and resisted in wider Chinese society.

Treating children's rights as "a historically and politically constructed concept that reflects the concerns and interests of those who construct and invoke it" (Svensson, 2002: 4), I explore the specific conditions that have led the Chinese government to grant its youngest citizens substantial and unprecedented rights and privileges under the law. I ask whether the CCP's use of "rights talk" in regards to children is merely a ruse, a way to pay homage to notions of "human rights" and "personal dignity" while strengthening, defending, and legitimizing a variety of repressive initiatives. And I try to determine whether it reflects a significant mutation in the governing logic and ruling style of the CCP, particularly in the post-1989 era.

This book will argue that the discussion of rights does indeed reflect an important change within the CCP. It will show how recent endeavors to elevate the status of Chinese children and to protect their individual rights in both the public and private spheres crucially intersect with processes of political, economic, and cultural restructuring in China of the post-socialist era. The emergence of a child-rights discourse, of child-centered pedagogies, and of lenient parental practices, I argue, is best understood not only as an epiphenomenon of the empowerment of urban singletons in the era of the One-Child policy, but also as a product of the growing influence of modern, global conceptualizations of the child and the person, of privacy and subjectivity in China. In making this argument, I do not suggest that the Chinese child-rights discourse is a local enactment (or simply an example) of a universal, progressive model of the child and the person. Rather, I regard contemporary Chinese conceptualizations of children's rights as products of cross-cultural translations of various projects of liberal modernity and of a middle-class civility. These projects reflect, in part, the emergence of new regimes of truth and power, as well as the rise of ever more refined technologies of self-conduct in China of the post-socialist era. However, these new modes of childrearing and pedagogy are also interwoven with more ancient, indigenous notions of familial and social order. Together, they create hybrid and at times contradictory models of governing the young. In presenting this claim, I seek to contribute to the rich body of work on the distinct forms of Chinese modernities (see, for example, King, 2002; Rofel, 1999; Ong, 1996; Yang Mayfair, 1994, 2004; Zhang Everett, 2011; Kipnis, 2012), and to highlight the sociological and anthropological study of childhood as a key component in the cultural construction of these unique modernities.

Throughout twentieth-century China, disputes over notions of children and childhood have been closely related to processes of modernization, nation-building, and state formation (Anagnost, 1997a; Farquhar Mary Ann, 1999; Jones, 2002). In contrast to Europe, where the state-making process preceded attempts at encouraging citizens to identify with and feel loyalty to the nation-state, in China, state-making was proclaimed within the framework of nationalism and related ideas of modernization (Duara, 1988: 2). In their quest for the formation of a powerful nation-state that could stand up to its imperial aggressors and later for the creation of a new type of socialist society, twentieth-century Chinese political leaders, reformers, and educators have been preoccupied with the steps that should be taken to transform the way in which children are viewed and educated in order to develop a "modern person (*xiandai ren*)" (see Henze, 1992: 104). This issue continues to preoccupy government officials, scholars, and education reformers in China to this day. It gives even apparently mundane issues, such as whether adults should respect children's privacy or employ corporal punishment as a disciplinary method, heavy significance as an "ideological showroom in which ideal images of citizens, communities, and even the nation are put on stage" (Thøgersen, 2002: 5). Early twentieth-century Chinese reformers and intellectuals of the May Fourth movement (1915–21) who sought to dismantle what they regarded as a decaying Confucian culture and to construct a powerful, modern nation-state tackled this problem by looking to the liberal, democratic West for new modes of thinking about domesticity, childrearing, and education (Anagnost, 1997a; Glosser, 2003; Farquhar Mary Ann, 1999; Jones, 2002; Pepper, 1996; Saari, 1990; Schwarcz, 1986). After the socialist revolution of 1949, these Western pedagogies and child-rearing models were attacked by Maoist educators (see for example, Chan Anita, 1985; Bastid, 1987), but their influence—even as abhorred "bourgeois" ideas—continued to be felt in public discussions about the proper way to treat and educate China's future generation of revolutionaries.

At the dawn of the twenty-first century, when China has reopened its gates to outside influences and is closer than ever to reaching its goal of becoming an economic and global political power, modern paradigms of childrearing and education, especially those identified with the liberal, capitalist West, once again loom large in current debates about the proper way to raise and educate Chinese children. Participants in these debates frequently employ the idioms of "individual rights," "science" and "modernity" while referring to global paradigms of childhood. To fully appreciate why a child-rights discourse is gaining increased popularity in contemporary China and to understand the distinct features of this discourse in a Chinese setting, we must therefore first consider the origins and contours of the modern and increasingly global child-rights movement.

In what follows, I place the central themes of the book in the larger field of childhood studies and sinology, and discuss how my own thinking about the origins, contents, and implications of China's emergent discourse of children's rights has been shaped by relevant theoretical developments. I further suggest how this book can contribute to a fuller understanding of the unique form of modern Chinese childhood and of the relationship between new social formations and changing conceptualizations of power and personhood in China today.

The emergence of the child-rights discourse in the modern era

A concept of childhood as a stage of life distinguishable from adulthood was present in all pre-modern, non-Western societies, including late imperial China (see Bai, 2005b; Hsiung, 2005; Kinney, 1995a; Nylan, 2003; Wicks and Avril, 2002). Yet it was by no means self-evident that children are persons of distinct interests and attributes, nor indeed that they constitute individuals with specific entitlements. As a rich body of work has shown, the notion of children as autonomous subjects with rights is the product of a particular moment and place in history: post-Enlightenment, rationalist, secular, Western, modern and capitalist.

Much of what we know about Western, liberal conceptions of the child rests on the work of Philippe Ariès, who has famously asserted that in pre-modern times, "nobody thought, as we ordinarily think today, that every child already contained a man's personality" (1962: 39). This keen observation was accompanied by the more provocative claim that "in medieval society the idea of childhood *did not exist*" (Ariès, 1962: 128, emphasis added). Since the publication of Ariès's 1962 landmark study of European social history, *Centuries of Childhood*, both these sweeping claims have come under substantial criticism (see for example, James *et al.*, 1998). Yet, in making such bold statements, Ariès was attempting to advance the notion that the conception of childhood as a unique stage of life, and of children as individuals with distinct needs and particular rights, was not a universal phenomenon but a product of specific historical and social circumstances.

As Ariès and others suggest, the concept of children as persons with unique needs and interests emerged in Europe between the fifteenth and eighteenth centuries, together with middle-class ideas of family, home, privacy, and individuality. Whereas in medieval Europe, children past the dependent stage of infancy (about the age of seven) were conceived and depicted as "miniature adults" and, for the most part, mingled freely with adults in everyday life (Ariès, 1962: 37), beginning in the seventeenth or eighteenth centuries, they began to occupy separate spaces both within and outside the domestic sphere. Among middle-class, European families, the allocation of separate spaces for the youngest members of the family within the house was held to be a sign of distinction. It further corresponded with the increasing autonomy of private people within a newly reconfigured modern public sphere (Habermas, 1991: 44–5).

As the appropriate treatment of children became separate from that of adults, and a division of adults' and children's dress, language, roles, and responsibilities began to appear, the recognition of children's special nature and distinct needs also drew heightened attention to childhood as a crucial stage in the individual's life cycle. In his 1762 work, *Émile*, Rousseau suggested that if only children were left to discover things for themselves and be educated according to the "natural unfolding of their character," they would do only good (Rousseau, 1964: 80). Nature, he further postulated, "wants children to be children before being adults," and therefore, "a child should be treated neither as an animal nor as a man, but as *a child*" (1964: 92, emphasis added). To Rousseau, children have their "own ways of seeing, thinking and feeling." Adults should leave the child's body "in its *natural* habits" and enable him to become "*a master of himself*" (1964: 80, emphasis added).

Rousseau's admonition to "respect childhood" (cited in Heywood, 2001: 24) left a deep mark on the modern conceptualization of the child. It introduced the notion that "childhood was worth the attention of intelligent adults" and encouraged "an interest in the process of growing up, rather than just the product" (James *et al.*, 1998: 13). Influenced by Rousseau's sentimental notion of children, the Romantics of the eighteenth and nineteenth centuries took the idea further by depicting childhood as "a lost realm that was nonetheless fundamental to the creation of the adult self" (Heywood, 2001: 24). They popularized the concept of childhood as an idealized site of play, freedom, creativity, and innocence (Field, 1995: 65; Heywood, 2001: 241; Stephens, 1995b: 14–15). At about the same time, the urban middle classes of modern Europe and North America began to embrace this idealized notion and to place an increasing emphasis on childhood as a site of domesticity and education rather than work or productivity. By the early twentieth century, the efforts of social reformers sought to extend this new status of children to working-class circles as well.

In parallel with these ideational currents, other more concrete features of modern social life have also sharpened the focus on children as independent persons. One is the well-documented change in the modern family structure from a collective unit to a coalescence of individuals (James *et al.*, 1998: 6). Another is the demographic shift to an aging population which provided the idea of the child with an increased scarcity value and therefore more deserving of "precious" attention. From the late nineteenth century onwards, children were increasingly transformed from "economically useful" to "economically useless" (Zelizer, 1985: 209). As their instrumental value to their parents decreased however, their emotional, expressive worth became ever more pronounced (Scheper-Hughes, 1987: 12), resulting in the creation of what sociologist Viviana Zelizer (1985: 211) has termed "the priceless child."

The rise in the emotional value of the individual child in modern, liberal societies was further facilitated by the emergence of modern psychological science. Identifying a new source of causality in human affairs, psychoanalytical theory and developmental psychology were largely responsible for modern adults' increasing preoccupation with childhood as a period and with children's "normal" progression through a sequence of successive stages (Walkerdine, 2005: 16–17; see also James *et al.*, 1998). Seeking to methodically describe (and, in effect to prescribe) the natural, normal course of a child's physical and emotional development, "psy" experts worked to transform the modern family into "a conductor of relational norms" (Donzelot, 1997[1979]: 209). They placed it into a matrix that symbolizes the structure and values of the bourgeois middle classes (Deleuze and Guattari, 1983[1977]: 93). In the course of the twentieth century, the normalization of a distinctly middle-class model of childhood was further advanced by the radical growth in popular advice literature offered in books, magazines, general newspapers, television, and most recently, the Internet, resulting in the contemporary worldwide "cult of child psychology" (Burman, 2005: 35; see also Illouz, 2008: 6).

In many respects, the recognition of the distinct emotional needs of children and the framing of these needs as necessary conditions for the healthy development and future success of the individual, served the interests of the modern, liberal nation-state. The recommendations of post-World War II psychologists that caregivers and educators allow children more freedom and autonomy, refrain from the use of violence, and instead exercise a mode of restraint or of "civilization" in their dealings with children, imposed a high degree of self-regulation and self-control on the part of adults as well as youngsters (Elias, 1998: 191, 209). That, in turn, enabled the production of self-governing citizens capable of and willing to contribute to the building of a modern liberal society (Hultqvist, 1998; Rose, 1989; Walkerdine, 2005). In this respect, the rise of a psychological discourse of the autonomous child may not be a progressive, enlightened evolution in the treatment of the young, but rather the effect of a shift from the use of naked power to more subtle, individualized forms of governance in modernity (see Foucault, 1991[1978]).

At the same time however, the scientific and popular constructions of the child as a self-directing, autonomous subject played a crucial role in the rise of a child-rights discourse in post-World War II, capitalist societies. Until the 1960s and 1970s, child rights were generally characterized and understood in Western thinking as "needs" children had, rather than "rights" children possessed, perceptions which were embodied in The League of Nations (1924) and the United Nations (1959) declarations on the rights of the child (Er, 2008: 34; see also Fass, 2011). Since the 1960s, however, the emergence of feminist critiques of the family, the "discovery" of child abuse in the West, and the linking of child protection with child rights contributed to a significant transformation in this regard (Archard, 2004; Er, 2008). Identifying the family as an oppressive institution to both women and children, 1960s feminist critiques of patriarchy depicted the respective oppressions of these two groups as mutually reinforcing (Archard, 2004; see also Fass, 2011). With the aid of pediatricians and psychological experts, feminist scholars and activists helped push for the passing of new legislation to protect children from abuse, while creating a link between psychological needs and moral and political "rights" (Illouz, 2008: 167–8).[1] Inspired by the feminist movement, some radical educators and child liberationists further protested against the deprivation of the child's personal freedom at the traditional school (see for example, Neill, 1960), and insisted that children be given all the rights currently possessed by adults, including the right to privacy, the right to freedom of speech and thought, and the right to make decisions for themselves (see for example, Adams *et al.*, 1971). Others contested this radical notion on the grounds that one can grant children "rights," but need not necessarily ascribe the same "packet of general rights" to children and adults who constitute different "kinds of beings" (Schoeman, 1980: 7).

Over the past several decades, these issues have been argued inconclusively by educators, philosophers, and legal scholars (see for example, Archard and Macleod, 2002). Since the 1980s and in particular the 1990s, sociologists and anthropologists have also contributed, suggesting that childhood shares similarities with subaltern classes and with the category of gender (see Hirschfeld, 2002). Indeed, it could be argued that in insisting that children be regarded as social actors in their own right and given voice in studies of and about them, sociological and anthropological literature has done much to consolidate and facilitate the global diffusion of the notion that children not only require protection, but also have agency (for noted examples, see Stephens, 1995a; James *et al.*, 1998; James and Prout, 1997[1990]; James, 2009; Schwartzman, 2001).

Since the 1980s, this new conviction has also been translated into legal practice in the form of successive international instruments and human rights events. These include the 1979 International Year of the Child; and most significantly, the 1989 UN Convention on the Rights of the Child (UNCRC). The Convention's legal principles have provided a focal point for the development of children's rights legislation and social policy at both the international and national levels (Boyden, 2001: 197). Since its promulgation, the UNCRC, which is a legally binding document, has also been hailed by children's advocacy groups, elicited policy commitments from UNICEF and other international agencies, and prompted numerous conferences dedicated to implementing the Convention's objectives (Stephens, 1995b: 35–6).

The contemporary child-rights discourse, embodied in the UNCRC, in national legislation, academic literature, and in the popular media has provided a new lexicon for the perceived entitlements and duties of children. It has contributed to a transformation in the emotional culture of the school and the family in liberal, capitalist societies and has helped to refine conceptions of children, schooling, and families worldwide (Archard, 2004: 58; see also Boyden, 2001). By incorporating theories of healthy child development, which constitute "psychological needs" as "moral rights," and in labeling third-world deviations from this logic as a "loss" and "contamination" of childhood (Stephens, 1995b: 19), the global discourse of rights can be said to facilitate the dissemination of a uniquely modern, middle-class view of childhood to non-Western, non-liberal societies. It has therefore been criticized as a form of "cultural imperialism" (for example, Alston, 1994; Daws and Cairns, 1998; Boyden, 2001; Burman, 1996; Panter-Brick, 2002).

This accusation may be an overstatement. Child-rights discourse is grounded in Western, liberal, post-Enlightenment thinking on childhood, citizenship, and subjectivity and it does have a tendency to reduce historical and local complexities of family and school life in different world regions. From a pragmatic point of view, however, the fact that the child-rights discourse "claims to be universal but is really the product of a specific cultural and historical origin" (Kennedy, 2004: 18) may be irrelevant. Just as the Western origins of the child-rights tradition may cause some people in non-Western countries to regard it with suspicion, for others, these specific origins make it all the more attractive. Moreover, children's rights "are not merely a product of deliberations that are fixed in international legislation." As Hanson and Nieuwenhuys (2012: 3) emphasize, many of their underlying ideas already exist before they are translated into legal principles" (2012: 3). The more interesting issue then is how various social actors in different national contexts creatively take up the notion of rights in answer to their contemporary needs (see Kennedy, 2004; Svensson, 2002).

Examining the cultural, social, and political conditions that are shaping the engagement of PRC officials, writers, educators and caregivers with the notion of children's rights provides a way to explore this issue in the particular case of China. Recent work on the activities of foreign NGOs in PRC children's welfare institutes demonstrates, for instance, the difficulty of 'imposing universal standards of childhood across all national contexts.' It suggests the salience of cultural differences and material limitations, even in those instances when Chinese and foreign parties are ready to adopt the individualistic, "middle-class" ethos of the global child-rights discourse (Wang Leslie, 2010: 149).

Though the present book centers on mainstream schools and on urban elite homes rather than on welfare facilities for marginalized populations, it too aims to explore the tensions and contradictions that arise when social actors in China engage with the child-rights discourse in their day-to-day practices. To fully understand the social construction of the Chinese discourse of children's rights, we must examine the distinct historical, economic, and political conditions which have shaped the nature of urban Chinese childhood. We must also ask how these conditions facilitate and sustain the rise and dissemination of a liberal discourse of childhood in contemporary China.

Childhood, rights, and citizenship in post-socialist urban China

Much of the scholarship on Chinese childrearing and education since 1978 has justifiably focused on the One-Child family policy and China's reintegration within the global market economy as the two most important developments shaping the lives of Chinese children and youth, and influencing notions of childhood (see for example, Anagnost, 1997b, 2008b; Goh, 2011; Fong, 2004b; Greenhalgh and Winckler, 2005; Woronov, 2008, 2009). However, few scholars have explored how these changes have facilitated the emergence of a child-rights discourse in post-socialist China, and how this discourse, in turn, has contributed to the further empowerment of Chinese children within the urban family and society at large. The present study explores these issues, while highlighting the key role of China's child-rights discourse in the broader human rights debates that have gained momentum in the country since 1989.

With singletons now making up about 80% of the children enrolled at primary schools, day-care centers, and boarding nurseries in Chinese cities (Jing, 2000b: 1), the impact of the government's population policy on city families has been dramatic. Popular and academic discourses have often portrayed the first wave of urban single children as a generation of "little emperors" (*xiao huangdi*), who are "showered with attention, toys, and treats by anxiously overindulgent adults," and who consequently are "insufferably spoiled, self-centered, and difficult to control" (Jing, 2000b: 2; Anagnost, 1997a: 216). Yet, a number of ethnographic studies have vividly revealed the plight of these urban singletons, who constitute the "only hope" of anxious parents and grandparents (Fong, 2004b; Goh, 2011; Jing, 2000a; Woronov, 2008). Most scholars also agree that since the introduction of the One-Child Policy in 1979, urban Chinese children—in particular boys but increasingly also girls— have in many respects become the sort of "precious commodities" described by Viviana Zelizer in her (1985) work on the emergence of the "priceless" child in Western, capitalist societies.

In post-socialist, urban China, parents as well as grandparents invest ever more heavily in their only child. They buy health- and education-related food and toys, and pay for "enrichment lessons" to ensure the educational and career success of their singleton in an increasingly competitive environment (Croll, 2006; Davis and Sensenbrenner, 2000; Fong, 2004b; Goh, 2011; Lozada, 2000; Milwertz, 1997; Rosen, 2004).

China's urban only children also hold much more power in the family compared to previous generations of youth, a fact illustrated in their ability to affect family consumption patterns (see for example, Croll, 2006; Fong, 2004b; Jing, 2000b). One study, by McNeal and Yeh (1997), estimates for instance that Chinese single-tons influence 68% of household purchases (as compared, for example, with around 45% for households in the United States). This influence extends beyond the consumption of toys, snacks, and fast food to include many of the family's everyday purchases and leisure activities, such as television viewing, shopping, vacations, and visits to parks and restaurants (Watson, 1997; Yan, 1997; Chee, 2000; Guo Yuhua, 2000; Lozada, 2000; Chan and McNeal, 2004). The growing role of Chinese single children in making individual and household consumer decisions, some scholars suggest, has turned these children into a new kind of independent, market-minded, "neo-liberal" young persons, who will later become self-governing global citizens (Greenhalgh, 2011: 155).

For its part, the Chinese government has been encouraging this development by promoting high "quality (*suzhi*)" health-care and "education for quality (*suzhi jiaoyu*)" programs for the nation's only children (Anagnost, 2004; Greenhalgh and Winckler, 2005; Jing, 2000b; Kipnis, 2006, 2011; Woronov, 2009). Since the early 1980s, a broad array of state policies, scientific research programs and social activities have been calling on the public "to reproduce less in order to nurture better" in order to "improve the quality of the popula-tion (*renkou suzhi*)" (Anagnost, 1995, 2004; Gottschang, 2000; Jing, 2000b). As part of this "quality" campaign, Chinese caregivers have been urged to invest in the upbringing of their only-child according to "modern, scientific" methods of childrearing. Children have been encouraged to exhibit "entrepreneurship, innovation, and flexibility"—in other words, the skills of a successful capitalist laborer and consumer (Greenhalgh and Winckler, 2005; Woronov, 2007, 2009).

Some scholars maintain that this new focus on the norm of quality (rather than mere quantity) in managing the population and the attempts to insert market discipline in young children through the promotion of self-governance, serves as an indication that the post-socialist state in China is seeking to produce "neoliberal subjects par-excellence" (Greenhalgh and Winckler, 2005: 236). They concede that in China, neoliberalism is not a coherent formation, but nonetheless posit that neoliberal ideology is on the rise in various areas of life (see for example, Rofel, 2007; Yan Hairong, 2003). In the realms of childrearing and education, in particular, the CCP is said to be moving from a "naked use of repression" (Jing, 2000b: 15), to a Foucauldian form of "bio-political" governmentality: a subtle yet effective mode of control that seeks to produce self-cultivating, individualized subjects "whose interests, desires, and choices align with those of a neoliberalizing market and state" (Greenhalgh and Winckler, 2005; see also Anagnost, 2004; Murphy, 2004; Woronov, 2007, 2009). In this view, the empowerment and individualization of children in contemporary China is only a manifestation of the shift to bio-political governmentality. It indicates the country's transformation into a "market-driven capitalist enterprise," with children as the emerging focus of this economy and as major players in a government-orchestrated "festival of consumption" (Donald, 2005: 52; Greenhalgh, 2011: 155).

While these studies have made a considerable contribution to our current understanding of shifting notions of Chinese childhood, power, and subjectivity in the period of economic reform and the One-Child policy, they do have several weaknesses. First, they fail to take into account (or tend to underestimate) the importance of alternatives to neoliberalism within Chinese discursive formulations of power and subjectivity, such as the indigenous moral logic of filial piety or the repressive logic of modern sovereign power (see Nonini, 2008; Kipnis, 2007, 2008; Yang Mayfair, 2011).

Second, and more specifically, previous studies on Chinese children have also downplayed the potentially subversive functions of the child-rights discourse in the context of an authoritarian regime. One of the main arguments I wish to make in this book is that although the notion of children's rights can—and is—appropriated by the Chinese government for its own purposes, it can also operate in some unexpected ways which may exceed the limits of state control or of market prescriptions. The idea that even the youngest members of society possess rights under the law; that children should be educated about these rights and about the laws which protect them; and that adults should abide by these laws and uphold youngsters' rights, enhances the legal- and rights-consciousness of Chinese children and youth. These children may in turn grow up to become not only innovative, entrepreneurial workers or avid consumers in a neoliberal market economy. They may also become self-assured citizens with a better ability to stand up to power and authority.

In making this claim, I follow a growing body of work on the emergence and deepening of rights-consciousness in contemporary Chinese society. For most of the post-1949 period, "individual human rights" (*geren quanli*) had been "a taboo subject" in Chinese political discourse and were "labeled a bourgeois slogan inappropriate and irrelevant for a socialist society" (Svensson, 2002: 1). Following the 1989 crackdown on the democracy movement in Tiananmen, the Chinese government has nonetheless begun to directly engage with the issue of human rights. In the face of rigorous and sustained multilateral and bilateral pressures on human rights issues, China has displayed increased activity in UN human rights forums, has hosted international delegations on the issue, and signed a series of international human rights charters.[2] In addition, the Chinese government has also shown strong domestic support for human rights research, conferences, and scholarly and official human rights publications (Kent, 1999: 233–4; see also Keith, 1997; Svensson, 2000, 2002).

This pro-active approach to the issue of human rights has also been part of a sustained attempt to accommodate an emergent market regime to satisfy the demands of global capitalism for transparency and legal protection. Since the 1990s, the Chinese government has increasingly exercised rational-legal means of control over the population; allowed ordinary people to sue local officials; and even amended its criminal laws and enhanced rights of due process

(Svensson, 2002: 1; Yang Mayfair, 2002: 469). Though some scholars have dismissed these developments as an inconsequential and cynical exercise on the part of the Chinese Party-state, others have argued that China is genuinely transforming its legal framework—once an unmistakable tool of the state—into a more flexible system. That system, at least on paper, may offer assistance for the protection of the individual's rights (Keith, 1997: 52; Kent, 1999: 242; Diamant *et al.*, 2005).

Furthermore, a growing number of studies published in the past decade or so document an expansion of rights-awareness among ordinary Chinese citizens from various walks of life (for example, Cai, 2005; Goldman, 2005; O'Brien and Li, 2006; Pei, 2010; Read, 2008; Yan Yunxiang, 2003, 2009). Members of different social groups in both rural and urban China often invoke the language of rights when protesting against the abuses of various predatory forces, such as developers, large companies and local government agencies (Yan Yunxiang, 2011: 44). Notably, many of these protests, whose numbers have steadily grown since 1989, target abuses associated with market reforms, attesting to the fact that market logic, including the logic of neoliberalism, is far from hegemonic in China (Nonini, 2008: 146).

While the notion of human rights can become a propaganda slogan or even an instrument of oppression in the hands of power holders, it can also function as a tool of resistance in legal and political struggles of ordinary citizens (Svensson, 2002: 11). Moreover, while rights practices in China may be severely limited by the tight control of the state, which encourages self-interest only in the realms of employment, private enterprise, and consumption (Ong and Zhang, 2008: 12), rights consciousness is never static. Individuals may assess the extent of the protection, exercise, and enjoyment of rights on the basis of various signals they receive not just from the governing elite but from society in general (Pei, 2010: 34). Indeed, groundbreaking work by anthropologist Yan Yunxiang (2003) in rural north China has shown the development of a new type of individualistic ethos in the private realm of the family. This discourse is particularly prevalent among young rural men and women who, as Yan finds, are quick to assert their right to privacy, intimacy, freedom and personal happiness vis-à-vis their families (see also Yan Yunxiang, 2009).

Building on the findings and insights of these studies, this book hopes to contribute to our understanding of the construction of China's contemporary rights discourse by looking at how urban educators and caregivers interpret and practice the concept of rights in their interactions with children. In discussing the unique features of the child-rights discourse in contemporary China, I consider the complex and at times contradictory role played by demographic changes, market reforms, and recent shifts in the governing rationality of the Chinese Party-state in shaping this discourse.

As we will see, Chinese official, academic, and media publications, as well as caregivers and educators often associate the notion of children's rights with "Western modernity." Rather than passively adopting real (or imagined) global notions of childhood and subjectivity, however, informants' constructions of the idea of children's rights take on unique forms through a process of interpretation and modification. Within this process, differences in social standing and in the historical and political conditions in which a generation of urban Chinese educators and caregivers were raised, shape actors' various forms of engagement with the notion of children's rights. This book therefore highlights the links between the emergence of a child-rights discourse; historical and generational factors; and the rise of new class formations in post-socialist, urban China.

Social and generational *habitus* in the formation of children's rights

The significance of social and generational factors in the shaping of individuals' views and practices has been well described. Scholars such as Karl Mannheim (2005 [1927]), have shown that membership in a particular "generation"—defined as a group of people born roughly at the same time who have experienced similar social and historical events during childhood and adolescence—may affect their interpretation of and interaction with cultural, social or political phenomena later in life (2005[1927]: 277). In China, recent ethnographic work of scholars such as Rofel (1999), Evans (2008), and Goh (2011), confirms the observation and illustrates the importance of generational factors in the shaping of contemporary Chinese views and practices of gender and the family. In particular, these studies have documented the commonalities in the worldviews of Chinese men and women who grew up under the tumultuous social and political conditions of the 1960s and 1970s, and shown how these differ from those of Chinese born before 1949 or after the introduction of liberal market reforms in 1978. The present study draws on these important observations and considers how Chinese teachers and parents of different age cohorts conceptualize the idea of children's rights in different ways. At the same time however, informants' affiliation to a certain age-cohort also intersects with their professional identity or social standing to create a unique view of children, power, and personhood.

In making this argument, I draw on Pierre Bourdieu's theoretical concept of *habitus*. In *Outline of a Theory of Practice* (1977), Bourdieu suggests that the interaction between one's membership in a certain social and generational grouping may result in a distinct *habitus*, a "system of internalized structures, schemes of perception, conception, and action" (Bourdieu, 1977: 86). Describing *habitus* as "history turned into nature" (1977: 78), Bourdieu calls our attention to the fact that each historical generation produces its own system of "durable dispositions" and that the unique conditions of a certain period impose "different definitions of the impossible, the possible, and the probable" on disparate individuals who happen "to share a similar location in the historical process" (Bourdieu, 1977: 78). However, Bourdieu (1984) also makes the crucial point that a person's relative standing in the social matrix significantly shapes thought and behavioral patterns that he or she may regard as natural or taken for granted.

Bourdieu's discussion of class *habitus* relies on empirical sociological studies of twentieth-century French class culture and emphasizes the historical *longue durée* in the formation of social structure. As such, Bourdieu's formulation may not be entirely applicable to the case of post-socialist China, in which processes of social formation occur in conditions of dramatic time compression and the cultural markers of class distinctions are not fully formed yet (see Donald and Zheng, 2009: 7). However, the notion of *habitus* may be useful to our understanding of the social factors which currently shape the conceptualization of children's rights especially among members of the new urban middle classes in China.

Current estimates put the Chinese middle class at somewhere between 10% and 25% of the total population, or 15%–40% of

China's urban population, depending on how this status is defined (see Li Cheng, 2010: 13–16). One Chinese study has found that 46.8% of respondents considered themselves "middle class" by various criteria (Li Cheng, 2010: 15). In other words, even though the size of the Chinese middle class is disputed and may still be relatively small, the *idea* of the middle class may serve as a powerful "dream image" for "a much larger aspiring segment of Chinese society through advertising, televisual fantasy, the housing market and the new private 'public' spaces of the shopping mall" (Anagnost, 2008a: 515).

Similarly to other studies, this book therefore regards China's contemporary middle classes not as a fixed entity with specific social and economic markers but rather as a cultural category that is imagined, staged and contested through the spheres of family, community and lifestyle (see Zhang Li, 2008: 24–5; see also Donald and Zheng, 2008, 2009; Wang Jing, 2005). Specifically, it finds that Shanghai caregivers who indulge themselves "in a social imaginary that fans their dream of being part of the global, 'cosmopolitan' culture" (Wang Jing, 2005: 539) also tend to see children as autonomous subjects with rights. Wishing to re-create themselves as "modern, civilized" subjects, these Shanghai caregivers display views and practices which resemble those of urban middle-class parents elsewhere in the industrial world. Following the recommendations of global child-experts, these Shanghai caregivers strive to use gentle persuasion methods and rational negotiation rather than a stern approach with their child. They also make systematic attempts to elicit their child's feelings, opinions, and thoughts in line with a "psychologized," rights-based conception of the self (see Hays, 1996; Lareau, 2003; Kusserow, 2004). In early twenty-first-century China, the "middle class" may still be "a discourse more than it is a reality" (Tomba, 2009a: 10). However, the notion of children's rights and its accompanying modes of conduct play an important role in the formation of this class discourse and in the emergence of a new middle-class *habitus.*

The process of individual- and social remaking is nonetheless a "messy business." New ideas, values and cultural models of the child and the person do not simply replace old ones but coexist with, incorporate and rework pre-existing cultural material (Illouz, 2008: 21). The Chinese family institution was founded on patriarchal and collective principles, some of which have survived the vicissitudes of the Maoist period (1949–76) (see Evans, 2008; Fong, 2004b, 2007; Goh, 2011; Kipnis, 2011). The implementation of the discourse of children's rights therefore requires a major modification in cultural meanings and practices, in particular those which are associated with the indigenous ethos of filial piety. Whereas the modern discourse of children's rights ushers a rational and quasi-economic approach to emotions in the familial sphere, the Chinese filial ethos requires self-sacrifice, particularly from the young. And whereas the traditional principle of filial piety assumes a series of reciprocal obligations "which focuses on rules of conduct constrained by status definitions," rights are in contrast "more analytically abstract and more inclusive." They define social and familial relations in terms of "entitlements that are universally shared" (Wilson, 1993: 112). These contradictions inevitably create tensions and confusion, even among caregivers and educators who are genuinely interested in implementing the idea of rights in their relationship with children.

One of the key questions this book aims to explore then is how Chinese parents and educators reconcile these tensions in their daily lives. Drawing on Swidler's (1986) notion of culture as a "tool kit" or "repertoire" from which social actors select differing pieces for constructing lines of action, I examine the interplay between the child-rights repertoire and pre-existing Chinese modes of childrearing and education. I show that even in this period of unsettling social change, people in China "do not build lines of action from scratch." Instead, they continue to rely on pre-existing cultural patterns which dictate particular behaviors and interaction styles (see Swidler, 1986: 277). As a result, the views and behavior of individual teachers and caregivers who subscribe to the child-rights discourse do not neatly converge into the global, neoliberal mode of governing children. Rather, they take their own characteristics, producing—to borrow Arjun Appadurai's (1990) phrasing—"distinct pragmatic configurations" rather than "exact translations" of modern, middle-class visions of the child and the person.

Research populations and research methods

My enquiry into the construction of children's rights in contemporary urban China draws on the results of eleven months (August

2004 to June 2005) of ethnographic fieldwork conducted in the eastern coastal city of Shanghai. Frequently described as "a world unto itself" by city residents and visitors alike, Shanghai is China's largest city and one of four municipalities with a status equivalent to a province. With a decade and a half of double-digit annual growth rates, it now constitutes a leading hub of Chinese capitalism and an important metropolis that exerts a powerful influence not only nationally but also globally. In many respects, conditions in Shanghai are far from representative of the rest of the country, or even from many hinterland cities in China. But conducting research in this site held the promise of glimpsing something of China's potential future in the twenty-first century.

Designated as an Open Coastal City and as the "Dragon head" of the Special Economic Zone (SEZ) of the Yangtze River Delta, Shanghai's government has since the early 1990s been accorded special powers and privileges. In order to attract foreign investment and create jobs for millions of migrant workers and city residents, Shanghai enjoys autonomy in all economic and administrative matters, making it a "zone of economic exception" (Ong, 2006). The city's unique political and economic status also means that it has been consistently allowed to introduce innovative educational policies that the central government has in turn instructed the rest of the country to follow. For instance, Shanghai has been allowed to alter its curriculum and textbooks earlier than others, has been a trail-blazer in terms of introducing innovative education methods to its schools, and has also been at the forefront of child-rights legislation in China.

As many of my interlocutors frequently reiterated, "Shanghai is like no other place in China." Just as the Shanghai of the 1920s and 1930s signified a "modern" universe set apart from the "traditional-ism" of the surrounding countryside (Lee, 1991: 164), the city is now regarded by many Chinese as "the best place to be if going abroad (*chuguo*) is not an option" (Sun Wanning, 2002: 43; see also Gamble, 2003). On their part, Shanghainese often pride themselves on being more sophisticated and refined than people in other parts of the country, especially the "country folk" (*xiangxiaren*) who have flocked to the city in search of work (Gamble, 2003: 78–9).

With new underground stations, highways crisscrossing the city, a sleek new airport, several giant bridges and a whole new city in

Pudong District, the Shanghai I encountered during my fieldwork in 2004–5 indeed seemed the emblem of a hyper-modern China set on shaking off its past and becoming a new global economic power. Yet it also contained a disorderly and sometimes jarring juxtaposition of so-called "Western" and "Asian" culture, "socialism" and "capitalism," "tradition" and "modernity." A building which had housed the first congress of the Chinese Communist Party overlooks the entrance to *Xintiandi* ("New Heaven and Earth"), a refurbished neighborhood in the former French Concession now home to expensive fashion boutiques, restaurants and night clubs. A giant billboard selling Levi's Jeans loomed over a revamped Buddhist temple where old and young Shanghainese came to worship on weekends. And each morning, crowds of workers lined the pavement to buy their *youtiao* (fried bread sticks) or *xiao long bao* (pork dumplings) around the corner from a Starbucks outlet, where suited businessmen and women sipped coffee while reading the newspaper.

These were but a few examples of the way in which "boundaries, both spatial and social" were constantly "being dismantled, fractured, and configured" (Gamble, 2003: xi) in early twenty-first-century Shanghai. And it is for this reason that Shanghai serves as an ideal testing ground for examining the uneasy effects of the introduction of the global discourse of children's rights among a population which considers itself the most open to "foreign" products, people and ideas.

The main bulk of the study took place in Shanghai schools and homes where I observed interactions between children and adults and where I interviewed parents and teachers on their thoughts and attitudes. In the first few months of fieldwork, I conducted participant-observations inside and outside of classrooms and talked to school administrators and frontline teachers at two Shanghai primary schools: the Affiliated School, and Whitewater School.[3] Situated near a noisy expressway in a neighborhood that could hardly be considered upscale, the Affiliated School is an elite institution which serves as an experimental base for educational research conducted at the adjacent university. Founded in 1952, the school caters to children aged 6–11 in grades one to five, many of whom come from families of university faculty and staff who lived nearby. The school's affiliation with one of Shanghai's top universities also meant that at the time of my study of its 60 teachers, a majority were Shanghai-born and had relatively high qualifications. Most possessed a BA degree, enjoyed many opportunities for in-service training and were encouraged to continue their studies for an advanced degree at the university. Most were also female.

Formerly a "key school,"[4] the Affiliated School's facilities as well as the quality of its teaching staff attracted children not only from the neighborhood but also from other parts of the city. Parents with connections to senior professors or top management staff at the university could enroll their children at the school provided they were able to pay a hefty "donation fee." The Affiliated School's reputation may have accounted for its large student body (900 altogether) and for the crowded classroom conditions, with each class containing 40 or more students.

The official motto at the Affiliated School is "Bringing out the vitality in each child," and "Seeking truth, perfection, flexibility, and uniqueness" ("*qiu shi, qiu jing, qiu huo, qiu xin*"). Yet what struck me most during my visits was the cheerless, unexceptional look of the campus. The school occupied two white-tiled buildings of several stories each. These surrounded a large courtyard paved with asphalt which also included a running track. Next to the courtyard stood a small playground that had seen better days; its fixtures were shabby and rusty. Teachers explained that they "preferred not to let children play there, for fear of their safety." There was little greenery in sight. Inside, the school and classroom walls were dirty and painted a drab gray. Next to pictures of scientific luminaries such as Newton and Einstein, hung a faded-looking poster of the famous Maoist-era figure, Lei Feng. Only students' artwork and essays, which decorated the long corridors on each floor, seemed to bring some color into the campus.

The second site in which I conducted my research, Whitewater School, was situated in a small, relatively quiet street on the other side of town, in an area of heavy-industry factories and densely populated residential buildings. It was founded in 1954 but had a refurbished look and prided itself on its special emphasis on art and music teaching. During my visits, the school grounds looked clean and well maintained. Its whitewashed buildings surrounded a small paved yard that contained trees and flowerbeds, and the school had a large grass lawn making for a much more cheerful atmosphere than at the Affiliated School.

Whitewater School employed 75 teachers, most of whom, again, were Shanghai-born women. The teaching profession—particularly at the primary school level—is in general considered a low-status, low-salary occupation in Shanghai as well as in other large cities in China. Indeed, several doctoral students in the field of education (and a young male teacher at the Affiliated School) observed that the "best students rarely choose to attend normal education institutes or become primary school teachers."[5] Significantly, a majority of those who do are female.

In contrast to the Affiliated School, many of the teachers at Whitewater School did not possess an academic degree, relying instead on a college or a high-school diploma. Their educational profile resembled that of the typical urban teacher in China. Under current government regulations, graduates from secondary teacher-training institutes are regarded as qualified primary school teachers,[6] a requirement many teachers fulfilled on the job.[7]

Whitewater Primary school catered to students aged from 6–11 from less affluent families who lived nearby. With a body of 800 students, classes at Whitewater were considerably smaller than those at the Affiliated School, averaging 20–25 students each. According to the vice-principal at Whitewater, the small class size was a result of recent demographic changes brought on by the introduction of the One-Child family policy. Yet I suspected that it might also have had to do with the fact that, unlike the Affiliated School, Whitewater School did not have a particularly good reputation for producing large numbers of students who continued their studies in top middle schools or in prestigious universities. As a result, it did not attract children from other parts of town as the Affiliated School had done.

Schools are difficult places to conduct research, methodologically as well as ethically. They have "gate-keepers" from whom permission must be secured. "They often require a difficult negotiation of structurally opposed interests and alliances, and such conditions may threaten the sustained observations and interviews needed to construct a compelling interpretation of the effects of schooling" (Levinson, 1999: 599). My initial experience at Shanghai primary schools largely confirmed this observation, and my identity as a foreign researcher from an American university further compounded the conditions of my research. During preliminary visits to the schools, I found the principals of both schools warm and forthcoming. Each assured me that their school had been successfully implementing the city's recent curriculum reforms for several years now, and that the teachers "all welcomed" the changes brought on by the government's reforms. Despite what seemed like a promising beginning, however, my work at the Affiliated and Whitewater primary schools did not go smoothly at first.

In the first several months of my research I was frequently cast in either of two equally undesirable roles: the "nosy" outsider who was about to tarnish the good name of the school and its teachers; or the "esteemed" education expert who was there to sing the praise of China's recent school reforms. Neither of these roles suited me. While the former led many teachers to regard me in deep suspicion and even avoid me altogether, the latter made them enthusiastically recite official slogans while evading any questions about practical matters or the concrete difficulties they faced.

When I shared my frustration at this situation with a local friend, a young Chinese woman who was herself pursuing a doctoral degree in comparative education, she was not at all surprised. As an academic researcher, she herself had often encountered similar reactions during her visits to schools, especially those outside Shanghai. "In China," she noted, "education has always had a very strong link to politics." Indeed, during the "anti-rightists" campaigns of the Maoist era (1949–76), Chinese schoolteachers were classified as "intellectuals" (*zhishi fenzi*). They served as primary targets for public denouncements, especially during the violent decade of the Cultural Revolution (1966–76). This complex history, suggested my informant, placed Chinese educators, even those who engaged in teaching art, math or science to first-graders, in a very sensitive position indeed.

My initial strategy in attempting to overcome informants' deeply ingrained suspicions was to assure my interlocutors that I was not there to judge and criticize but to document practices and elicit views and opinions. I promised that teachers' identities would remain protected, and guaranteed that under no circumstances would I divulge their names or views to their superiors or to the authorities. While these clarifications did help to clear teachers' doubts, I suspect that what made the real difference was the dozens of apparently trivial chats during lunch breaks and between classes.

Drinking cup after cup of *Woolong* tea in teachers' offices, I answered repeated inquiries about the number of children couples in America were allowed to have and how many my husband and I were planning. Other topics of interest included the size of our California apartment compared to the one we were renting in Shanghai, the sort of appliances we had here and there, and the amount of rent we were currently paying (everyone assured me that being foreigners, we were "thoroughly duped.")

Conversing about these topics to teachers at both schools—most of whom were, like myself, women in their thirties—gradually allowed us to move away from the tension-laden relationships of "foreigner/Chinese" and "researcher/objects of study." We began to interact as "young women" or "wives." With time, most of my school interlocutors became much more relaxed even during our more formal conversations. Many of them trusted me enough to openly describe their difficulties in implementing the city's recent school reform, to criticize the government's overall educational policies, and to allow me to put their criticisms on tape. Yet people never forgot that I was a "Western" researcher who was there to collect data for an ethnographic study, as their replies to the interview questions frequently reflected. In this respect, my work in Shanghai schools produced partial and "situated knowledge" (Haraway, 1991: 190–1), constrained by my historicized and social location and embedded in the differing visions of the "West"—and particularly of the United States—among the educators I met.

In addition to interviews with more than 50 schoolteachers and staff at both schools, I also conducted close to 100 hours of classroom observations across subjects and grades. I took part in participant-observations in teachers' offices, during teachers' meetings and lunch breaks, and in school-wide ceremonies and school outings where I watched dozens of formal and informal interactions between teachers and students and among teachers themselves. Another important venue for observing teachers' interactions with their colleagues and superiors were teacher-training seminars. During my fieldwork, I was able to attend several of these full-day colloquiums during which I listened to speeches of local education officials, sat in lectures and observed exemplary lessons along with the other participants: school administrators and frontline teachers from different parts of the city. The informal conversations I held on theses occasions with teachers who worked with different populations, including for instance, children of migrant workers or children of highly affluent families, considerably broadened my perspective on the views and attitudes of contemporary Shanghai teachers.

Toward the end of my fieldwork, I was also able to visit one of Shanghai's teacher-training institutes where I held lengthy conversations with several trainers. In addition, I was fortunate enough to meet with two Shanghai professors, both of whom were involved in the planning and implementation of the city's recent curriculum reforms. My conversations with these professors and with the teacher trainers offered valuable insights into the general direction and implications of the government's school reform plan, at both the city and national levels. These conversations revealed the intricate relationship between political ideology and educational practice in present-day urban China.

The second part of my fieldwork was spent talking to mothers of schoolchildren. My initial experience with teachers convinced me that if I wanted to hold relatively candid, pressure-free conversations with parents of different backgrounds, I needed to find informants without soliciting the help of the school authorities. With the assistance of several of the teachers I knew, as well as friends and acquaintances, I located 20 mothers, aged 33–52 (with an average age of 39), whose children were aged 6–14 (with an average age of 9). More than half of these Shanghai mothers were educated, white-collar workers. Three had at least a middle school education; two had a college diploma; nine had a Bachelors' degree; and one possessed a PhD. In addition, I also interviewed two market vendors, two homemakers, and a former factory worker. Mothers of this group had relatively lower levels of education. While three had a middle school diploma, one had completed only nine years of schooling, while another—a recent migrant from the countryside—had only attended primary school.

Most of my informants reached reproductive age after the introduction of the government's population policy in 1979 so a majority had only one child. There were a few exceptions, however. One mother had given birth to twin girls; another, the wife of a wealthy entrepreneur, had two boys—apparently, the couple was able to afford the hefty fine for having a second child.[8] In addition, two of my interviewees were originally from the countryside and had recently migrated to Shanghai in search of work. Since the state's birth policies are less stringent in rural areas, these migrant women had two children each—in both cases an older daughter and a younger son.

Overall, my interactions with Shanghai mothers were friendly and relatively relaxed. No one's career was on the line and the subject of the interview— raising children—was clearly a favorite among the women I met. It also helped that I was initially introduced to these women as a "foreign friend (*pengyou*)" rather than a "foreign researcher." While some of the interviews took place at the child's school or at the mother's workplace, I met a majority of women at their homes, where we sometimes chatted for several hours, and where I was able to observe their interactions with their children and with other household members. In some cases, it was understood that, in exchange for the interview, I would practice English with the child (many well-educated women wanted their school-aged child to be able to not only read and write, but also to converse in English). I gladly complied with these requests, which also allowed me to interact informally with several children.

Toward the end of my fieldwork, I was fortunate to meet with five grandmothers, all of whom were in their early- to late-sixties. My group interview with this lively bunch of retired women took place one afternoon at the end of a dance class they had all been attending at a local pensioners' club, and was immensely productive. While this book does not focus on the particular role of grandparents in the rearing and educating of Chinese urban singletons, my conversations with these elderly women shed important light on differences and similarities between Maoist and post-Maoist notions of childhood. It further brought home the importance of historical *habitus* to the shaping of practices of childrearing and education in China.

During the interviews with educators, mothers, and grandmothers, my interlocutors sometimes referred to television ads, newspaper articles, popular child-rearing guides and, in the case of highly educated parents, Internet websites they browsed while looking for parenting guidance and information. I therefore complemented my ethnographic work with an extensive survey of textual and visual media items published in China from the 1980s to the mid-2000s. I also looked at policy statements and law codes mentioned by informants; at teacher-training manuals; at school textbooks; and at Chinese scholarly work on childrearing and education. Analyzing these materials provided a fuller, more nuanced understanding of the various elements which shaped Shanghai caregivers' and educators' views toward children and childhood.

Two caveats are in order. First, my study focused on the perspectives of mothers rather than fathers. Although the views and practices of fathers form a crucial aspect of any inquiry into childrearing and family life, the study's exclusive emphasis on women's perspectives can be justified by the fact that an array of social and cultural forces in China currently focuses on mothers as the main bearers of responsibility for raising and educating children. During the Maoist period (1949–76), state propaganda stressed gender equality and for the most part, promoted the idea of the "iron girl" (*tie guniang*), who could compete successfully in the public sphere long dominated by men. In contrast, post-1978 China has seen a renewed political and cultural emphasis on gender differences, on the "natural" inequality of men and women and correspondingly on women's role in caring for the young (Anagnost, 2008b; Brownell and Wasserstrom, 2002; Evans, 1997, 2008; Honig and Hershatter, 1988). Many of the mothers I met in Shanghai seemed to have internalized these messages. While a majority worked outside the home, virtually all of them regarded themselves as the main caretakers of their school-aged child.

Finally, my work in Shanghai did not include systematic interviews with children. While children's opinions form a crucial component in understanding the changing nature of childrearing and education in contemporary urban China, the goal of my project was to focus on the perception of children's rights in the eyes of adults: in this case, parents, grandparents and educators. The study therefore did not include a methodical inquiry into the thoughts and views of children. It does however incorporate children's perspectives on the issue of rights, transmitted through informal exchanges I had with children in schools and at homes, and reflected in the many anecdotes parents and educators had related to me. These offered much valuable information regarding the role of the young in shaping contemporary notions of childhood and rights in post-socialist China.

Outline of the book

I begin the book with an overview of the development of the child-rights discourse in China of the post-socialist era. Chapter 1 discusses the social, political, and economic conditions which have contributed to the formation of this discourse, and identifies the political and social institutions involved in its production and dissemination since the early 1990s. Tracing the promotion of the child-rights discourse through Chinese legislative codes, academic works, popular media publications and pedagogic materials, I suggest that despite notable differences between these various strains of discourse, they all share a commonality: a decidedly modern conceptualization of children as separate, autonomous subjects with a right to make decisions and to express their views and opinions in matters which concern them.

Chapter 1 further describes how Shanghai educators and caregivers engage with this new idea at home and at school. It shows that young teachers born or raised after the introduction of market reforms in 1978 and elite parents of the rising middle classes are keenest on embracing the notion that children should be given a voice, and that this voice should be heard. Some believe that outspoken children will become successful, entrepreneurial future workers in a global market economy. Others hope that respecting children's opinions at home and school will ultimately produce more assertive citizens who will be able to defend their interests against power and authority when they grow up. Respect for the dignity and integrity of the child's person further entails respect for his/her privacy, or in other words, for the child's control over his/her body and individual possessions.

In Chapter 2 I trace the articulation of this particular notion in Chinese legislative measures, pedagogic materials and media publications of the past two decades or so. I note the economic developments and ideational currents which have contributed to its emergence in contemporary China. I further argue that the increasing popularity of the idea that even the very young have a right to self-ownership, which also includes the right to protection against violence, reflects a sharpening of boundaries between individuals, and a requirement of a higher degree of self-regulation and self-control from adults and children alike. As Chapter 2 will show, this requirement is once again accepted most readily by a younger generation of teachers and by well-educated parents. Educators and caregivers of these two social groups also seek to employ the more modern, "rational", and "civilized" code of conduct recommended by contemporary child psychologists in China.

Chapter 3 further explores the link between China's child-rights discourse and the growing popularity of psychological knowledge in contemporary urban China. It argues that the reconceptualization of Chinese children as autonomous subjects with rights has been facilitated by the rise of an imported psychological discourse of childhood. The discourse of child psychology associates developmental "needs" with individual "rights" and seeks to redefine and recover "the proper meaning" of childhood in China. In Chapter 3, I describe how Shanghai teachers and caregivers consume this psychological discourse and attempt to implement its principles in their daily interactions with youngsters. I argue that in China, the association between "rights talk" and the discourse of developmental needs, both of which rest on an individualistic, rational logic of conduct, serves to legitimize the idea of children as autonomous subjects with rights. This is especially true among a younger generation of Chinese teachers and among elite urban parents who place much stock in the principles of modern science. Although they are willing to embrace some of the basic tenets of the scientific-*cum*-moral discourse of children's rights, some parents in Shanghai are nonetheless selective about its implementation. Middle-aged school teachers also express uneasiness about the possible effects of introducing the notion of rights to the classroom.

Chapter 4 considers the reasons for informants' ambivalence about children's rights. It suggests that their doubts stem from both pragmatic concerns as well as from a moral anxiety about the inherent contradiction between the individualistic, contract-based notion of rights and the more traditional ethos of filial piety grounded in the logic of self-sacrifice and reciprocity. The discourse of children's rights is gaining ground among both a younger generation of teachers and among parents who wish to associate themselves with a modern, middle-class *habitus*. The rapid pace of social, economic, and demographic transformations, however, as well as concerns about the integrity of Chinese cultural and national identity in an age of increased globalization, lead some educators and caregivers to revert to the ethos of filial piety in familial and school relations. But it is a refashioned ethos to which they turn, one that has been accommodated to suit the social conditions and new subjectivities of twenty-first-century urban China.

I end the book with a chapter summarizing the dialectic relationship between the meanings of "global" and "local," "modern" and "traditional" in the construction of the child-rights discourse in present-day China. I discuss the implications of the emergent rights discourse for contemporary Chinese conceptualizations of family, childhood, and subjectivity, and consider the role of this discourse in present as well as future mutations in the state-citizenry relationship. I conclude by noting some of the limitations of the present study and by pointing out future lines of research into the discourse of children's rights in post-socialist China.

1

Recasting Children as Autonomous Persons: Children as Future Citizens and Workers

"Respect for the independent rights of children is the hallmark of any modern, civilized society.... From this day onward, when parents behave in a way that violates these rights, children will be able to voice their objections knowing that the law is on their side" (Cheng and Ren, 2004). So declared a top Shanghai government official following the adoption of a landmark piece of legislation designed to protect the rights of minors in one of China's largest, most cosmopolitan cities. Shanghai's 2004 Municipal Regulations on the Protection of Minors (*Weichengnian ren baohu tiaoli*) urge caregivers and teachers to respect children's "human dignity" (*renge zunyan*) and individual personality, and to safeguard their "legitimate rights and interests" (*hefa quanyi*). These entitlements include the right to "personal privacy" (*geren yinsi*); to protection from "verbal abuse" (*ruma*) and "physical punishment" (*tifa*); and the right to "adequate rest and leisure time" as prescribed by children's unique physical and psychological characteristics. At the time of their introduction, Shanghai's Municipal Regulations on the Protection of Minors appeared innovative in both language and scope. They are nonetheless representative of a new and increasingly influential strain of discourse about children and their entitlements in post-socialist China.

In this chapter, I discuss the social, political, and economic conditions which have contributed to the formation of China's child-rights discourse. I identify the political and social institutions currently involved in the production and dissemination of that discourse, and I describe how national and local legislation, academic works, popular media publications, and pedagogic materials have been promoting discussions about children's rights since the early 1990s. I argue that despite notable differences between the various strains of discourse about children and their entitlements in contemporary China, there are a number of important commonalities in the vision of the child they promote. First, the Chinese discussion reflects the decidedly modern recognition of children as a structurally differentiated group within society whose members must be allowed to develop "happily and healthily" according to the principles of modern psychological science. Second, it mirrors a new conceptualization of children as distinct and independent persons with identities of their own, not simply as parts of their family, society or the nation. Rather than "objects" or potential victims of various forms of harmful treatment, Chinese children are increasingly regarded in contemporary government and public discourse as "subjects or agents, capable of exercising for themselves certain fundamental powers" (Archard, 2004: 60). For the first time in the history of PRC legislation, these powers include the right to make decisions and to express their views and opinions in matters which may affect children's lives.

Child-rights legislation "always represents an unstable translation of ideas of right and wrong that exist in the real world and are based on lived experiences" (Hanson and Nieuwenhuys, 2012: 3). The discussion in this and the following chapters therefore considers not only the juridical and official discourse of children's rights but also how the lived experiences of contemporary Chinese teachers, caregivers and children shape their understandings of this discourse. In the present chapter, in particular, I examine how Shanghai educators and caregivers currently engage with the idea that even young children are able to make independent choices; can "speak (rather than be silenced);" and should be "heard (rather than ignored)" (Archard, 2004: 66).

Drawing on interviews and observations conducted in Shanghai schools and homes, the following discussion addresses this issue while tending to the specific role of social and generational *habitus* in the formation of China's contemporary child-rights discourse. As we shall see, it is particularly young teachers and well-educated, elite parents who tend to embrace the new concept of children as autonomous persons with rights, including the right to their own opinions. Their largely positive reception of the child-rights notion partly stems from pragmatic calculations concerning the desirable qualities of a successful future worker in the global market economy. At the same time, however, it also reflects the rising importance of an "individualistic ethic of autonomy" (see Yan Yunxiang, 2011; Zhang Li, 2008) among a younger generation of teachers and among the rising middle classes in China, who are beginning to re-conceptualize the relationship not only between children and adults but also between the Chinese state and its citizenry.

The legal discourse of children's rights in China

Public attention to children's rights in China is not an entirely new phenomenon. In the early decades of the twentieth century, Chinese intellectuals of the May Fourth Movement had argued strongly for children's autonomy and their freedom from authoritarian, patriarchal forces, though they often rationalized their program with the need to achieve national survival and social progress (Anagnost, 1997a; Farquhar Mary Ann, 1999; Jones, 2002; Thøgersen, 2002). Influenced by this modern agenda and by the Marxist notion that the state rather than the family was to assume care for all children in an idealized egalitarian society (Engels, 1978[1884]), the Chinese Communist Party (CCP) likewise sought to assign children and youth a greater role in social and political processes and to strengthen their status vis-à-vis their parents and extended families. The regulations of marriage promulgated in the Jiangxi Soviet in 1931 and later in the Shanxi-Hebei-Shandong-Henan Border Region in 1942, expressly acknowledged that the welfare of children, "the future masters of society," had been consistently neglected in the past. Regulations in these "liberated areas" also made several specific provisions for the protection of children born out of wedlock and affected by divorce (Sheng *et al.*, 1989: 426). This new attention to children's wellbeing and the attempt to fundamentally change their status within Chinese society was further reflected in legislative measures introduced by the socialist state after the revolution of 1949.

Notably, China's new Marriage Law of 1950 attempted to abolish the "arbitrary and compulsory feudal marriage system" which was said to ignore the interests of women as well as children. The law banned such practices as arranged marriages, polygyny, concubinage and minor marriage (defined as marriage between men under the age of 20 and women under 18). While reasserting the duty of adult children "to support and assist their parents," China's 1950 Marriage Law also emphasized the duties of parents toward their offspring, particularly children's right to survival and to adequate treatment.

The Maoist state further sought to limit the patriarchal power associated with three-generation households in China by a systematic attack on the structure of the patrilineage. After 1949, lineage property was confiscated in the name of land redistribution and collectivization. Collectives and party cadres gradually replaced the political and economic functions of lineages (Potter and Potter, 1990: 255; Yan Yunxiang, 2003: 213; see also Yang C.K., 1959). The destruction of the economic basis of lineage power was accompanied by a frontal attack on ancestor worship and on the Confucian notion of filial piety. In a direct strike against the cultural and religious core of the adult-child relationship in China, Maoist official campaigns attempted to reduce the past prerogatives of the elderly by removing state sanctions for these traditional beliefs and rituals. Consequently, it became harder for parents to invoke the threat of supernatural punishment against children who failed to respect them (Davis-Friedmann, 1991; Davis and Harrell, 1993). The systematic attempt to shift power from the old to the young in post-1949 Chinese society (Yang C.K., 1959; Diamant, 2000; Yan Yunxiang, 2003), reached its apogee during the tumultuous decade of the "Cultural Revolution" (1966–76) in which Chinese children and youth were called upon to publicly critique and strictly denounce their elders and seniors who were accused of "counter-revolutionary" thinking.

Following the end of the Cultural Revolution in 1976 and the introduction of liberal economic reforms in 1979, the official drive to empower and protect children through legal measures became even more pronounced as the Chinese state began to emphasize the principle of government by law. A new marriage law, introduced in 1980 to replace the previous law from 1950,[1] reiterated, and to some extent expanded, the prohibition on domestic violence and maltreatment and "desertion of one family member by another." The 1980 PRC Marriage Law emphasized the duty of parents "to bring up and educate their children" and contained the notion that adult family members should "cherish the young" (PRC National People's Congress, 2001). Notably, the law also employed new and evocative language in asserting the "lawful rights and interests" of women and children, thereby challenging the past dominance of the concept of moral "obligations" in PRC legal constructions of familial relations (see Keith, 1997: 38).

Despite this new emphasis, the 1980 Marriage Law also attempts to balance minors' rights with those of adult caregivers. It requires children to "respect the old" and to "support and assist" their parents as well as their grandparents (both paternal and maternal), a stipulation that did not appear in the 1950 Law. The 1980 law also grants parents the right to "subject their children who are minors to discipline," and demands that both parents and children do their best to "maintain equal, harmonious and civilized...family relations" (PRC National People's Congress, 2001). Similar language appears in China's Constitution, adopted in 1982 and amended four times since (in 1988, 1993, 1999, and 2004). Like China's Marriage Law, the Constitution recognizes children as a category of "weak" social persons whose lawful rights and interests require the state's special protection. However, in affirming the duties of adult children toward their parents, the Constitution is as concerned with the promotion of reciprocal harmonious relations within the family as with the guarantee of children's individual rights (see Information Office of the State Council of the PRC, 1996).

The legislative measures of the early 1980s in China emphasize the equal status of children within the family and highlight the role of the law in regulating family affairs. At the same time, however, the new Marriage Law and the Constitution also seek to limit children's rights vis-à-vis their parents while rehabilitating the traditional notion of filial piety. That notion is now presented as a precondition to the maintenance of "harmonious" family relations, one of the hallmarks of a Confucian family ethos that had been thoroughly challenged during the first three decades of socialist rule. In part a response to the social disruptions that occurred in family life during the Cultural Revolution these provisions indicate growing anxiety in reform-era China over rising social instability and the "declining health" of the family in the age of market reforms (Keith, 1997: 30). The new emphasis on children's duties toward parents may further reflect economic calculations on the part of the Chinese government which recognized that it could not possibly provide welfare support for the growing sector of the elderly, especially in the age of the One-Child Policy (see Wolf, 1985; Cook, 1989: 395).

Beginning in the early 1990s however, we see a discernible shift in Chinese legal formulations of children and their entitlements within the family and society, together with a reconceptualization of the *type* of rights which children ought to possess. An important milestone in this respect was China's ratification of the 1989 UN Convention on the Rights of the Child (UNCRC). A legally binding document, the UNCRC grants children the "right to survival; to development to the fullest; and to protection from harmful influences, abuse, and exploitation." Unlike previous formulations such as the 1959 UN Declaration of the Rights of the Child, the 1989 UNCRC also recognizes children's autonomy, the importance of children's views and the concept of children's empowerment by assuring their right to "freedom of expression and thought," "privacy," and "freedom of association" (UNICEF, 2007; see also Freeman, 2000).[2] China reportedly played a significant role in the shaping of this international charter and was one of the countries that raised the draft resolution for the approval of the Convention in the UN.[3] The Chinese government formally ratified the UNCRC in 1990 and has since submitted periodic reports to the UN Committee on the Rights of the Child, the international body responsible for monitoring its implementation.

China's ratification of the UNCRC is significant in several ways. First, it indicates the Chinese government's readiness to adopt a canon that (presumably) represents universally agreed norms for children's development (Naftali, 2009). Second, it reflects the distinctly modern recognition that minors constitute a different social category—"if children were simply viewed as human beings, albeit smaller and younger human beings" (see Archard, 2004: 60; Boyden, 2001: 191), they would already have certain rights under China's existing laws. Lastly, China's ratification of the UNCRC also indicates the Party-state's acknowledgment that children are in fact individual subjects, and as such, possess fundamental entitlements under the law.

Following the adoption of the UN Convention on the Rights of the Child, China promulgated its own set of regulations dedicated to children's rights. The first article of China's 1992 Law on the Protection of Minors (*Weichengnian baohu fa*) echoes socialist-era rhetoric by emphasizing the importance of training children to become "successors to the socialist cause with lofty ideals, sound morality [...], and discipline" by educating them "in patriotism, collectivism and socialism" (All-China Women's Federation, 2006). However, an examination of the rest of the document, the first of its kind in the history of PRC legislation, reveals a distinctively new way of thinking and talking about children and their entitlements.

Like China's Marriage Law and its Constitution, the 1992 Law on the Protection of Minors (amended in 2006), prohibits the maltreatment of children at school or in the family, thereby recognizing that minors form a group "whose members experience the exercise of power differently to adults" (James *et al.*, 1998: 211). Notably however, the stated goals of China's new law, whose contents have been disseminated through various media campaigns over the past two decades or so, are to safeguard minors' "lawful rights and interests" while upholding their "personal dignity *(renge zunyan)*," a new, important term which does not appear in earlier legal formulations concerning children (All-China Women's Federation, 2006). The 1992 law thereby acknowledges that minors (defined as persons under the age of 18) are not ancillary to their families but constitute a separate social group that is entitled not only to protection but also to respect as human beings.

Addressing a child's basic welfare rights to survival, provision, and education,[4] China's Law on the Protection of Minors also details specific protection rights to which underage citizens are entitled. These include the right to protection against "domestic violence" *(jiating baoli)*, corporal punishment, and "any act which degrades" children's "dignity" at school. For the first time in PRC history, the law further asserts children's right to personal privacy *(geren yinse)* and to receive adequate time for "sleep and entertainment" according to their mental and physical developmental requirements.

One of the pivotal questions underlying any discussion of children's rights is whether children actually have the capacity to make choices on their own and to clearly express these choices (Archard, 2004: 54; see also Schoeman, 1983). While the UNCRC details a series of civil and political "participation rights," and strongly advocates the idea that children are capable of taking part in decisions which affect their lives (at least when they reach a certain age and level of maturity), China's Law on the Protection of Minors lacks such a clear assertion; the law only stipulates children's right "to express their views in matters concerning them" within the family and requires educators to foster students' "ability for independent thinking" at school. In effect, however, the Chinese law promotes a new, liberal conceptualization of the child, as an autonomous person with a separate identity and individual interests which adults must respect and attend to.

Chinese legislation in the areas of family and criminal law since the 1992 Law on the Protection of Minors has also started to reflect this position. A child who has become involved in judicial proceedings is now allowed "to express his/her personal views" and when parental custody is disputed in divorce cases, courts in China are now instructed to hear "the opinions of children aged 10 and above" and consider these opinions as "decisive factors in [their] eventual judgment." The same is true of adoption proceedings involving a child 10 years of age or older: the child's opinions about the adoption must also "be taken into account" (United Nations Committee on the Rights of the Child, 2005a: 18).

Local governments in China have likewise started to promote the idea that children should be allowed to take part in decision-making processes in matters which concern them—including the promulgation of child-related legislation.[5] Prior to the introduction of its 2004 Municipal Regulations on the Protection of Minors, the city of Shanghai's top legislative panel sought "comments and suggestions" from primary and middle school students in the city. Shanghai People's Congress member, Xia Xiurong (whose observation opened this chapter) explained the rationale behind the city's initiative by stating that it "is necessary for us to listen to children directly because the law will eventually serve them" (Cheng and Ren, 2004). This move was hailed in local media reports as indicating the recognition that children are "independent individuals (*duli de geti*)" who have "a right to speak up and express their views (*shuohua de quanli*)" (see for example, Zhang Rong, 2004; Zhang Jun, 2004; Shanghai Star, 2004). A government report on the state of Shanghai children from the same period further celebrated the city's acknowledgement that "children should be heard," calling it an important departure from "traditional beliefs," which hold that youngsters lack sufficient ability to form their own judgment and therefore must be closely "guided by parents and teachers" (Wu and Zhao, 2003; Hu Shen, 2000).

Some academics in China similarly regard the passing of child-rights legislation as a positive and even inevitable development in Chinese thinking about children. A 2001 scholarly article published in the *Zhongguo jiaoyuxue kan* [*Journal of the Chinese Society of Education*] argues, for instance, that contemporary Chinese children "have a better capacity to form their own judgments, views and positions," along with "the necessary cognitive and emotional capabilities" to enjoy and "even *demand* new rights at a relatively early age" (Tang Zhisong, 2001: 13; emphasis added). In a 2000 volume, Chinese Education philosopher, Hu Shen, likewise observes that Chinese children, particularly those residing in cities, currently "possess rich knowledge and a broad worldview," since they are increasingly exposed to alternative, diverse sources of information disseminated by the mass media and the developing information technology. Unlike children of previous generations, he and other writers suggest, Chinese youngsters of the early twenty-first century have a better "view of the rule of law (*fazhi guannian*)" and a better ability to acquire a so-called "democratic consciousness (*minzhu yishi*)" (Hu Shen, 2000: 117; see also Wang Peng, 2002: 111–12). What these liberal Chinese scholars seem to suggest is that the emergence of the notion of children's rights is a natural, inescapable development which reflects the new subjectivities of contemporary Chinese children. Yet the political context in which they operate impels us to read their pronouncements as something more: as the expression of a desire to transform not only the relationship between youngsters and adults but also between the Chinese state and its citizenry while strengthening the rule of law in the PRC.

"Children are masters of their own lives"

The idea that children have both the ability and the right to express their own views appears not only in legislative codes, media publications, and academic works, but also in China's Education for Quality (*suzhi jiaoyu*) reform plan. Throughout the 1990s, several provinces and municipalities in China, including the city of Shanghai, implemented "education for quality" experiments in their schools, the results of which were reported in Chinese educational journals. In June 1999, the Chinese Ministry of Education incorporated the principles of these various reform programs into a

nationwide policy (Anagnost, 1997b; Kipnis, 2001, 2006; Woronov, 2007). Described by contemporary Chinese scholars as "a turning point in the history of education reform" and as "the most pressing task every educator currently faces" (Sun Lichun, 2001: 1), the "education for quality" plan aims to address the excesses of "traditional," "exam-oriented education" which is said to have stifled creativity, dulled students' minds and led to numerous social and psychological problems among China's youth (Communist Party of China, 2000: 232).

As noted by a number of scholars, Chinese pedagogy has traditionally been "directed towards finding methods of effective control." Discipline, loyalty, and submission in children have been instilled through the use of exemplary models and the learning techniques of imitation and repetition (Bakken, 1999: 96; see also Wu David, 1996; Landsberger, 2001; Kipnis, 2011; Woronov, 2008). China's Education for Quality reform plan can be seen as an attempt to counter this tendency. It mandates the replacement of passive learning, mechanical drills, memorization and repetition of the textbook or the teacher's words with more diverse instructional activities. Children take part in small group work, "discussion-style" teaching, "learning by doing (*zuo zhong xue*)", and "learning through discovery and enquiry (*tanjiu*)" (Cui Xianglu, 1999: 73–6). These new methods, say PRC reform materials, currently prevail in schools of "Western, developed countries," and if implemented in China would allow students to make their own decisions and provide them with sufficient "time and space" to exercise independent learning and develop innovative ways of thinking (Zeng, 2004: 61; *Xiaoxuesheng xinli*, 2000: 8–9).

One of the main targets of the national Education for Quality program, and of local reform plans initiated in its wake, has been the transformation of the teacher-student relationship. Citing traditional sayings such as "a teacher for one day is a father for a lifetime" (*"yi ri wei shi, zong shen wei fu"*), contemporary reform texts in China criticize the "long-held" notion that just like parents, teachers should exert strict control over children, and that students need to respect and obey their teachers who are their "elders and seniors" (Huang *et al.*, 2001: 88; Zhou, 2005).

At the two Shanghai primary schools in which I worked, teachers and school staff born before the introduction of market reforms in

1978 still seemed to hold onto these precepts. "In China, we believe that children are like young saplings," one middle-aged math teacher at Whitewater School told me. "They should not be given too much freedom but instead require constant trimming, watering and cultivating if they are to grow the right way."
In contrast, a younger computer teacher in her early twenties related with unhidden scorn how the former principal at her school, a woman who came of age during the Maoist period (1949–76), used to tell her: "Little children don't have the ability to control themselves, so they have to rely on others to control them."
Critiquing these "backwards" views concerning young children and their capacities, Chinese academic works published in the 2000s have been calling for a "humanization" (*renbenhua*) of students and a "democratization" of the classroom (see for example, Cui and Huang, 2002: 20; Zeng, 2004; Tang, 2001). Teachers, they argue, should regard themselves not as students' "governors" or "caretakers," but as "facilitators," "partners" and "fellow investigators" (Huang *et al.*, 2001: 88; Zhou, 2005). They should set learning goals together with the students and encourage children to speak freely, make suggestions, and ask questions (Zeng, 2004: 93; Li, 2003: 12). For their part, students should take charge of the learning process and occupy a so-called "subject" (*zhuti*) position within the classroom (Zhang Hua, 1997, 2002). Moreover, students should be allowed, even encouraged, to correct their teachers whenever they make a mistake, instead of "automatically accepting what the teacher says as dictated by the Confucian ethos of filial piety" (Cui and Huang, 2002: 190; Zhou, 2005; see also *Xiaoxuesheng xinli*, 2000: 42–3). As Zhou Feng, a Guangdong education scholar, put it in an argument typical of the Education for Quality literature:

> Children are masters of their own lives (*ziji shengming de zhuren*) and have *a right* to develop and learn.... Too often, we adults force children to submit to our will and do not allow them to make mistakes.... When students make the smallest error, we punish them severely and use different methods to publicly humiliate them. These practices force children to imitate adults and inevitably make students into the [teachers'] "yes men" ("*ying sheng chong*") or "mouthpieces." Only if we

establish children's *subject position* (*zhuti diwei*) and nurture their ability to take initiative and be active, would we be able to help them develop themselves.... The implementation of Education for Quality "requires first and foremost the *liberation of students' bodies and minds*" (Zhou Feng, 1998: 75; emphasis added).

To many of my school informants in Shanghai, the current attempts to introduce reforms which would liberate students' "bodies and minds" have been directly related to the promotion of the "putting people first" or "people-centered" (*"yi ren wei ben"*) principle, touted by the CCP since the early 2000s. The advancement of the "people-centered" ruling principle has been part of a drive by China's former president (2002–12), Hu Jintao and his Premier, Wen Jiabao, to construct a "harmonious society (*hexie shehui*)" based on a "scientific concept of development."[6] As part of this program, the Chinese government has, in the course of the 2000s, tried to employ a more "humanistic," "compassionate" governing style which seeks to replace a focus on GDP growth with greater attention to "the needs, interests, and wishes of ordinary citizens" (Chai, 2004; Ching, 2004; People's Daily, 2004a, 2004b, 2006b). In education, "putting people first" has been translated into "children-first" (*ertong weiben*)." According to Chinese education scholars this requires teachers to respect students' interests and wishes by treating them as "the axis of the learning process" and by allowing children "to be free and make their own choices" (see for example, Huang Shuguang *et al.*, 2001; Li Chongli, 2003; Zhang Hua, 2002: 5–6; Zhong Qiquan *et al.*, 2001; Zhou Shizhang, 2005).

In a candid interview I conducted with Professor Chen, a senior education scholar who spent time at an American Ivy League institute and who in recent years has been advising the Chinese government's school reforms, the link between recent transformations in the CCP's governing ideology and the introduction of liberal school pedagogies received a strong emphasis.

Professor Chen observed that "from a Western viewpoint" the principle of regarding the student as a subject (*yi xuesheng wei zhuti*)," an idea promoted in Shanghai schools, "may seem absurd." In the "West," he explained, this particular issue has already been resolved about 100 years ago. In America, for example, it is obvious that a student is a person. Generally speaking, this is not a problematic notion in Western, democratic countries, where every person is respected and each person's value is regarded as important...but here in China it is not so self-evident. On the one hand, we idolize scientific technology and industrialization because we are still a developing country ourselves. We believe that if only we achieve development, we will be able to solve all our other problems. On the other hand, China's centralized political system does not regard every person as a subject (*zhuti*). This is especially true when dealing with people of low social status, poor people, or children.... Chinese children have long been treated...merely as means to get ahead in society and not as "persons" in the full sense of the word.

The notion of treating students as subjects, added Professor Chen, signifies an important departure from previous Chinese thinking about the nature of the education process. Maoist-era pedagogues, he noted, accorded teachers the role of "subjects" while students received the passive role of "objects." Children were thought "to lack consciousness of themselves (*ziji de yishi*)" and were therefore considered "products" to be worked rather than autonomous persons. China's contemporary school reforms, Professor Chen told me, constitute a welcome attempt to align local views of children and personhood with those which exist in "more developed, demo-cratic nations."

Reflecting the continual fascination of modern Chinese intellectu-als with children as "a class of social inferiors" (Chow, 1995: 114), Professor Chen's remarks further exemplify the tendency of contem-porary liberal thinkers in China to promote human rights as a form of legal and political modernization based on "a fantasy about the modern/liberal/capitalist West" (see also Kennedy, 2004: 20). Yet Professor Chen's critique of authoritarian modes of governing chil-dren is also notable in that it represents a prominent strain of thought in China's contemporary education literature. Within this strain of thinking, the development of children's strong self-consciousness, self-respect, and a spirit of freedom may ultimately lead to the emergence of a liberal political system in China (Kipnis, 2011: 72–3).

To my surprise, the Communist Party Secretary at Shanghai's Whitewater Primary School expressed a similar view. A bubbly young woman with a taste for miniskirts (rather than the grim-looking commissar her title might have suggested), Ms. Qu described how in the past, the "ideal student" was "obedient, disciplined (*tinghua*), and respectful of his/her elders and seniors." However, this sort of attitude was not as desirable in present-day China, she said, adding that in "a modern, advanced" society, "students do not have to agree with everything their teachers say" but rather—"have a right (*quanli*) to their own opinions." This message also appeared in the textbooks Shanghai's primary school children are studying.

In a 2001 "Society" (*Shehui*) textbook taught in Whitewater Primary School at the time I conducted my fieldwork, fifth-grade students read not only about the history of the Chinese Communist Party, the Chinese military, or the "socialist features of China's economic system," but also about the country's legal system, including its Law on the Protection of Minors (*Weichengnianren baohu fa*), "designed by the country's experts in order to safeguard [minors'] rights and interests (*quanyi*)." The book emphasizes that parents and teachers must abide by the law and avoid "any act that humiliates (*wuru*)" the child. It also urges children to become familiar with the laws designed for their protection (*Shehui, wu nianji diyi xueqi*, 2001: 119–23). Similar exhortations are evident in the Chinese government's public campaign on the topic of children's rights. Significantly then, both the textbook and media campaign attempt to teach adults and children in China that youngsters are not merely weak social persons who require protection but empowered agents who can actively safeguard their personal interests by drawing on the law.

A more recent, experimental edition of the same textbook, published in Shanghai under the new title "Morality and Society" (*Pinde yu Shehui*), allots an even larger amount of space to the issue of children's rights. Moreover, it highlights the link between the empowerment of contemporary Chinese children via legal means and the emergence of the global discourse on the rights of the child, as illustrated by the promulgation of the 1989 UNCRC. The textbook explains that "like other international conventions, the contents of the UNCRC derive from a global consensus" and signify an attempt to establish a "new international order" which would ensure children's protection worldwide. What children need to be protected from is made clear, too. Fifth-graders in Shanghai read about deplorable phenomena such as child-soldiers, street children, and child laborers which the UNCRC attempts to prevent. They also hear that they have "a right to participate in family and social activities and make suggestions in relation to these activities," and that parents cannot simply dismiss their opinions on the grounds that "little children should not interfere in adults' business." For their homework assignment, Shanghai fifth-graders are asked to list the rights they currently possess and to contemplate whether these rights are actually respected or violated (*Pinde yu Shehui*, 2007: 67).

Teachers and school staff at both the Affiliated and Whitewater Primary Schools in Shanghai echoed these messages by emphasizing the importance of listening to students' views and opinions. "We need to believe in students," argued Ms Feng, a young animated Math and Class teacher at Whitewater Primary School. "We shouldn't say: 'A child is small, so he's probably wrong. He doesn't understand.'"

Ms Pan, 31, and the assistant to the principal at the Affiliated School, likewise stated that teachers at her school are encouraged "to consider problems not only from their point of view but also from their students' perspectives."

"Children may be small," said another teacher at the same school, "but they already have ideas of their own...and you can reason with them." Observations at both schools revealed that these were not mere slogans. In many of the classes I attended, teachers, particularly those in their twenties or early thirties, did in fact encourage students to ask questions, make suggestions and debate different solutions to a given problem instead of simply providing the textbook answer as would have been required of them in the past.

On some occasions, children were even asked to evaluate their peers' work, a measure which according to current academic literature in China would do much to encourage their ability to form independent judgments and assume responsibility for the learning process from an early age (see for example, Zhao Shiping, 2002:

180). Some teachers, especially those in their twenties, followed the current recommendation that they kneel down when speaking to individual children in order to address them from their own level rather than from a position of power.

Despite these features which, I was told, were mostly introduced after the launch of Shanghai's current phase of school reforms, in the early 2000s, I could not help but notice that in a majority of lessons, students seldom directly challenged their teachers or questioned their textbooks. That is perhaps not surprising considering that some teachers, particularly those in their mid-30s to mid-40s, still made it a point to criticize those students who had failed to follow the prescribed guidelines. In one Crafts lesson at the Affiliated Primary School, for example, second-graders were asked to make 3D glasses from cardboard and cellophane paper. The children were following directions shown in an experimental textbook, which had been introduced to a number of Shanghai schools with the goal of fostering independent, imaginative thinking among students.

As was often the case in "non-academic" lessons, such as Art or Crafts, the class atmosphere was relatively light and relaxed: while some students were sitting on the back of their chairs, others were dangling their feet, humming to themselves or conversing with each other freely. I was surprised then when, toward the end of the lesson, the teacher—a man in his mid-40s—began to approach various students and audibly evaluate their work as either "pretty" (*haokan*) or "ugly" (*bu haokan*). One boy, seated not far from where I was situated, had decorated his glasses in a distinct way that did not quite match the model shown in the textbook. Obviously proud of his creation, the boy raised his hand and asked the teacher to take a look at it. Briefly examining the student's handiwork, the teacher clearly looked displeased. Offering the boy no words of praise, he merely put the glasses back on the desk and walked away with a disapproving frown. Minutes later, he approached the desk of another student, a timid-looking girl who, despite repeated attempts, had encountered some trouble putting her glasses together. Briefly examining her work, the teacher sternly reproached the girl for "not doing it right" and then proceeded to tear the glasses apart in front of her and her classmates.

While this teacher seemed to treat students of both genders in an equally harsh manner, conversations with other teachers revealed a gender bias when it came to the issue of allowing students to express their own views and wishes. Several of the mostly female middle-aged teachers with whom I spoke agreed that it was "quite important to allow children to voice their ideas in the classroom," but added that it was *especially* crucial in the case of boys. When I asked why, 37-year-old Teacher Gong reflected:

> These days, many [boys] are quite fragile (*cuiruo*) because most of them are only-children and everyone in their families spoils them. Not only that, but it is mainly mothers who take care of children. Men don't participate so much in raising children nowadays...so boys are becoming more and more like girls. When they come across all sorts of problems at school, they have no idea what to do and will often start crying. That's not good at all.

Her 35-year-old colleague, Teacher Fong agreed, adding that these days "there are so many female teachers at the primary school level" that there is "a real danger that boys will grow up to be *too gentle and soft* (*wenrou*)."[7] Since the shift to a market economy, the competition over jobs has become quite fierce, she continued. Therefore, it is particularly important to teach boys how to "toughen up" and help them develop assertiveness and independence.

As these anecdotes and statements reveal, Shanghai primary school teachers held complex views regarding the notion of children's rights. The youngest cohort of teachers, those born and educated after 1978, generally acknowledged the principle of "treating students as subjects" and even attempted to implement it in their classroom practices. In contrast, teachers who were born in the mid-1960s to early-1970s and who had received at least part of their formal education before the beginning of the reform period, were more likely to express a different attitude. They sometimes professed an educational worldview and implemented teaching practices which did not quite match the idea that children are autonomous persons with a right to their own views. Remarks concerning the perceived differences between male and female students also reveal that, in the minds of at least some educators, the principle of children as independent persons was not necessarily applicable to all students. In short, teachers' generational *habitus* was a decisive factor in determining their views of the child-rights discourse; for Shanghai parents, class aspirations and social *habitus* played an equally important role.

Creating a democratic family environment

"Respect for children," suggests a 2004 article published on the Chinese Internet website, *Baba Mama Wang* [Mom and Dad's Network], should start before they reach school, ideally "from the day they are born." Before parents change the baby's diaper, for instance, they "should explain what they are about to do, apologize to the baby, and ask him/her to be patient."

Such advice may seem a bit extreme, but academic publications, mass media reports and popular childrearing guides published in China in the past decade or so have been echoing recommendations that parents respect children's rights, allow them to voice their opinions, and treat these opinions with consideration (Fu Daoqun, 2002; Hu Shen, 2000; Wang Shuguang, 2004).

This approach was becoming rather popular among the well-educated Shanghai parents I met. An accountant married to a university professor told me, for instance, that she and her husband "believed that a child has his own ideas and views" and therefore parents must not impose their will on him.

"My husband says that this is what parents in America do," she added.

Asked what sort of relationship she wanted with her child, Ms Bo, a 33-year-old suburban homemaker with a high-school education, was clear.

"A friendly one (*gen pengyou yiyang*)," she told me, as she waited to meet with her son's teacher on Parents' Day.

"Can you give me an example?" I asked.

"Well, I let him make all sorts of decisions on his own," she explained after a moment's thought.

"What kind of decisions?" I persisted.

This time, she did not reply. Instead, she turned to her son, who was standing nearby, and asked him what *he* thought. Could he give me an example of the sort of decisions he makes on his own? Pausing for a second, the boy, a shy-looking 10-year-old, regained his courage and explained that since he liked "sports," his mom let him "choose sports lessons as an after-school activity."

These statements matched the recommendations of teachers' manuals, childrearing guides, and Chinese parenting magazines which suggest that caregivers create a "democratic family environment." Some of these experts recommend, for instance, holding regular family meetings in which children as young as 6 or 7 can participate, and which—according to one publication—would "help the child prepare for the future exercise of his/her democratic rights (*minzhu quanli*)" (Yan and Li, 2001: 12; Tang Hong, 2005: 25–7; *Xiaoxuesheng xinli suzhi peiyang: Si nianji jiaoshi yongshu*, 2000: 31–3). Many of the well-educated, high-earning Shanghai mothers I met with did in fact report that they let their school-age children make decisions on various issues, including which clothes to wear; what they liked to eat for dinner; which books to read and television shows to watch; and in some cases, how to spend their allowance. Several mothers even stated that they and their husbands were in the habit of consulting with their child on issues that affected the household at large.

One afternoon, I visited the home of a well-educated, 45-year-old office worker at a Shanghai finance company. Married to a successful entrepreneur, Ms Gui and her husband lived in a new, upscale apartment complex located in Xuhui district, a relatively upper-class residential neighborhood in downtown Shanghai and home to many foreign consulates. Our interview took place in a spacious living room in the presence of the couple's live-in domestic helper (*a-yi*), who was busy polishing furniture that to me looked spotless.

Well-spoken and forthcoming, Ms Gui told me that she believed parents should trust their child's judgment and not try to control everything he does. Until recently, she added, she and her husband had made all the decisions for their 11-year-old son, but "now that he is older," they "discuss all sort of things with him and respect his wishes," even if these contradict his parents' will. Before she and her husband had purchased their current apartment, she told me, they consulted their son and asked for his opinion, making sure he liked the place as much as they did.[8]

Ms Zhong, a middle-aged book editor, went as far as signing a "contract" (*xieyi*) which summarized her child's entitlements and responsibilities. The terms of the contract were decided through a consultation between the child, her husband, and herself when the boy first entered primary school. The child's duties included doing his homework, arranging his schoolbag, and dressing himself. Rewards in the form of a monthly allowance if he performed these tasks in a satisfactory manner were also listed. Impressed by this systematic record keeping, I asked Ms Zhong how she came up with the idea of signing a pact with her child.

"Well," she told me, "my husband and I had read about this particular method in a parenting magazine and thought it might be a good way to teach our son how to become more independent and self-reliant."

"You see, in China," she continued, "mothers often do things for their children, for example, homework assignments or arranging the schoolbag, but I think that this is my son's business, not mine."

Family contracts (*jiating xieyi*) like the one signed by Ms Zhong and her son were apparently becoming increasingly fashionable. Indeed, they even served as the subject of an episode on the popular CCTV talk show, "*Shi hua shi shuo*" ["Tell it like it is"] which aired in the 2000s. While the host doubted the ability of small children to grasp the meaning of a legal contract, a psychologist invited to the studio endorsed this "innovative" method of setting house rules, while criticizing "traditional" childrearing practices for dictating that "parents manage (*guan*) their children's affairs until they [themselves] have children of their own." One of the show's guests, who had signed an agreement with her 7-year-old son, assured the television audience that the contract had not only improved her relationship with her child, but also increased the boy's confidence and independence, qualities which she noted "were seriously lacking in many contemporary only children" in China (*Shi hua shi shuo*, 2001). A few of the Shanghai mothers I spoke with—especially those who had a son—agreed. They emphasized the importance of fostering self-confidence and independence among boys, since, as one woman explained: "Society is quite cruel these days, so it's best that boys learn how to face difficult situations from an early age."[9]

Children's empowerment and the quality of the nation

Concern for an apparent lack of independence among contemporary Chinese singletons (of both genders) was apparent in the childrearing guides, media articles, and academic publications cited earlier. Some of these publications not only encouraged parents to allow children to express their wishes, but also warned them against over-indulging their only child by doing everything for him or her, including, for instance, "tying the child's shoelaces or feeding her long after he or she is quite capable of accomplishing these tasks on his/her own" (Zhao Shiping, 2002: 182–3).

During my own fieldwork in Shanghai I frequently saw examples of excessive doting. At the end of each school day, for instance, scores of parents and, in some cases elderly grandparents, would wait outside the gate for their children. Once a child was in sight, those waiting would rush to his or her side, grab the child's school bag, and mount it on their own backs. Parents and grandparents would then turn away, continuing to carry the young learner's burden while the child in question was hopping happily by their side. This applied not only to 6- or 7-year-olds who may have been too frail to carry a school bag filled with books, but also with older students more capable than their grandparents of carrying a school-bag. Daily observations outside a middle school adjacent to my Shanghai apartment revealed that parents and grandparents of more robust 13- and 14-year-olds behaved in a similar manner.

Lamenting such practices, contemporary media and academic writers in China recommend that instead of "guarding the child's every move," as dictated by "traditional" childrearing practices, parents should encourage the child to exercise his/her autonomy. Not only should they allow their children to tie their own shoelaces or carry their school bags, they should also allow them to arrange their own after-school schedules. The result, promise these contemporary publications, would be a child better able to "manage his/herself (*zi li*)" both now and in the future (see for example, Chen Peiling, 2004; Cui Yutao, 2005: 40; Zhao Yanyan, 2002: 170–3).

The perceived inability of contemporary Chinese children to act for themselves was a cause for concern to many of the Shanghai educators I met. Ms Huang, a 35-year-old arts teacher at Shanghai's Whitewater Primary School, complained:

> These days, everything revolves around the child (*weizhe haizi zhuan*). I don't know if you have noticed this or not, but many parents and grandparents now walk the child right up to the

school entrance and also wait outside the gate at the end of the school day.... Why, some even help their grandchildren clean the classroom after school![10] No wonder children today can't do things by themselves!"

Ms Hu, a Chinese and Moral Education teacher at Whitewater Primary School, agreed: "Our children work very hard at their studies, but lack ability to do things on their own or take care of themselves. They find it hard to handle even simple life-skills tasks... If parents aren't at home, for instance, children often go hungry because they don't know how to prepare a meal on their own!"[11] One of my youngest school informers, 24-year-old Teacher Wang, further commented on Chinese children's lack of independent thinking. Recalling her own childhood at a "model" primary school, "foreign dignitaries" who visited the school would often ask the children what they "wanted to study." The question baffled Wang and her classmates.

"We didn't understand what they meant," she told me with an embarrassed smile, "so we simply answered: 'We want to study whatever the teacher teaches us!'"

It is precisely this sort of passive attitude and inability to think for oneself, she and other young teachers reiterated, which places so many contemporary Chinese students at a disadvantage. "We Chinese are good at copying things," mourned many of my school informants, but "fall behind countries such as America, Japan, and South Korea when it comes to showing creativity and innovation." The responsibility, they admitted, was partly theirs. China's education system has long been "exam-oriented" with a focus on selecting outstanding students through the testing of "book knowledge." Unfortunately, the result has been the phenomenon of "high grades, low ability" (*gao fen di neng*).

"If we want more Chinese to win Nobel Prizes," reasoned my interlocutors without noting the irony, "we must transform our education system by borrowing and learning from others."[12]

Concerns about Chinese children's deficiencies in independent thinking and action were also apparent in contemporary guidebooks comparing local educational practices to those thought to exist in other countries, particularly in the United States. One of the best selling works in this genre, *Suzhi jiaoyu zai Meiguo* [Education for

Quality in the U.S.], criticizes Chinese education for its emphasis on respect for authority while praising American pedagogies for emphasizing the ability of children "to recognize and express their own needs and desires." American attitudes, suggests the author, educational consultant Huang Quanyu, contribute to the production of "confident," "entrepreneurial" subjects who possess an increased ability to creatively express themselves (cited in Woronov, 2007: 40–3). In a similar work, educator Shen Ning contrasts what he describes as "outdated" Chinese concepts concerning the "limited rational capacities of children" with "American notions of childhood," which deem that even young children possess the ability to make judgments in matters concerning them. Chinese parents and teachers are well advised to adopt such a stance, argues the author, not only because it is more "scientifically correct," but also because China's shift to a market economy requires workers to exhibit qualities such as "independence," "individuality," and "self-awareness" (cited in Hu Shen, 2000: 154).

As these examples reveal, Chinese official, academic and media conceptualizations of children and their rights abound with contradictions. The calls to allow Chinese children to display independence and initiative both at home and at school at times merge with an instrumentalist discourse concerned with the production of "self-regulating" workers and consumers needed to fuel market growth. Alongside a humanistic discourse that seeks to liberate and empower the individual child sits a more collectivist strain of thinking which connects the interests of the young to those of the nation. These contradictions are equally evident in the views of educators, school staff, and parents in Shanghai. Some informants viewed the idea that children have a right to voice their opinions as a pre-condition for the fostering of competitive and enterprising workers and consumers who would be successfully integrated into the global market economy. Others regarded the empowerment of children as a means to counter the conceived weakness of character among contemporary urban only-children, especially boys. Still others maintained that allowing children more freedom to make choices and decisions in matters concerning them is an important component in the creation of a new type of a "modern" citizen, one who is aware of his/her rights under the law and who can assert these rights when these are violated.

Concluding remarks

China's ratification of the UNCRC in 1991 and the subsequent intro-duction of child-specific legislation at the national and local levels attest to the growing influence of a global discourse of children's rights in a country which, in the past few decades, has increasingly subscribed to the logic of market capitalism but which still retains its authoritarian regime. This chapter has argued that the proliferation of this globally-inspired "rights talk" in PRC legislation, academic works, pedagogic materials, and media publications reflect a substan-tial shift in Chinese official and popular conceptualizations not only of children, but also of citizenship and subjectivity.

It is certainly true that in China the notion of children's rights, and in particular the idea that children constitute autonomous indi-viduals, is subject to capture by the government's on-going project of "raising the quality of the population" or of building a strong, prosperous nation through the production of enterprising, self-governing citizens. As this chapter has shown, however, it is also the case that the Chinese child-rights discourse provides educators and caregivers with a new lexicon for speaking and thinking about youngsters and their entitlements. Drawing inspiration from the modern, worldwide movement of children's rights, the Chinese dis-cussion of children's rights seeks to recast the young in the role of autonomous persons with an ability to make judgments, voice their opinions, and enter into rational contracts with those around them. It attempts to constitute Chinese children "as competent people" who are "encouraged and enabled to participate in society, to act as citizens in the here and now" (James, 2011: 171). As such, it also inscribes a liberal, individualistic logic of conduct and lays the ground for a reconceptualization of the adult-child relationship as well as the relationships between citizens and the state in China.

This chapter has further shown that in Shanghai schools, it is par-ticularly the youngest cohort of teachers who embrace this indi-vidualistic view of the child and the person, and who enthusiastically employ novel techniques designed to encourage students to display independent thinking and become actively involved in the learning process. The willingness of young teachers to take up the notion of children's rights may reflect the particular characteristics of their generation. Previous studies have observed that members of the post-1980s generation in China (the *balinghou*, as they are called) are generally marked by the "pursuit of freedom, choice, and self-interest" (Kleinmen *et al.*, 2011: 9; see also Hoffman, 2010; Rosen, 2009). My work among Shanghai teachers largely confirms this observation. It shows that informants who were born in the mid-1970s or later and who, for the most part, received their education after the introduction of reforms in 1978, tended to embrace a more liberal, individualistic notion of the child and the person. Teachers' support for the idea that children's views should be respected both inside and outside the classroom may also reflect their common professional socialization. Many of the younger teachers I met with have been taught and continue to receive training from professors and teacher-trainers who had spent time in foreign universities. In the past three decades or so, sending students and scholars abroad "to seek modern knowledge" has become not only permissible but also somewhat of a national policy in China (see Ye and Ma, 2005: xxi). While some scholars have stayed on and settled in their host countries, others have chosen to return, bringing with them global ways of thinking, including the idea of children's rights, which they deem more appropriate for a society that wishes to become "modern" and "civilized" (see Naftali, 2008).

Well-educated and relatively wealthy Shanghai parents likewise showed consideration toward children's views and wishes in small and large matters, and tended to grant youngsters much power in family decision-making. Noting the growing power of only children within the contemporary urban Chinese family, many scholars (for example, Croll, 2006; Davis and Sensenbrenner, 2000; Fong, 2004b; Goh, 2011; Lozada, 2000; Milwertz, 1997; Rosen, 2004) have suggested that this development is mainly a product of the government's One-Child Policy, which in a period of merely three decades, has made Chinese children into "precious commodities" of the sort found in Western, capitalist societies of the modern era (Zelizer, 1985).

While I do not seek to challenge this important thesis, the findings of the present chapter nonetheless suggest that if we are to truly understand the roots of Chinese children's recent empowerment within the urban family, we must pay attention not only to the role of demographic changes but also to the way in which these changes intersect with current transformations in public and popular conceptualizations of childhood and personhood. In other words, we must consider how the increasing usage of the language of rights in regards to children in China sharpens "the moral boundaries which separate people" and emphasizes the appropriateness of seeing other persons, adults and children alike, "as independent and autonomous agents" (Schoeman, 1980: 8). This distinction between individuals is equally evident in the idea that children are not only free to voice their own opinions but also have a right to self-ownership over their bodies and personal possessions. As the next chapter will reveal, the notion that children have a right to privacy and to protection from physical violence is the product of both material transformations and the growing influence of modern, liberal ideologies in post-socialist China, especially among the post-1980s generation and the rising urban middle classes.

2
Children's Right to Self-Ownership: Space, Privacy, and Punishment

"When we were parents, children usually wanted what you wanted," one Shanghai grandmother told me after an afternoon dance class at a local pensioners' club. To vigorous nods of approval from her classmates, some of whom were still busy collecting their breaths after dancing across the room for the last hour or so, she continued to describe the differences between contemporary and Maoist-era ideas of childrearing and education. "Back then [i.e., in the 1960s and 1970s], children were more disciplined and agreed with you on everything... But these days, kids are smarter. They have a broader awareness... [They] know that adults can't go through their drawers or look in their schoolbags without permission."

The remarks of this Shanghai grandmother, a retired school principal now in her late sixties, reflect the common sentiment that in present-day urban China, the parent-child relationship is dramatically different to what it had been merely two or three decades ago. More specifically, her observations also point to a substantial shift in Chinese conceptualizations of children's right to self-ownership and in popular beliefs concerning the ability of youngsters to express their will in relation to their body, to other things, and to other people.

Modern notions of privacy and self-ownership have their roots in respect for the dignity and integrity of the person (Boling, 1996; Benn, 1984; Moore, 1984; Westin, 1984). In Western legal formulations, these notions play a particularly important role in fostering equality, political freedom, and individual autonomy (Yan Yunxiang, 2003: 135). When applied to children, the notion of self-ownership can translate into the presumption that parents and educators do not have the right "to access the private world" of children without permission (or worse, without the child's knowledge), an act that would deny the child "a separate identity" (Flekkoy and Kaufman, 1997: 39–40). By extension, the modern, liberal notion of children's right to self-ownership may also imply a ban on corporal punishment in school or at home since the use of violence as a disciplinary tool encroaches upon the child's right to "control access" to one's body which in turn is central to the protection of the child's "human dignity, moral autonomy, and the notion that one belongs to oneself" (Boling, 1996: 30).

Drawing on these theoretical understandings, this chapter describes the social construction of children's right to self-ownership in China in the sense of protection of access to a child's personal space, including one's own room or other space perceived as being under the child's control; protection of access to information about the child (through a diary or personal correspondence, for example); and protection against bodily intrusion, which might include various forms of physical violence (Flekkoy and Kaufman, 1997: 39–40). I examine how legal, academic, educational, and media publications in contemporary China have been promoting these various meanings of self-ownership in regards to children; and further explore how Shanghai teachers and caregivers currently engage with the notion that children are entitled to privacy and to protection from physical violence at school and at home. My work in Shanghai schools and homes documents the rising popularity of the idea that children have a right to self-ownership in both a psychological and a physical sense. This change is in turn crucial to the broader development of new notions of privacy and individuality in post-socialist, urban China.

Recent studies suggest there is a well-established tradition of private property and privacy values in China (McDougall, 2005: 98; see also McDougall and Hansson, 2002; Wang Hao, 2011). However, scholars are also in agreement that up until the early twentieth century, and to some extent, even beyond this point, privacy in China "was not a legal right but a flexible privilege, the boundary of which varied according to one's social status in specific contexts" (Yan Yunxiang, 2003: 137; see also Zarrow, 2002; Wang Hao, 2011). Being social inferiors, Chinese children, in particular, enjoyed very little privacy in late imperial Chinese society.

The status of Chinese children within the family and society experienced a dramatic rise in the course of the twentieth century but the idea that youngsters have a right to self-ownership nonetheless remained highly ambiguous. In the first three decades of socialist rule, the concept of "privacy" and its various connotations were overwhelmingly negative, and the domain of the private was generally used as one of the many labels to denigrate those guilty of the "selfish individualism" of bourgeois society (McDougall, 2005: 98; Evans, 2008: 103). In the realm of childcare, this negative attitude translated into a rejection of the notion that children were the private property of their families in favor of the idea that youngsters belonged to the state and to the "revolutionary masses."

The economic reforms introduced to China in 1978 have, in contrast, led to the "reemergence of the realm of the private" (Hershatter, 2004: 313; Schell and Shambaugh, 1999: 261; see also Ong and Zhang, 2008; Yan Yunxiang, 2011; Wang Hao, 2011). As a result of the intensification of market reforms and the reduction and elimination of socialist-era welfare provisions, particularly since the 1990s, Chinese citizens are increasingly called upon to stop 'relying on the state' (*kao guojia*) and start 'relying on yourself' (*kao ziji*)" (Ong and Zhang, 2008: 8; Anagnost, 2008b: 59; Woronov, 2007: 30). The promotion of the household as a locus for consumption and the official endorsement of private enterprise and private property in constitutional amendments and in the new civil code of 2002 likewise indicate the renewed legitimacy of the private domain in the eyes of the Chinese government. Correspondingly, Chinese popular culture of the post-socialist era has been celebrating intimate life, and a wide range of activities is increasingly accepted in China as "private, and desirably private, to individuals or families" (McDougall, 2005: 112; see also Rofel, 2007).

The promotion of *children's* right to privacy is, I suggest, an extension of this broader development and may in fact indicate the deepening awareness of the idea of self-ownership in contemporary urban Chinese society. As we shall see, in the past two decades or so, government, academic, and media publications in China have been promoting the idea that even the youngest members of society are entitled to a personal space, in both a psychological and a physical sense. They further recommend that adults refrain from the use of violence against children and instead exercise a mode of restraint or "civilization" in their dealings with youngsters. In so doing, government officials, academics, and media writers in China seek to re-draw the current boundaries between the old and the young. In the process, they also aim to impose a higher degree of self-regulation and self-control on both adults and children—a demand that has characterized the formation of the urban middle classes in modern, industrial societies elsewhere in the world (Elias, 1998: 191, 209).

In this respect then, the emergent notion of children's right to self-ownership in post-socialist urban China may be seen as part of a broader drive to produce a new type of modern neoliberal, middle-class citizen, one who is capable of and willing to contribute to the building of society, which includes the task of building up the subject itself (Hultqvist, 1998; Rose, 1989; Walkerdine, 2005). In China as elsewhere, however, privacy and self-ownership are also attributes of power, as "those in powerful positions hide their private affairs from public view while at the same time depriving the less privileged of rights" to privacy (McDougall, 2005: 109). Drawing on this crucial observation, this chapter further suggests that the enhanced ability of urban Chinese youngsters to control access to their bodies and their personal possessions at school or at home enhances their present—and perhaps also their future—capacity to resist acts of violence or any other infringement of their interests by those in authority.

Children and privacy in Chinese modernity

Children's privacy within society and the family is a distinctively modern phenomenon. In pre-modern societies, for instance, "only the very rich could manage to give children their own beds," and in general, people did not think of isolating youngsters from adults by reserving their own room for them (Elias, 1998: 197; see also Ariès, 1962). The development of a new concept of childhood in modern Europe was demonstrated, among other things, by the appearance of children's private rooms. Notably, this transformation of the domestic space was part of a broader process of a "privatization of life" (Habermas, 1991: 44–5). Within this process, "the solitarization of the family members even within the house was held to be a sign of distinction" among middle-class European families. It further cor-responded with the increasing autonomy of private people within a newly reconfigured public sphere—an autonomy that was "founded on a right to property and...realized in the participation in a market economy" (Habermas, 1991: 44–5).

Unlike western, post-Enlightenment concepts of the private sphere, in late imperial Chinese usage, the term 'private' (*si*) generally harbored negative connotations, associated with "selfishness," "the ignoble" and "immoral desires" (Zarrow, 2002: 121; see also Wang Hao, 2011). In traditional Chinese homes, rooms often lacked doors, and "parents had absolute rights to enter their children's private space" (Dutton, 1998: 210). This domestic design reflected the notion that the unit of privacy was not the individual but the lineage and clan (McDougall, 2002: 6; Tang and Dong, 2006: 288). As the youngest members of their extended kinship group, children were more likely to be conceived of as the private property of the patrilineage than as autonomous individuals entitled to a private space of their own (Kinney, 1995b; Bray, 1997; Waltner, 1995). Moreover, individual privacy existed in a strictly hierarchical context. In the traditional parent-child relationship, a parent—the dominant party of the dyad—could acquire the information he/she wanted from the child, but the reversal was considered an offence (Yan Yunxiang, 2003: 137; Chan Ying-Keung, 2000: 5).

In the early decades of the twentieth century, Chinese notions of family, childhood, and privacy began to undergo a significant transformation. In the reformist, modernizing discourse of the May Fourth period (1915–21), the notion of "private" acquired a positive association and became increasingly attached to the individual and to the nuclear family (Glosser, 2003). As noted, early twentieth-century Chinese reformers also promoted the idea that children constitute a distinct social group which must be allowed to assert its separate existence and private wishes in relation to parents and the extended family (Anagnost, 1997a; Farquhar Mary Ann, 1999; Jones, 2002; Pease, 1995).

After 1949, Maoist-era rhetoric continued to emphasize the autonomy of the young, as well as the special role of children as successors to the socialist revolution (Donald, 1999; Farquhar Mary Ann, 1999). At the same time, this period witnessed sustained attack on the notion of individual as well as family privacy. In the new socialist society, there was no room for the "absurd and barbaric notion" that a child constitutes "the private property (*sichan*) of his/her parents," explained a 1955 article in the CCP's mouthpiece, the People's Daily [*Renmin ribao*]. Rather, parents had to recognize that "from the time a child lets out its first cry coming into this world, he/she has already become a future citizen of the socialist state" (Xiao, 1955: 3).[1] This recasting of children as "assets of the whole society" (Sheng *et al.*, 1989: 427) can be seen as part of the period's ban on private property and the general abhorrence for the cultivation of personal desires, including the desire for personal space (Ong and Zhang, 2008: 6; Hershatter, 2004: 311).

Few children in post-1949 China could say that they possessed a room of their own. In the cities, this state of affairs was also due to material shortages and the scarcity of housing. In Shanghai of the 1980s, for instance, the average living space per urban resident was approximately six square meters (Davis, 1993: 56). Until the 1990s, urban Chinese families, many consisting of three generations, resided in government housing where they had to share a kitchen and bathroom with several other households (Lu, 2000: 134).

The past few decades have seen a dramatic change in Chinese evaluations of privacy and, particularly since the late 1990s, also in adults' and children's ability to achieve it. Increasing privatization of the housing market, growing household incomes, the rise of consumerism, and the reduction in family size due to the effects of the government's population policy, have enabled a growing number of urban families to purchase their own, more spacious apartments. Many families have also been able to renovate their existing residence by separating adjoining households and by reconfiguring interior spaces in order to provide themselves—and their children—with more privacy (Davis, 2000: 3; Lu, 2000: 134).[2]

"Each person has his own piece of the sky"

In practically every Shanghai residence I visited in 2004–5, children had a room of their own. Notably, most of these homes belonged to parents of means, yet even in the case of less affluent families, the importance of giving children their own space was evident in parents' views and practices. Ms Tan, a rural migrant with only a primary school education, lived with her husband and youngest child in the small area above their family store which was located on a relatively noisy street. Her eldest child, a lower-middle school student, had been left in the care of her paternal grandparents back in the countryside. Despite their meager resources, Ms Tan made a point of telling me that she and her husband had recently managed to rent a room for their younger, 11-year-old son, where the boy, she said, could "study in peace" without being interrupted by either his parents or the shop's customers.

Consideration for children's privacy can be seen not only in the allocation of a separate space, but also in the importance of allowing children to exercise independent judgment regarding this space and their personal belongings. In a recent discussion on perceptions of privacy in present-day China, legal scholar Wang Hao notes in passing that due to a genuine wish to protect children, Chinese parents generally believe that youngsters should keep no secrets from them. Many see no fault with reading their children's diary or entering their room without permission. Wang also observes, however, that in contemporary China and particularly in urban areas, children have started to protest these parental practices, and increasingly demand to "live in their own world" (2011: 42).

A recent academic survey conducted among more than 300 Shanghai junior and senior high-school students and their parents reveals that urban caregivers are beginning to heed these calls and to change their view towards children's privacy. It shows for instance that parents to children aged 13–16 express relatively high levels of support for the notion that they should "knock before entering children's rooms" or "search children's rooms, backpacks, or purses" (Tang and Dong, 2006: 291). Significantly, my own ethnographic study among Shanghai parents to primary school students reveals a similar finding even in regards to younger children, aged 6–12.

This is particularly true in the case of well-educated professionals. A middle-aged office administrator and university graduate told me, for instance, that she and her husband were careful not to touch their 12-year-old son's belongings without his permission. An editor with a doctoral degree similarly explained that her nine-year-old son was "solely responsible for his room, his toys, and his books," and emphasized that neither she nor her husband could enter his room and move his stuff without the child's authorization.

The idea that children require a space of their own was prevalent in the child-rearing literature these well-educated mothers reported reading. The 2001 parenting guide, *Raising a Happy, Healthy Child*, emphasizes, for instance, that caregivers must respect the child's "integral rights as an individual," including her "right to privacy (*yinsi*)," and to "a free, personal space (*ziji de ziyou kongjian*)" (Yan and Li, 2001: 96–8). Describing privacy as a developmental need necessary for the formation of independence and responsibility in the child, the authors recommended that caregivers make every effort to create a separate space for their son or daughter, preferably by allowing them to have their own room. If that is not possible, they should give the child a personal corner, a desk drawer, "or even a box." Regardless of the size and location of this space, children should be allowed to decorate it as they see fit and place whatever "secret," personal object in it they wish. Parents and other family members need to respect the privacy of the child's space and take care not to invade it in any way, emphasize the authors. They "must knock before entering their son or daughter's room" and they should "always seek permission before touching or using the child's belongings" (Yan and Li, 2001: 96–8).

Significantly, the idea that although a child may be young, he or she is already a "free individual" (*ziyou de geti*) who requires "a personal space of his/her own (*geren kongjian*)" (*Baba mama wang*, 2004), has also found its expression in government literature. Official pronouncements, legislative codes, and school textbooks introduced to Shanghai schools over the past two decades all emphasize the importance of a child's privacy. China's 1992 Law on the Protection of Minors uses language similar to that of Article 16 of the 1989 UN Convention on the Rights of the Child (UNCRC), which prohibits "arbitrary or unlawful interference with a child's privacy...or correspondence." (UNICEF, 2007). The PRC Law on the Protection of Minors strictly bans any "organization or individual" from disclosing the personal secrets of children and from opening, concealing, or destroying the mail of any minor (All-China Women's Federation, 2006). Local legislation measures, such as Shanghai's 2004 Municipal Regulations on the Protection of Minors, similarly emphasize the importance of protecting access to personal information about children.

These legal prescriptions have been accompanied by a number of educational measures. According to a PRC government report submitted to the UN Committee on the Rights of the Child in 2003, authorities in China have been trying to ensure that information on a child's physical or mental health remains confidential. They have also forbidden Chinese teachers and schools "to disclose information on a child's academic performance to anyone but the child or his parents"; and have instructed parents that children's diaries "are not to be read without their consent" (United Nations Committee on the Rights of the Child, 2005a: 5).

Even the state-run media has become involved, popularizing the notion that children need their privacy. An article published in the CCP mouthpiece, the People's Daily, two years after the introduction of the 1992 Law on the Protection of Minors, declares that in order to establish a "modern, civilized (*xiandai wenming*)" parent-child relationship, suitable for an advanced industrial society, Chinese parents must refrain from such "backwards" practices as "peeping into their child's diary" or "eavesdropping on his/her phone conversations" (Li Yixian, 1992). More than a decade later, school textbooks in Shanghai repeated this notion. At the beginning of the fifth-grade lesson on "Children's Rights," the city's students were told about Lingling, a fifth-grader who liked to write a diary:

> Every day, after she got back from school and finished her homework, she would sit quietly at her desk and write about personal issues in her diary. To Lingling, this diary was her small personal secret. One day, she accidentally discovered that her mother touched her diary. She asked her mother: "Why did you look in my diary?" and told her: "What you did violates my right to privacy (*yinsi quan*)." Her mother disagreed by saying: "you're so young, what right to privacy do you have?" She then added: "I'm your mother. Why can't I look in your diary?" As a result, the mother and daughter were both angry at each other.

The authors of the textbook ask the students for their thoughts regarding Lingling's argument with her mother. They then present the concept of children's rights to the young readers and ask students to re-consider their view of the story while keeping in mind their legal entitlements (*Pinde yu shehui* [Morality and Society], 2007: 67).

In addition to using media and pedagogic publications to spread the notion of children's privacy, China's Ministry of Education has also banned the "decades-old ritual" of publicly praising or rebuking young school students for their test scores (People's Daily, 2006a). At the Whitewater and Affiliated Primary Schools in Shanghai, I was told that the practice of calling out children's test results in front of their classmates, as well as the public ranking of students based on their test scores, was no longer allowed. Following the recommendation of teacher's manuals, educators instead held a more discreet, "private consultation" with the student "to protect his or her feelings" (*Xiaoxuesheng xinli suzhi peiyang: Yi nianji jiaoshi yongshu,* 2001). There is evidence that teachers across the country generally support the change. Commenting in a teachers' forum posted on a Chinese website dedicated to basic education, a teacher nicknamed "*Ai shu*" reminded her colleagues in 2004 that "after all, children are only children...a low grade ranking can really devastate a child with poor psychological ability." A teacher from Shandong agreed:

> Publicly ranking students according to their test results has always been one of the hallmarks of Chinese culture...From what I heard, foreign countries don't have this system, however. I think their methods are relatively advanced, and we should certainly learn from them, which is exactly what we're doing now with the new [school] reforms.

Among members of the general public, support for a more private approach to student ranking is growing too. In 2006, more than half of the 1,500 comments left on Sina.com, one of China's biggest news websites, approved of the government's ban on the public ranking of students.

According to Chinese media reports, children themselves have become more aware of the privacy issues that affect them. A 2007 article which appeared in the state-run *Zhongguo qingnian bao* [China Youth Daily] noted that the protection of "individual privacy (*geren yinsi*)" was one of the top concerns of school students who had attended a Youth Development Forum held in Guangzhou the same year. Students who took part in one of the panels reportedly expressed the wish that parents do not "arbitrarily look at their diaries, letters, or online chats, nor listen in to their private phone conversations." Or, as one Guangzhou primary school student put it: "We know that Mom and Dad love us, but each person has his/her own piece of the sky (*geren dou you shuyu ziji de yibian tiankong*), and parents should respect our privacy (*yinsi quan*)!" (cited in Shu, 2007).[3]

Children's right to bodily privacy and physical integrity

The employment of physical force as a disciplinary measure constitutes another, extreme, form of a violation of children's bodily privacy and physical integrity. Corporal punishment is also closely bound with a particular concept of the use of violence toward weak social categories, such as children (Flekkoy and Kaufman, 1997: 40). The UN Committee on the Rights of the Child defines "corporal" or "physical" punishment as "any punishment in which physical force is used and intended to cause some degree of pain or discomfort, however light." Most involves hitting children with the hand or with an implement. But it can also involve, for example, "kicking, shaking or throwing children, scratching, pinching, biting, pulling hair or boxing ears, forcing children to stay in uncomfortable positions, burning and scalding." In the view of the Committee, corporal punishment is invariably degrading. In addition, there are other non-physical forms of punishment that are also cruel and degrading and thus incompatible with the Convention of the Right of the Child. These include, for example, "punishment which belittles, humiliates, denigrates, scapegoats, threatens, scares or ridicules the child" (United Nations Committee on the Rights of the Child, 2007: 3–4).

Already in the Maoist Period (1949–76), Chinese official discourse strongly condemned the use of such degrading forms of punishment against children—a relatively common practice in late imperial and Republican-era schools and homes. During the 1950s, physical punishment and harsh scolding were banned in Chinese schools on the grounds that these were "feudal practices," which only served "to stifle creativity" and "encouraged resentment and unreasonableness in a child" (cited in Chan Anita, 1985: 12; see also Thøgersen, 2002: 246; Wolf, 1985: 115). Field studies from the last twenty years or so reveals, however, that several decades of official exhortations may not have been entirely successful in eradicating corporal punishment in China, particularly in family settings, and in rural areas even in schools.

A 2011 qualitative study conducted in a northern rural county in China reports, for instance, that physical punishment was ubiquitous and indeed "valued" by virtually all adult participants, including teachers and caregivers (see Katz *et al.*, 2011: 99). A number of ethnographic works, including Martin Schoenhals' (1993) study of middle schools in a northeastern Chinese city; Teresa Kuan's (2011) study of middle-class urban Chinese mothers, and Esther C.L. Goh's (2011) work on childrearing in urban Xiamen, have all documented that in post-socialist urban China, caregivers of various socioeconomic backgrounds and levels of education have continued to practice corporal punishment at home.

There are currently no national statistics that show the extent of physical punishment of children across the country, but Qiao and Chan (2005: 21) cite a number of large-scale surveys which throw light on the scale of the practice. A 1999 study conducted in Beijing found that 60% of students had experienced physical punishment and disguised physical punishment from their teachers. A 2005 survey of more than 3,500 adolescents undertaken by the All-China Women's Federation (ACWF), Beijing University, and UNICEF, found that physical punishment was a common practice at Chinese schools and that more than 50% of males and one-third of females included in the study had been hit or kicked as children (Reuters, 2005). Another survey, conducted in the mid-2000s by the China Legal Studies Association (a quasi-governmental organization), revealed that "more than 60 percent of Chinese children have suffered corporal punishment, with most of the victims being girls" (China Daily, 2004b). According to this study, widely discussed in the state-run newspaper, the China Daily, two-thirds of the urban residents surveyed had endured "some form of domestic violence" during their childhood. Many recalled, for instance, "being badly scolded and being forced to kneel...as a way of contemplating one's wrongdoings, showing remorse and seeking forgiveness." Other respondents reported being "thrown out of their homes" or even "tied up" by their parents (China Daily, 2004b). In 2010, a web-based survey of more than 2,000 participants conducted by the Chinese State Council and the People's (*Renmin*) University,[4] again documented that close to 70% of respondents (a majority of which were urban and well-educated) reported hitting their children when they "lied, acted rudely, disobeyed their instructions, or performed badly in school."

One should note that the reported rates of the use of corporal punishment in China are relatively similar to those documented elsewhere in the world, including South Korea, India, the Philippines, Brazil, the US, and the UK.[5] A major UNICEF study of child discipline within the home in more than 30 low- and middle-income countries likewise finds that on average 75% of children experienced violent discipline, with 17% experiencing severe physical punishment (being hit or slapped on the face, head or ears or being hit over and over with an implement) (UNICEF, 2010). Over the past two decades or so, the general media and the academic establishment in China have nonetheless shown increasing attention to the phenomenon of corporal punishment and to the idea that youngsters have a right to protection against violence.

In 2011, for instance, a book entitled *"Suoyi, Beida xiongmei"* ("That's Why They Go to Beijing University,"), published by Shanghai Sanlian Shudian, generated a great deal of public discussion in China. The book followed the success of Amy Chua's volume, "Battle Hymn of the Tiger Mom" and describes how author and Hong Kong businessman Xiao Baiyou (whom the Chinese media quickly dubbed "Wolf Dad,") beat his children into China's top school, Beijing University. Xiao relates, for instance, that even in preschool his children would spend "days reciting Chinese classics ranging from poetry to philosophy. If they failed to meet his standards, the children would be beaten with a feather duster on the legs or the palm of the hand" (cited in *Xinhua*, 2011; see also Lim, 2011).

The book became a bestseller in China and Xiao's methods were heavily discussed. Some parents were quoted in the press as saying that they "fully understand why Xiao administers physical punishment to his children." Other caregivers, as well as most education experts in China, argued however that "too many beatings...can lead to psychological problems for children," and that the root of the problem was a way of thinking that ignores "children's personal choices and feelings" (cited in *Xinhua*, 2011).

This ongoing public debate received further attention when, in the same year, a small booklet authored by two Beijing ten-year olds was posted on *Weibo*, a widely-popular micro-blogging site in China. Filled with primitive line drawings, the small, scrappy book, entitled "The Complete Book of Combat with Mum," contained twenty strategies that children could use to avoid a scolding from their mothers, one of which included "running to Mom and throwing yourself on her" in an attempt to make her "heart go soft." The young authors of the booklet reportedly picked up many sympathetic reactions on the Chinese Internet. The children's parents also started to take note of the possible adverse effects of using corporal punishment, though according to reports, did not stop the practice altogether. In a media interview, Mr. Chen, the father of one of the book's young authors, explained that although he and his wife did occasionally spank their daughter, a practice which prompted her to compile this booklet with her friend, "mostly we respect her decisions and treat her as an equal.... I don't want her to be an obedient child. It just means you're in the system, you can only follow orders" (cited in Lim, 2011).

The father's ambivalent feelings towards corporal punishment—and his daughter's individualism—were echoed in a conversation I had with a well-educated mother in Shanghai. Though expressing general support for the notion that children have a right to privacy and to expressing their own views, the mother—who worked in the media business—was somewhat skeptic about the possibility of banning corporal punishment in China. She then proceeded to recount a famous fable told to her by her own grandmother about a man who had not received proper disciplining while he was young and, as a result, grew up to become a murderer. This Shanghai mother then explained:

> Chinese parents beat their children not because they are angry with them. It's because they believe it's for the child's own good.... In China, if you hit a child, it means that you love him. Western people don't understand this point at all! I have noticed that from watching many Western films and TV shows.

In Chinese popular psychology and academic literature of the past decade or so, the notion that a child who has not been beaten when young "will grow up to be an unfilial son (or daughter) who will never amount to much" is often put down to the persistence of so-called "feudal beliefs," according to which children are "not separate individuals, but a part of their parents" (Wang Peng, 2002: 105). These beliefs, argue PRC child-rearing and education experts, lead caregivers to treat their children as nothing more than "punching bags" or "small lackeys," while sanctioning "psychologically damaging behaviors" such as corporal punishment, verbal humiliation and ridicule (Liu Ying, 1992: 3; Hu Shen, 2000: 263–4; Zhang Suying, 1995: 6).

Notably, both academic and popular media publications draw a link between the frequent use of corporal punishment and children's psychological health, and argue that the protection of the "mental health" of China's young is "a major priority for this new century." Scholars such as Gu Xiaobo, Tianjin professor of Psychological Health Education, urge Chinese parents and teachers to recognize that "though a child may be young, he/she already possesses a sense of shame and self-respect" which adults must protect (Gu, 2002: 191–2; see also Hu Shen, 2000: 262). The 2001 popular parenting guide, *Raising a Happy, Healthy Child*, written by two Shanghai psychologists, likewise suggests that if parents feel a need to punish or criticize their son or daughter they should do so in "a calm, controlled manner so as not to harm the child physically or emotionally" (Yan and Li, 2001: 2, 25). Official media publications in China reiterate this point and recommend that parents and teachers replace verbal and physical violence against children with "gentle persuasion by means of reason and encouragement" (see China Daily, 2004b).

Significantly, the increasing preoccupation with the issue of physical violence at school or in the family is also evident in government policies and legislative measures of the last two decades or so. China's 1992 Law on the Protection of Minors prohibits "teachers and administrative staff in schools and kindergartens" from "enforcing corporal punishment...or any other act that humiliates" students (All-China Women's Federation, 2006). The law mirrors Article 19 of the UNCRC, which affirms the duty of states to protect children from all forms of physical or mental violence. A similar ban appears in the 1993 PRC Teachers' Law which mentions "a persistent use of corporal punishment" as a cause for termination of a teacher's employment (Qi and Tang, 2004). China's revised Compulsory Education Law, in effect since 2006, further requires teachers refrain from "any sort of degrading disciplinary measures, including physical punishment and physical punishment in disguised form," clauses that were notably absent from the previous, 1986 version of the law (Ministry of Education, 2006).

The Chinese Law on the Protection of Minors, however, is relatively vague on the topic of physical abuse against children within the family. Although the 1992 law refers to Article 182 of the PRC Criminal Law which details criminal punishment for abuse of minors by family members (Keith, 1997: 45), it does not include an explicit prohibition of physical punishment within the family, an issue which did not escape the attention of the UN Committee on the Rights of the Child (United Nations Committee on the Rights of the Child, 2005b: 9).[6] To date, the Law on the Protection of Minors has not been amended and no formal child protection system exists in China. Cases are dealt with through the criminal justice system, and there is no network of social services or any system to support "at risk" families (Hesketh *et al.*, 2000; Katz *et al.*, 2011). As a result, several scholars (for example, Qiao and Chan, 2005; Katz *et al.*, 2011) have concluded that in contemporary China, violence against children remains an "unacknowledged" problem that does not receive a sufficiently active response from government officials, health care professionals, educators, or indeed caregivers themselves.

There are, however, some signs of change. An explicit ban on violence against children within the family does appear in some local regulations. In 2004, the city of Shanghai prohibited the use of "corporal punishment *(tifa)*" and "verbal abuse *(ruma)*" at the hands of both teachers and parents (Shanghai People's Congress Standing Committee, 2004). A number of projects, implemented in some of China's provinces since the mid-2000s with the support of Chinese government and international organizations such as UNICEF, have sought to prevent child abuse and neglect both in schools and medical institutions, as well as in homes. In 2011, the "China Human Rights Development Fund," a state-sponsored organization, further announced the launching of a new "Harmonious family" project, which reportedly aims to promote education against "soft" and "hard" violence within the family.

It's questionable whether such projects and legal prohibitions can prevent actual cases of child abuse, especially in the absence of a mandatory reporting system. But my work in Shanghai does reveal an increasing awareness of the issue of violence against children and of youngsters' right to protect themselves. That awareness is present among both Shanghai educators and caregivers, and also among the children themselves.

"What right do you have to reproach him?"

In my conversations with Shanghai primary school teachers, old and young alike recalled how their own teachers used to hit students who disobeyed them. This was no longer the case, they assured me, since these days, schoolteachers "can no longer hit (*da*), verbally abuse (*ma*), or order students about (*mingling*)." Ms Huang, a 35-year-old art teacher at Whitewater Primary School explained: "We all realize now that a student is also a person, even though he/she may be smaller than you. Therefore, what right do you have to reproach him/her (*ni you shenme quanli qu zhize ta*)?"

The gap between recognition and action, however, was evident in a story recounted by Ms. Zhang, a 29-year-old Music teacher at the Affiliated School. Once, she recalled, she had taught a student who often misbehaved at school. "No one liked him at home either," she noted.

One day, she told me, the boy came to class "with his face all covered in bruises." When Ms. Zhang asked the boy what had happened, he replied that he "didn't listen (*bu tinghua*) to his parents," so they gave him "a beating."

"I felt so sorry for him," Ms. Zhang sighed. "I thought to myself: 'He might be a naughty (*wanpi*) kid, but this isn't right.' I could never treat a child like that. When a child misbehaves, you need to give him extra love and attention. That's the only way to improve his behavior."

Teacher Zhang did not define what the parents had done as a form of "abuse," nor did she feel obligated to report the incident to her superiors or to the authorities. While denouncing the violent nature of the parents' disciplinary measures, she kept her criticism to herself. However, her account does reflect the growing recognition, expressed by many of my school informants, that beating a child was no longer a lauded practice, not at school and perhaps not even at home.

Indeed, when I discussed the use of corporal punishment at school with a Shanghai teacher trainer, she stated explicitly that physical punishment "had been banned in Chinese schools since the 1990s." Most present-day Shanghai teachers abide by these regulations, she assured me, although "a small minority" may still employ harsh disciplinary measures, often "in a covert manner" (for instance, by making children stand for long periods or instructing a student to copy a text dozens of times as a form of punishment).

Professor Chen, the Shanghai education scholar who has published extensively on school reforms in China and served as an adviser to the government, observed that while "some teachers in China continued to humiliate students both verbally and physically," the situation in Shanghai was "decidedly better."[7]

My own observations at the Affiliated and Whitewater Primary Schools largely corroborated these claims. In nearly one hundred hours of observations both in and outside the classroom, I never once saw a teacher employing overt corporal punishment[8] although I did happen to witness various forms of physical reprimand. For instance, some teachers, particularly those in their mid-30s to mid-40s, knocked on children's heads with a pen or a book to stop them from talking. Other middle-aged teachers ordered tardy students to stand in front of the classroom for almost half the lesson, sometimes as long as twenty minutes or so. Stories related to me by Shanghai parents whose children attended schools in different locations across the city, demonstrated that these were by no means isolated incidents. Sitting in the teachers' office between and after classes, I also happened to observe middle-aged teachers shouting at and, in several cases, even forcefully pushing students who were called there on account of misbehavior or mistakes in their homework. These teachers were not reluctant to employ physical force even though they were aware of my presence in the room.

"We now have a law that protects us!"

Shanghai teachers, especially those in their mid-30s to mid-40s, were certainly aware of the notion that children had a right to protection from violence but they did not always respect that right completely either in or outside the classroom. Similarly, more than half of the mothers I talked to also reported using physical punishment, for instance, when their son or daughter "did something wrong," such as get into a fight, neglect a homework assignment or disobey them in any way. This was true for mothers of various occupations and levels of education. Ms An, a 53-year-old retired factory worker whose daughter was in ninth grade, related that she used to beat her child "until she was about twelve or so." When I asked why she had chosen to use corporal punishment, she explained: "When children are young, they don't understand things. They rely on adults to guide them. As a parent, your job is to discipline and control the child. If my daughter did something wrong and I didn't hit her, she would just repeat her mistakes in the future." Tan, a recent migrant from the countryside who sold window and door frames at a Shanghai market similarly mentioned corporal punishment as an effective disciplinary tool. "Just the other day," she recalled, "I caught my son watching cartoons instead of doing his homework," so I had him "kneel on the floor for about an hour or so to think about what he had done."

Corporal punishment was even employed by well-educated mothers who generally described their relationship with their child as "friendly" and "democratic."[9] Ms Deng, a middle-aged academic who worked as a university language instructor argued that "parents should allow their child the freedom to be happy (*ziyou xingfu*)...and encourage him to have his own thoughts and views." Later in our conversation, however, she noted that when "it came to matters of principle," she could be quite "stern (*yanli*)" with her six-year-old son. One day, she related, the boy was repeatedly nagging her to buy him a toy he had just seen in a store window.

"I told him he couldn't have it...but it didn't do any good," she recalled. "He started crying in the middle of the street, so I slapped him and told him I wouldn't buy it for him even if he cried his head off."

Several mothers, particularly those of white-collar occupations and higher levels of education who also reported consuming child-rearing literature, held a different view. It is best not to hit children, they suggested, because it "only stirs up rebellious emotions and resentment" in them, and also because "children's feelings can easily get hurt." After all, "small children don't mean to do any harm," reasoned Ms Jiang, an academic who works in the media industry, "so what good would it do to hit them?" An accountant married to a university professor, stated that they never hit or punish their son. "Sometimes, when he doesn't listen to us, we ask him why."

Interestingly, of those mothers who reported hitting their child on occasion, several saw fit to add that they "knew it was wrong" to do so. Ms Qian, a 37-year-old native of Shanghai who worked as an editor at a government publishing house stated:

> In the past, parents in China didn't think there was anything wrong [with beating your child]. They felt that if the child disobeyed them, they should hit him...we have this old saying: *"gunbang chu xiao zi"* ["a stick produces filial sons"]. In other words, you have to hit children because that is the only way to teach them right from wrong. But nowadays, most parents, especially those who are civilized/cultured (*you wenhua*) and well-educated, don't agree with this idea anymore.

While she herself admitted that she "sometimes" hit her eight-year-old son, especially when she "couldn't control" herself anymore, Ms Qian nonetheless went to great lengths to assure me that she "did not" support corporal punishment by any means: "I know it's not a good method," she commented. "It's better to explain things to your child rather than punish him."

According to another Shanghai-born mother, who told me she frequently consulted child-rearing manuals and magazines, this attitude was not typical of parents in other parts of the country. In China's more "backward (*luohou*)" areas, she noted, "people treat their children in shocking ways," which she herself "couldn't really understand." Unlike these parents, she assured me, "we [in Shanghai] raise our children *with great care.*"

Ms Tan, herself a recent migrant from the countryside, didn't entirely disagree. After informing me that she sometimes hit her son, she added somewhat apologetically that parents "like her"— with "little education"—"don't really have a choice because children won't listen to them any other way."

Statements such as these convey the fact that subjecting children to brutal disciplinary measures was still prevalent in many Chinese homes, yet was becoming a less *accepted* practice, especially among those who wished to associate themselves with a middle-class civility and a more "modern, scientific" parenting style.

In yet other instances, however, a mother's change in perception came about because of her child's broadening consciousness of his or her new entitlements under the law. Already in the beginning of the 2000s, primary school children in Shanghai were made aware of their rights through their textbooks. One class assignment prompted fifth-graders to recognize that a "father who frequently hits and scolds his child while saying: 'I brought you into this world...and therefore, I can beat you to death if I like,'" is in fact breaking the law (*Shehui, wu nianji diyi xueqi*, 2001: 122).

Some Shanghai students successfully internalized the lesson. Ms Gui, the academic married to a wealthy entrepreneur, remarked that her child's school had "really made some changes" in the curriculum.

"These days," she noted, "schools teach students not only how to respect other people or how to behave in public, but also how to protect themselves. I'm not sure what children actually get from this but I can tell you one thing: they certainly know what it means to protect their own interests!"

She then explained by telling me a story:

> "The other day, my son came home from school and told me: 'Mom, you know how you sometimes shout and swear (*ma*) at me when I do something wrong? Well, you can't do that anymore!'
>
> 'Why not?' I asked.
>
> 'It says so in our schoolbook,' he told me. 'We now have a law that says you can't abuse or hit children anymore (*bu neng da ma haizi*).'
>
> 'Well, if I'm not allowed to shout or hit you, how would you know when you've done something wrong?' I said.
>
> Do you know what he told me? He said: 'You can persuade me (*shuofu*) or reason with me (*jiang daoli*) instead!'"

Ms Gui was surprised but also visibly proud of her son's newfound assertiveness. She wasn't the only mother who discovered that her school-aged child was ready to demand his or her rights to protection from violence. Ms Fei, a 37-year-old native of Xinjiang Province who had arrived in Shanghai to pursue a Master's degree, admitted that she "sometimes hit" her eight-year-old son when he disobeyed her, but hastened to add: "It only happens when I really can't control myself anymore. You see, now that my son is older, he can really 'give me a lesson' and tell me that what I am doing is a form of 'domestic violence (*jiating baoli*).' So even if I'm upset about what he says or does, I need to make sure I don't do anything wrong."[10]

Even Shanghai grandmothers have noticed the new ability of children to resist parental violence. One group of women in their late sixties told me that this change came about "not only because of the introduction of the Law on the Protection of Minors" but also because contemporary Chinese children were so "different" to their predecessors. "Today's children are much smarter," one grandmother said, echoing the observation of the former principal which started this chapter. "You can reason (*jiang daoli*) with them and they actually understand what you're saying, so there's no need to hit them anymore." Another grandmother, who worked as a teacher before her retirement, chimed in: "Nowadays, all the books say you need to reason with children and educate them using persuasion (*shuofu jiaoyu*), rather than force."

What these observations suggest is that a new conceptualization of children, their capacities, and their entitlements, expressed in the contents of PRC laws, media publications and textbooks, may in turn have prompted a new sense of subjectivity and an increased "rights consciousness" in children themselves. The grandmothers' observations also point to the fact that well-educated parents in Shanghai no longer subscribed in the full to the notion that corporal punishment is crucial for the successful upbringing of a "good" child. Like a child's right to voice his/her opinions and a child's right to privacy, some informants held that abstaining from corporal punishment was key to raising an independent-minded, creative person, who could later compete in the global, market economy. Others came to believe that even young children are autonomous persons with rights, and therefore they should reason and negotiate with the child, instead of using brutal force in an attempt to control his/her thoughts and behavior.

Discussion and conclusion

Contemporary educators and caregivers in Shanghai are increasingly aware of children's right to self-ownership in both a physical and a psychological sense. They exhibit more respect for children's private possessions and personal space, and are more doubtful about the use of physical force in the disciplining of the young. In this respect then, younger Shanghai teachers and elite caregivers display similar behavioral patterns as their counterparts in highly complex, modern societies. *but how about other places*

As noted by historian Norbert Elias (1998: 191), contemporary, industrial societies are generally characterized by a greater degree of self-regulation and self-restraint, or "civility" in social relationships, illustrated for instance by the rejection of the use of force against children. While the relationship between parents and children might once have been characterized by parents' clear authority, twentieth-century middle-class caregivers, notes Elias, are far more skeptical about the notion that the unconditional power of adults and the unconditional obedience of children" is "the best, healthiest, most productive social arrangement" from the standpoint of adults or indeed of children themselves.) *skeptical ab traditional th anythh*

As this chapter has shown, in the fast-modernizing, increasingly complex society of twenty-first-century Shanghai, some adults have come to believe that they need to exercise a greater degree of caution and restraint when dealing with the young. Recent ethnographic studies by Kuan (2011) and Goh (2011) have documented that (corporal punishment remains a common enough practice *still* among contemporary urban Chinese families of various socioeconomic backgrounds. My own study records a similar finding among Shanghai families yet also reveals that the use of force is becoming less acceptable as an educational measure, particularly among educated professionals who associate the use of violence with a lack of education or "culture" (*wenhua*), or wish to distinguish themselves from China's more "backward masses" by adopting more "modern," "civilized" modes of social interaction.) *however in Shanghai*

This shift in elite attitudes toward corporal punishment is further sustained by the new recognition that children have a right to self-ownership: a modern, "neoliberal value, which expands and transforms the meaning of the private" in contemporary China (Ong, 2008: 187). As was the case in modern Europe, the Chinese discourse on children's right to privacy is the product of material transformations, including the rise of a market economy; the emergence of new propertied social classes, particularly since the 1990s, and the falling family size of these urban, middle-class families. Tang and Dong's (2006) survey finds, for instance, a clear relationship between family size and parents' degree of respect for the privacy of high-school students: the larger the family size, the less likely the parents were to value their teenage children's privacy (p. 294). Unfortunately, the authors of this study did not furnish an explanation for this finding. However, we can speculate that smaller urban

Chinese families, who in recent years have seen their disposable incomes rise, are now able to allocate their child a space of his or her own in which he/she may be able to exercise a right to privacy. New economic and demographic realities in turn interact with new imaginings of privacy and subjectivity. To paraphrase Habermas (1991: 45), the growing autonomy of property owners in post-socialist, urban China finds a parallel expression in the presentation of children as psychologically emancipated subjects within the private realm. Chinese youngsters, who traditionally were regarded as inseparable parts of their parents and their families, and in the first 30 years of the People's Republic were presented as the property of the Party-state or of the revolutionary masses, are now recast in the role of distinct, autonomous individuals. They have a right to control their possessions and to protect the privacy of their bodies from the intrusion of others. *but how they know their rights*

This new conceptualization of children's right to self-ownership is particularly evident among well-educated, high-earning mothers who consume the child-rearing advice currently circulating on the Chinese Internet and in contemporary books and magazines. Various psychology professionals generally recommend that Chinese caregivers respect the autonomy and privacy of their child in order to foster his or her sense of individual identity and separateness, and suggest that caregivers use reasoning and negotiation instead of violence as mechanisms of parental control. In so doing, these publications create a direct link between the notion of children's moral *rights* and the notion of children's developmental *needs*. The next chapter will explore this link in depth and consider how the growing popularity of a modern, psychological discourse of childhood among particular sections of urban society sustains and enables the dissemination of the idea of children's rights to autonomy and self-ownership in contemporary China.

3
Constituting Rights as Needs: Psychology and the Rise of Middle-Class Childhood

"Are children persons (*ren*) or objects (*wu*)?" inquires the author of an essay entitled "Avoiding Erroneous Views of the Child in Family Education" (*"Zai jiating jiaoyu zhong quzou ertong guan de wuqu"*). The question might seem peculiar, but the writer, who is also the former Deputy Head of the Wuhan Education Research Institute in China, is not being rhetorical. In fact, he observes, many contemporary Chinese parents are not entirely sure of the answer. Deploring the commonplace tendency "to treat children as the showcase of the family" while pressuring them to devote a majority of their time to academic work and skill-enhancement activities, the author pleads with caregivers to "advance with the times" and to recognize that children are "not small-sized adults," but persons with *"unique emotional needs which vary according to their age"* (Wang Peng, 2002: 104; emphasis added).

Part of an edited volume published by China's Ministry of Education (MOE), The Communist Youth League, and the ACWF, the essay illustrates the growing significance of a psychological discourse of childhood in Chinese academic and official publications over the past two decades. Placing children's unique needs and healthy emotional development at center stage, this psychological discourse is present in many of the legal codes, pedagogic materials, media products, and parenting literature surveyed in the previous two chapters. These contemporary Chinese publications often incorporate the notion of children as rights-bearing subjects with psychological theories of healthy child development. Drawing their inspiration from global articulations of children's rights, which emphasize "individual rather than collective wants and needs," and label Third-World deviations from this logic "as a loss and contamination of childhood" (Stephens, 1995b: 19), PRC publications on children's entitlements often link moral *rights* with developmental *needs*. They present the fulfillment of the former as a condition to the satisfaction of the latter, while implying that respecting children's rights is a crucial component of modern parenting and pedagogical science.

Since the introduction of the One-Child Policy in 1979, urban Chinese singletons have frequently been forced to bear the entire weight of their parents' (and grandparents') hopes, expectations, and aspirations, primarily in the area of schoolwork and academic achievements (Croll, 2006: 201; Anagnost, 1997a, 2008b; Chee, 2000; Fong, 2004b, 2007; Milwertz, 1997; Woronov, 2007). Urban families, and in particular elite urban families, are showing an "increased attentiveness to the exhaustive use of children's time." After-school hours are now filled with extracurricular activities designed to enhance the bodily, cognitive, and emotional capabilities of the only child (Anagnost, 1997a: 196; see also Champagne, 1992; Fong, 2004b).

In the past decade, in particular, Chinese child-rearing and pedagogical literature has emphasized the promotion of children's "creativity and enterprise." These qualities, say the authors, can be developed by individuals who engage in responsible self-making and who continuously scrutinize their own actions and words in order to maintain emotional wellbeing (Kuan, 2011: 80; see also Woronov, 2008, 2009). To some scholars, these attempts to improve the "quality" (*suzhi*) of Chinese children's mentality and physique signify the ascendance of a neoliberal discourse of subject formation in post-socialist urban China. Like their peers elsewhere in the world, suggest these scholars, Chinese only children are now encouraged to become self-governing subjects who can responsibly manage their emotional problems, and later become successful, self-reliant laborers and consumers in a global market economy (Anagnost, 2004; Greenhalgh and Winckler, 2005; Woronov, 2007). In the process, however, children's lives are said to undergo intensive "regimentation" and "managerialization," while Chinese childhood is arguably "in danger of becoming a time of ceaseless labor and struggle" (Anagnost, 2008b: 64; Greenhalgh and Winckler, 2005).[1]

The present chapter builds on these important observations but seeks to highlight the significance of a different type of universalizing logic of child-rearing and their education. Alongside—or indeed, in response to—the "production of a highly disciplined childhood" dedicated to improving the "entrepreneurial" qualities of the Chinese only child (Greenhalgh and Winckler, 2005: 243), an alternative strain of thinking has also emerged. This strain of thinking seeks to challenge existing pedagogical practices in China. It fuses the language of "rights" with the language of "needs," and rationalizes Chinese children's right to a separate identity, to self-ownership, and to experiencing a stress-free childhood by invoking the scientific principles of modern, developmental psychology.

The emergence of this alternative discourse should not simply be taken as a welcome attempt to acknowledge the "true needs" of children or to recover the "proper" nature of childhood in China. To make such an assumption would be to ignore the fact that a concept of childhood as a joyful, carefree time or of children as autonomous individuals is in itself a product of Western middle-class modernity rather than a necessary feature of childhood everywhere (Burman, 1996: 49; Field, 1995: 65; James *et al.*, 1998: 19; Stephens, 1995b: 14–15; Heywood, 2001: 24; Walkerdine, 2005: 16–17; Woodhead, 1997). Instead, we should view the rising popularity of psychological knowledge in China as part of an ongoing transformation in the conceptualization of childhood, power, and subjectivity among a younger generation of urban teachers and elite caregivers.

The following discussion regards the psychological discourse of childhood both as "a formal and specialized body of knowledge produced by professionals," and as "a cultural framework diffused through a variety of local and global institutions that define perceptions of self and others" (Illouz, 2008: 10). It suggests that the emergence of a psychological discourse of childhood in contemporary urban China facilitates the promotion of a particular logic of child-rearing and education. This logic equates the fulfillment of personal "needs" with the exercise of individual "rights." It places the wants, wishes, and happiness of the individual child at the center of attention, while presenting youngsters' rights as natural, developmental requirements which must be catered to if the child is to become a healthy, functioning adult.

To young Chinese teachers raised in the age of market reforms and to elite urban caregivers who wish to adopt a "middle-class" *habitus*, this individualizing logic is especially attractive. It functions as a token of membership in a certain social group: educated, modern, and global-minded (see Illouz, 2008: 222). This logic is also closely associated with liberal, less repressive forms of governing the child and the person. As Nikolas Rose has shown, the growth of the intellectual and practical technologies of psychology since the late nineteenth century "has been intrinsically linked with transformations in the exercise of political power" (1996: 11). This observation was made in the context of the liberal-capitalist democracies of Western Europe and North America. However, it may be equally relevant to post-socialist urban Chinese society. The emergence of a Chinese psychological discourse of childhood reflects a reconfiguration in the exercise of political power in China. Some may even argue that it indicates a shift from repressive to neoliberal techniques of governmentality (Naftali, 2010b). Rather than converging with global, neoliberal models of childrearing and education, however, this transformation takes on distinct characteristics and is fraught with contradictions.

Young educators and elite urban caregivers in Shanghai may be keen to follow the advice of psychologists and allow children to spend at least some of their time playing freely and creatively rather than memorizing lessons in preparation for endless exams. As we shall see, however, many educators and caregivers nonetheless feel obligated to push children to excel at their studies for fear they would be "left behind." Yet others are deeply troubled about the destabilizing effects of introducing a highly rational, individualistic logic of "rights" and "needs" to the school and to the realm of family relations.

The psychological discourse of childhood in modern China

Late imperial Chinese society saw children as different to adults and recognized childhood as a separate stage of life. However, until the turn of the twentieth century, Confucian discourses generally placed little value on the stage of childhood itself. Aimless play and unrestrained activity were frequently discouraged even in the very young, and it was often stressed that education should instill adult standards in children as early as possible, ideally from the age of seven or eight *sui* (six- or seven-years-old) (Bai, 2005a: 10; Dardess, 1991: 79; Hsiung, 2005: 119; Kinney, 1995b: 12; Saari, 1990: 45; Wicks and Avril, 2002: 4).

It was only in the late nineteenth and early twentieth centuries, suggest a number of studies, that a modern conceptualization of childhood as a series of normalized developmental stages, and of children as a unique type of persons who require prolonged periods of playful, spontaneous activities to maintain their healthy growth, were introduced to China from the West (Anagnost, 1997a; Fernsebner, 2003; Jones, 2002; Leung, 1995; Nylan, 2003). At a time of major national crisis and semi-colonial occupation, leading May Fourth intellectuals regarded the proper rearing and development of China's young as a necessary condition for nation-building and modernization (Jones, 2002: 700; Farquhar Mary Ann, 1999: 30, 61; Pease, 1995: 287). It was also at this time that Chen Heqin and other Chinese pioneers of child psychology sought to establish that "a child is not just 'a small man,' but possesses a 'psychology [that] is different from that of adults'" (cited in Borevskaya, 2001: 36).

Psychological principles, particularly those grounded in Soviet theories, continued to guide Chinese pedagogical thinking for a brief period after the establishment of the People's Republic (Chan Anita, 1985; Liu Fan, 1982; Tardif and Miao, 2000). Yet the notion that children possess unique needs or that childhood ought to be a time of amusement and leisure were soon to be eclipsed by the radical ideology of class struggle. During the chaotic decade of the Cultural Revolution (1966–76), even young children were called upon to play the role of "vanguard fighters" in the struggle for the construction of a new socialist society (Donald, 1999: 82, 95). Moreover, emotional problems in both children and adults were frequently cast as issues of deviant political and moral thinking to be addressed through re-education or work therapy rather than through psychological care (Chang *et al.*, 2005; Lee, 2011: 180; Liu, 1982; Tardif and Miao, 2000).

However in 1978, when the CCP turned from an emphasis on socialism and revolution to science and modernity, psychology once again gained ground in China. University departments of psychology, shut down during the Cultural Revolution, have started to train qualified psychologists (Tardif and Miao, 2000: 68). Indeed, in recent years, large numbers of Chinese in Shanghai, Beijing, and other major cities, have become interested in obtaining certificates in counseling and psychotherapy, both out of a desire to help others, and due to a new attentiveness to the exploration of one's selfhood (Kleinman *et al.*, 2011: 28; Lee, 2011: 209).

At the same time, a demand for Western-style talk therapy that allows for emotional release and psychological development has been increasing among the new middle classes in China. With the advancement of liberal economic reforms and rising standards of living in urban areas, increasing numbers of well-educated professionals are turning to psychological counseling in order to grapple with their personal and family problems—problems that are said to stem from the weakening of communal support networks and the increased competitive and stressful lives generated by the market economy (Zhang, 2008; Chang *et al.*, 2005; see also *Xinhua* News Agency, 2008). Although most urbanites, including those who may be classified as members of the new middle classes, still cannot afford the relatively high costs of psychotherapy, various public and private counseling clinics have opened in the cities. Among health workers, teachers, and self-labeled psychologists, seminars and courses on psychological treatment have become increasingly popular (Lee, 2011: 208–9). Hotlines, radio call-in programs and professional advice literature have also grown exponentially in China during the past two decades or so, and the psychology sections in general bookstores now contain an impressive number of publications, ranging from self-help titles to professional books on psychology and psychoanalysis, including translations of European and American authors (Erwin, 2000; Farquhar Judith, 2001; Kleinman *et al.*, 2011).

This intensified interest in "emotions, personality, and self-development" has spilled over to the educational and familial domains as well (Kleinman *et al.*, 2011: 29). Urban Chinese caregivers are now swamped with psychological child-rearing advice through lectures, books, websites, newspapers, and magazines. Television talk shows such as *Tell It Like It Is* (*shi hua shi shuo*) on CCTV stations have also started to devote episodes to discussing parenting issues with the help of "psy" professionals (Kuan, 2011: 79–80). Together, these new sources of psychological help signify the emergence of a new middle-class culture "that centers itself on the outer and interior furnishings of a new Chinese self" (Kleinman *et al.*, 2011: 29).

A survey of government, academic, and media sources published in China in the past decade or so reveals that this 'new culture of the self' is often associated with a novel conceptualization of childhood. Chinese psychological experts emphasize that children are not "short, light-bodied adults," as the writer whose words opened the present chapter suggests, but "constitute human beings in a class by themselves." As such, they are said to possess unique emotional features that must be understood and catered to (see for example, China Daily, 2005; Cui and Huang, 2002; Wang Peng, 2002; Xu Minqiang, 2004; Zeng, 2004; Zhou, 1998). The recognition of children's distinct psychological needs is in turn presented as a crucial step in solving what is thought to be one of the most pressing problems facing Chinese singletons today: emotional difficulties caused by excessive pressure at school and high expectations at home.

Recognizing children's developmental needs

Attending a dinner one evening at a restaurant with the parents of a Shanghai friend, I was introduced to a number of her relatives. One of them was a young boy, shy, quiet, and aged about five or six. The waiter took our orders and, at his parents' urging, the boy produced a violin from a case. He then worked his way through an almost flawless rendition of "Auld Lang Syne." If the boy had been at all embarrassed by his parents' request, he did not show it. What was certainly clear however, was that the boy's parents and grandparents (who had also been present) were extremely proud of the child's skill. They saw no harm—indeed, they derived visible pleasure—in having him exhibit his abilities to a "foreign guest" in a public restaurant.

To contemporary child-experts in China, this scene would have been disconcerting in more than one way. Parents who publicly flaunt a child's talents, suggests education scholar Wang Peng, should not treat their sons and daughters "as little different to puppies and kittens" or "high-quality living and talking toys." Such practices, he says, cause children "to cease being children" altogether (2002: 104–5, 109). Instead of regarding children as their "private property (*ziji de siyou caichan*)",[2] and attempting to mold them according to adult expectations, note other academic and media writers, parents ought to consider the child's distinct "developmental needs" and make a true effort to gain an understanding of his/her "unique inner world," and of the way in which this inner world changes according to the child's age (see for example, Tang Jing, 2003; Wang Lingyu, 2002; Wang Shuguang, 2004; Xiong, 2003; Xu Shan, 2004; Zeng, 2004).

This emphasis on children's unique emotional needs is also evident in China's state-run media reports on what is depicted as a national malaise of "too much homework, frequent testing, and heavy parental demands," all of which are said to be detrimental to the "mental health" of the nation's children. Quoting statistical surveys and scientific studies which show that China's urban young now suffer from a range of acute mental problems (from "internet addiction," to "psychosomatic skin diseases," to "suicidal tendencies"), a growing number of alarmist reports in Chinese as well as foreign media further suggest that these problems stem from the fact that a "majority [of Chinese urban children] spend longer hours at school than their parents spend at work," have "little time to play," and consequently "are experiencing *joyless childhoods*" (People's Daily, 2007b, emphasis added; see also AFP, 2004; China Daily, 2005; Cha, 2007; Guo Zi, 2004; People's Daily, 2005; Reynolds, 2008).

Some children apparently do not hesitate to publicly voice their objections (a fact which the Chinese media highlights in its reports). In the same year I conducted my fieldwork in Shanghai (2004–5) a large number of participants at the city's Fifth Conference of the national youth movement, the Young Pioneers, submitted public petitions in which they reportedly "voiced demands that parents and school officials start listening to the experts," "let up the pressure," and provide them with "an easier environment for study and life," allowing them "*to have a childhood*" (cited in China Daily, 2004a, emphasis added). In 2011, the same state-run newspaper published another story on the continuous plight of Chinese school students. After a fight with her mother who insisted that she finish a math worksheet, a 12-year-old from Nanjing had reportedly published a poem on the Internet entitled "Mom, I'm under such pressure." According to the newspaper, the poem contained the lines: "Mom, I'm under such pressure...I want to explore each blade of grass and every flower...Mom, I promise I will not fail you when I grow up. Please don't cut me from nature. Please give me a break." The author of the article highlighted the child's explanation that the quarrel with her mother was "a fight for the right" (China Daily, 2011).

The media's attention to the pressure placed on children corresponds to new official policies in China. Over the last ten years, China's central government has begun to introduce various measures to alleviate academic pressure and protect the "mental health of schoolchildren" in accordance with the "development characteristics...of [their] growth" (Communist Party of China, 2000: 231–2). Such measures, says the government, are necessary not only so that individual students would be able to "develop lively and actively" but also because children's psychological and physical health constitutes a "precondition" and "a manifestation of the strong vitality of the Chinese nation" (Communist Party of China, 2000: 231–2).

Since the mid-2000s, the state-run media in China have also begun to frame the problem of children's "poor psychological health" as a major obstacle to the successful construction of a socialist "harmonious society" (*hexie shehui*)—a key term in CCP policy statements and directives to cadres under the former administration of Hu Jintao and Wen Jiabao (Tian, 2005). The discourse of harmony as the ultimate goal of social policies in China frequently portrays individual behavior and responsible self-governance as key. Harmony, government statements say, is essential to the removal of the economic, social, or behavioral causes of underlying contradictions and threatening social problems (Tomba, 2009b).

Contemporary psychologists in China have been following suit by arguing that the formation of a politically stable society, where there are few negative social conflicts, is ultimately bound up with the creation of a "harmonious (*hexie*) personality." That personality is characterized by such features as "high levels of self-awareness," "emotional stability," "an optimistic outlook," and "appropriate behavioral responses" to frustrating situations in familial, social, and professional life (see, for example, He, 2007; Zhang and Zhou, 2008; *Guangdong sheng kepu xinxi zhongxin*, 2008).

The promotion of balanced mental development among Chinese citizens, old and young alike, in turn requires the introduction of systematic psychological tutoring. According to official statistics, China has fewer than two psychiatrists for every 100,000 people, far lower than the world average of four doctors for every 100,000 people (China Daily, 2010). Participants at a 2007 Chinese Academy of Social Sciences (CASS) colloquium on "Psychology and Harmonious Society" expressed concern about these figures and urged the establishment of a more effective psychological service system in the country.[3] Such a system, they suggested, would be conducive not only to the rise of the public health level and to improving the living quality of Chinese citizens but also to "upgrading working productivity...ensuring the society's stability and unity...and promoting its harmony" (CASS, 2007; see also CAST, 2007).[4]

New legal codes and school reforms introduced in Shanghai are already providing part of that system. For instance, Shanghai's 2004 Municipal Regulations on the Protection of Minors urge teachers and caregivers to "pay attention to children's physical and emotional changes according to the different age stages they are in." The regulations further assert that children's healthy development requires that they "receive sufficient time for rest and recreation (*yule*)" (Shanghai People's Congress Standing Committee, 2004). These general guidelines have been translated into specific measures. In 2004, Shanghai primary schools were instructed to start the day half an hour later (at 8 am rather than 7:30 am) and to reduce the duration of each lesson from 45 to 35 minutes so that children will have "more free time to play and relax" (Yang Lifei, 2004). But it is not just the importance of rest and recreation that is being emphasized. A central theme in Shanghai's school reforms, as well as in other reform plans introduced across China under the banner of Education for Quality (*suzhi jiaoyu*), is the notion that if children are to experience "a happy childhood," they should be allowed to enjoy their learning experience.

Learning should be fun

This new stress on the importance of allowing children a "joyful education" (*kuaile jiaoyu*) is part of a broader shift in Chinese thinking about the characteristics of childhood and the unique developmental needs of children. Studies conducted in China during the 1980s show that the prevalent notion among Chinese teachers was that "school is a place for learning, not for fun" (Wu, 1996: 13). An interview I conducted with Professor Ai, a Shanghai education scholar who has studied the impact of introducing innovative math teaching methods to the city's schools, reveals that this notion continued to dominate the thinking of Chinese educators throughout the 1990s and perhaps into the 2000s as well.

"Until recently," Professor Ai explained, "Chinese primary schools used to be almost indistinguishable from middle schools."

Just like their older colleagues, six-, seven-, and eight-year-olds, had to spend long hours in the classroom, received a heavy load of homework assignments and faced a large number of tests. The situation, said the professor, was slowly changing. Chinese educators "have now come to realize that they need to adjust the curriculum and instructional activities to the unique interests and developmental needs of children," she noted.

A survey of contemporary academic literature in China confirms this observation. Chinese pedagogy, a 2001 teacher training manual argues, has traditionally stressed the "knowledge (*zhi*)" aspect of learning, while ignoring its "emotional (*qing*)" side (Fu and Xu, 2001: 43). However, the manual suggests, "modern, psychological research" has shown that the latter aspect is in fact equally important. Teachers should pay attention not only to students' grades but also to their "emotional states," while striving to create a "relaxed, cheerful" class atmosphere that fits the unique attributes of young learners (Cui and Huang, 2002: 227–9, 233–43; Cui Xianglu, 1999: 73–6; Wei, 2000: 48; Zeng, 2004).

In conversations with primary school teachers at the two Shanghai schools I studied, I heard similar statements, particularly from informants in their twenties, the youngest cohort of educators.

Young children, explained these teachers, have short attention spans and cannot force themselves to study. Therefore, I was told, it is particularly important that they have fun in the classroom.

Many of these younger teachers played tapes, showed the children colorful pictures or used toys to bring the material to life. Games, storytelling, dancing, singing, performance of sketches, and hands-on experimentation were also common across the grades, especially in English, Math, Natural Science, Chinese, and Moral Education classes.

The new stress on children's need to enjoy their learning experience found an expression in the contents of lessons as well. Ms Ye, who taught Chinese to third-graders and who also served as assistant to the vice-principal at Whitewater Primary school told me that in the past, she would assign her students essay topics such as "the importance of doing good deeds." Today however, she would ask children to write about things that "actually interested them," such as their favorite cartoon figure.

Class textbooks were likewise beginning to undergo visible changes. During my work at the Affiliated Primary School, for instance, I came across an experimental version of a Moral Education textbook for first-graders. The book had been produced at the adjacent university as part of the attempt to make schoolbooks in Shanghai "more appealing and relevant to young children's lives" (*Jiefang ribao*, 2004). A comparison of the new book with its older version, which was still in use at the other school I studied (and at a majority of other Shanghai schools), reveals telling differences in tone and format, as well as in thematic content.

Titled *Sixiang pinde* [Ideology and Moral Character], the older book, in use since 1993, employs a heavy political tone, exhorts students to maintain order and respect for authority, and includes lesson plans on such topics as "A Good Child Loves to Labor" or the importance of "Cherishing Food." In contrast, the more recent, experimental edition, which has conspicuously dropped the term "ideology" from its title, lacks these socialist, frugal themes.[5] While it still includes sections on the importance of showing respect for fellow students, helping a friend in need, and cooperating with others, the new textbook, published in 2002, sets out to teach young learners moral development "through children's own lives and activities in order to encourage children to develop their own values and beliefs" (Qi and Tang, 2004: 466, 477).

The new edition no longer contains simple morality tales followed by explicit ethical codes.[6] Instead, it presents young readers with attractive cartoon figures and colorful drawings made by children themselves. It also offers a large number of hands-on activities designed to help children familiarize themselves with their new environment and enjoy their time at school. One lesson, entitled

psychological file (*xinli dang'an*) compiled for each child (Cui and Huang, 2002: 253; Zhou Shizhang, 2005). This personal file, suggest the authors of a 2002 academic volume, *Theories of Psychological Education for Quality*, should consist of "the circumstances of the student's family members"; the child's "individual history (in terms of academic achievements, behavior, thinking/ideology [*sixiang*], and illnesses)"; "an analysis of the student's personal character, cognitive abilities, and emotional tendencies"; as well as a "psychological consultation log" (Cui and Huang, 2002: 253).

For their part, children should prepare a list of their abilities and shortcomings based on their subjective evaluations, and then compare their responses to the assessments of their teachers, class peers, and parents. According to a teacher's manual on how "to nurture the psychological quality of fourth-grade students," exercises such as these will not only instruct Chinese children to "objectively analyze their personality and their relationship with others" but also help them to better "control their emotions and behavior" (*Xiaoxuesheng xinli*, 2000).[9] In order to further assist young learners in the development of correct self-awareness and self-consciousness, schools in Shanghai and Beijing have additionally been required to introduce "psychological training classes" to the regular curriculum (Shanghai People's Congress Standing Committee, 2004; *Xinhua* News Agency, 2003; see also Borevskaya, 2001: 46). These classes, suggest Chinese pedagogic literature, would strengthen students' mental health and encourage them to "happily receive psychological guidance throughout their lives" (Wei, 2000: 50; Sun Lichun, 2001: 65; *Xiaoxuesheng xinli*, 2000: 1–6).

Neither of the two primary schools I studied in Shanghai offered students psychological training lessons at the time I conducted my fieldwork in 2004–5, though one vice-principal proudly pointed to a new sign above a room designated to become the school's "psychology office" (*xinli shi*). Conversations I held with Shanghai school staff and frontline teachers nonetheless reflected informants' increasing recognition that they must pay attention not only to students' grades but also to their psychological well-being. A good teacher, several interlocutors explained, is "sensitive to children's emotional needs" and provides them not only with knowledge but also with the proper tools to "better understand themselves" and to attain "healthy emotional development."

When I asked for examples of how a teacher can achieve this goal, several informants explained that when a student is doing badly at school, a teacher should avoid the previously common habit of publicly shaming the child in front of his/her peers and instead "try to understand the unique circumstances" that may have led to the student's poor performance. Has the child lost faith in her ability to succeed due to some recent setbacks? Or is there some trouble at home that may be affecting her emotional state and consequently her ability to focus on her schoolwork? This new consideration for students' feelings was frequently linked to the idea that teachers should avoid any act that may humiliate children and damage their sense of personal worth.

Not all teachers spared children's feelings in class however. In particular, teachers in their mid-30s to late 40s sometimes reverted to older, more familiar methods of teaching. In one Math lesson, for instance, the teacher, a woman in her late 30s, asked all those who had received a lower-than-average mark to stand up. Half a dozen seven-year-olds quickly complied, their faces visibly reddening with shame. She then proceeded to scold these children for "not studying hard enough" and for "disgracing their parents" by getting a low grade on the exam. Judging by parents' anecdotes, public shaming of students continued in other Shanghai schools as well. A mother who worked at a publishing house for children and youth, recounted:

> The other day, my son came home from school and told me that his teacher had criticized one of the other children for getting a "70" on an exam. It turns out that most of the other kids had gotten a "90", so the teacher told that boy off for making the entire class "lose face"...I think what she did was really wrong. When a teacher publicly criticizes a student like that, it puts the child under tremendous pressure and can really hurt his self-esteem. From what I know about recent reforms in Shanghai, teachers are not supposed to do that that anymore. They are supposed to respect students and pay attention not only to their grades and studies, but also to their feelings. Still, you might say things are a little bit better now than they used be. When I was at school, teachers also criticized children in front of the whole class. At least nowadays they *know* what they are doing is wrong,

even if they don't always practice it. Back then, teachers weren't even *aware* of it.

My own work at Whitewater and the Affiliated Primary Schools showed that teachers, especially those born or raised after 1978, did for the most part subscribe to the notion that tending to students' individual emotional needs is preferable to rushing to scold the child in front of his/her peers. This recognition complemented the idea that teachers should respect students' personal dignity as well as their right to privacy. In the minds of these younger teachers, there was a crucial link between the promotion of children's rights in the moral sense and the maintenance of their emotional and developmental needs as defined by the principles of psychological science. If teachers were to ignore students' rights to autonomy and self-agency, they reasoned, they may end up hindering their healthy emotional development as well.

Tending to children's emotional development does not end with the school day. According to the psychological discourse of child-hood currently circulating in legal, academic, and media publications in China, emotional care is primarily the task of parents and grandparents who must familiarize themselves with rational, scientific principles of childrearing and education based on the "systematic, objective" perspectives of psychological science (Hu Shen, 2000: 261; Wang Peng, 2002: 110; Wang Lingyu, 2002: 15; Xu Minqiang, 2004: 12; Zhou Feng, 1998: 311). One institute in charge of the crucial task of instructing caregivers on psychological science is the state-sponsored "parent school" (*jiazhang xuexiao*).

Located mostly in urban areas and operated by departments of education, institutions for family education research, schools, hospitals, women's federations, and various other community associations, China's "parent schools" offer caregivers of children aged up to 18 free or subsidized lectures, consultation services, and year-long courses. Typical class topics include: "Main factors influencing children's growth within families"; "Psychology of family education"; and "Features of children at different ages" (Ma and Guo, 1995: 11; *Zhongguo funü wang*, 2007). The purported aims of these state-sponsored classes are to "challenge feudal standards of conduct," which stress obedience of children and to teach caregivers, especially those of lower levels of education, how to raise their children "in a more logical manner" while maintaining an "open mode" of communication and a "give-and-take cycle of interaction" (Ma and Guo, 1995: 10–11; *Xinhua* News Agency, 2001; Eastday.com, 2001). The parent schools are not alone in attempting to turn the contemporary Chinese family into a conductor of relational norms associated with a middle-class *habitus*. In the past two decades or so, a burgeoning private sector made up of teachers, psychologists, and sociologists has also begun to offer urban parents consultations to help them master scientific child-rearing methods. One example of such a market-based service, which operated at the time I conducted my fieldwork, was a company called "Mother's Helper." According to reports in the general media, this service sought to offer Chinese caregivers (especially mothers), various techniques of coping with the "contradictions between traditional ways of parenting and *the demands of contemporary children for independence and individuality*" (*Xinhua* News Agency, 2003, emphasis added). Such professional help does not come cheap. In the mid-2000s, Mother's Helper charged between a few hundred to more than 1,000 Yuan (US$120) a month for its services. That is a hefty sum for most Chinese parents, even in urban areas. Not surprisingly, none of the mothers I talked to in Shanghai reported using such a service. Many did mention, however, turning to specialized Internet sites, books, and magazines in search of parenting advice.

Necessary reading for parents

One example of a popular parenting magazine frequently mentioned by my interlocutors is *Fumu bi du* (literally: "Necessary reading for parents," though the English masthead reads "Parenting Science"). First launched in Beijing in 1980, *Fumu bi du* is now a joint publication with the French-language magazine, *Enfant*, and carries both translated and locally produced articles. The monthly magazine, whose target audience consists of urban parents aged 25–40, aims to teach caregivers how to "objectively analyze and judge children's behavior, feelings and abilities according to their developmental stage." Armed with a staff of Chinese and foreign child psychologists, educators, and pediatricians, the publication also instructs and encourages parents to "respect and unearth each child's unique individual qualities" while "constantly growing, developing, and adjusting to the child's changing circumstances" (*Fumu bi du*, 2002).

A survey of articles published in the magazine in the year 2004–5 reveals a frequent appeal to readers to pay attention "not only to what the child eats, drinks and wears," but also to his/her emotional needs, thereby helping the child "to construct a positive self-image, strong self-confidence, and a sense of personal worth." One way caregivers can achieve this goal, argues a 2005 feature, is to avoid traditional parenting roles, such as those of "commander (*zhihui guan*)"; "moralist (*daode jia*)"; "judge (*faguan*)" or "critic (*piping zhe*)," all of which are said to hinder healthy communication between parents and children. Parents, advises the article, should offer their child frequent praise and rewards, and avoid criticism and punishments which only "damage children's self-respect and make them feel unloved" (*Fumu bi du*, 2005).

Several of my informants, especially well-educated women in white-collar professions, appeared to take this type of advice seriously and even tried to implement it. Ms Ma worked as an administrator at a local government office in Shanghai. A native of Heilongjiang, she had arrived in the city two years earlier with her husband and son, then an eighth grader. During our conversation, which took place at the family's spacious living room, she confessed that her son, whom she described as "a very helpful, honest, and kind-hearted boy," was experiencing some difficulty at his Math and Science classes since he "was not very smart." At first she had scolded the boy for his disappointing academic achievements. Later however, Ms Ma came across a translated work entitled *Ai de jiaoyu* [Education based on love], which recommended a more sensitive approach toward children's education. She and her husband, a media reporter, had decided to adopt the book's advice and to acknowledge the boy's efforts even if these did not produce the high marks his parents had been hoping for. The result, she said, was surprisingly "effective."

Ms Qian, who worked at a government publishing house, likewise reported that she and her husband, an academic who worked in the private sector, had decided to adopt some of the recommendations which appeared in a book on the differences between Chinese and American parenting methods. "This book really opened new ways of thinking for us," she told me. "We realized that a child develops a sense of self-esteem from an early age…[so] you shouldn't criticize him in public, only behind closed doors or in his room."

Many of the well-educated mothers I spoke to, especially those who reported consuming psychological advice literature, voiced similar opinions. Some felt that in adopting the recommendation that they respect their child's personal dignity and privacy or show consideration for his/her emotional needs, they were in fact displaying a higher "quality" (*suzhi*) and a more "civilized" parenting style than that of parents with lower levels of education who did not consume this sort of scientific advice. At a primary school located in a small market town not far from Shanghai, a teacher told me that while child-rearing guides and magazines are certainly more available to Chinese parents today, they were not read by everyone. For the mothers of children at her school, most of whom were "simple workers" with "relatively low levels of education," they held little attraction. "What you read about in these books and magazines is just not relevant to them. It simply doesn't reflect their lives," insisted the teacher.

My own conversations with several Shanghai mothers who worked in blue-collar occupations, had no more than high-school education, and were born and raised in either a rural area or a small town outside Shanghai, revealed that such mothers were indeed more likely to report that they had *never* read books or magazines on childrearing and education.[10] Notably, women like Ms Tan, who worked at a small store together with her husband, or Ms Cheng, who sold tofu at a local Shanghai market, also did not display the same sort of concern for their child's feelings or self-esteem as recommended by these publications. Instead, they were more likely to use commands and corporal punishment with their children, and to voice the concern that if they used lax methods, their children would not work hard enough at school, and consequently "not amount to much later in life."

"You can barely call it a childhood"

Some of the well-educated mothers I spoke to, though, did voice similar fears to those expressed by the less educated mothers. They also reported purchasing extra exercise books and worksheets for their sons or daughters, enrolling them in complementary after-school lessons, and sending them to special classes designed to develop their only child's talents and abilities.

A 37-year-old Shanghai academic, who regularly consumed psychological child-rearing advice published in books and magazines, told me that she believed parents should "pay attention to children's emotional needs" and "respect children's right to voice their wishes and opinions." Yet she also mentioned that her eight-year-old son was currently participating in a number of after-school classes, including drawing, calligraphy, computers, and English lessons. ("He used to learn the piano, but didn't have time for it anymore," she noted).[11]

A Shanghai book editor in her late thirties similarly told me she often consulted Chinese and foreign advice literature on issues related to childrearing and education and stated that "unlike other parents," she and her husband placed their child's "happiness" and "unfettered development" over his academic success. Yet like the previous informant, this mother also enrolled her seven-year-old son in various enrichment classes. Between regular school assignments, studying for exams, taking lessons in art and conversational English, and competing in Chinese chess tournaments during the weekends, the boy—whose room was filled with games and toys—in fact had little time left for spontaneous play.[12]

Shanghai teachers and mothers I spoke to certainly acknowledged children's plight. A statement I repeatedly heard during my conversations with Shanghai interlocutors was: "Chinese children suffer too much nowadays!" ("*Zhongguo de haizi tai ku le!*"). Despite the city's attempts to alleviate the workload of primary school, it was obvious that many Shanghai children continued to endure heavy academic pressure, long schooldays, and large amounts of homework. By the time they reached fourth grade many children were failing to finish their schoolwork before nine in the evening, sometimes even having to wake up early in the morning to complete their tasks. As a result, complained my informants, children were in "a state of constant exhaustion."

Part of the problem lay in the fact that in many Shanghai schools, the directions from above did not conform to the reality below. "They talk about reducing students' workload (*jianfu*)," complained Mr Liu, a computer teacher and one of the few male instructors I met at Whitewater Primary School, but children are still required to learn "too many things in too short a time." Promising to "reveal the whole truth" about China's recent education reforms as long as I did not record our conversation, Mr Liu went on to explain that schools in the city continuously tested children on their knowledge of the material, forcing teachers to assign large amounts of homework and focus on exam preparation rather than on making the learning experience more enjoyable for children. In reality, he noted, many teachers followed the principle of *"Suzhi jiaoyu hande honghong lielie, yingshi jiaoyu zhuade zhazha shishi"* (literally: "Vigorously hail Education for Quality, hold firmly to exam-oriented education").

Shanghai teachers also argued that parents shared an equal responsibility for the excessive pressure experienced by their children. Several informants related that when they had done their best to reduce students' homework in order to comply with the new guidelines, parents objected that they were jeopardizing their child's chances of succeeding in future exams. Apparently, some mothers even started to assign their children extra homework to "keep them on their toes."[13]

Ms Xu, a 50-year-old volunteer at a Parents School in Shanghai, described how ten or fifteen years ago, parental pressure only began when children started middle school as they were preparing to enter university. Today, she said, it starts at kindergarten.

> The only form of entertainment kids have nowadays is playing the piano, and even that is forced on them. Some parents think that if their child can't play the piano, he is not as good as the neighbors' child. I've even heard of children who cut their hands so that they wouldn't have to play anymore. If you ask children today what they are going to do during the school break, they'll tell you all they want to do is sleep.... Sleep is children's way of having fun now! Their childhood years are so unhappy you can barely call it a "childhood" anymore!

As she and others noted, and as documented in recent ethnographic studies by Fong (2004b), Woronov (2007, 2008, 2009), and Kuan (2011), the highly competitive nature of China's selection and evaluation system drove many parents to push their children to excel in their studies. In order to get into a good university, a student had to do well on the National College Entrance Examination (the NCEE, or the *gao kao*). But to achieve that coveted goal, he or she first had to attend a good middle school, which was allocated based on the results of the middle school entrance examination (the *zhong kao*). Doing well on the NCEE presumably determined not only one's chances of entering a top university in China, but also of securing a good position later in life. In reality, that was not always true,[14] but many parents nonetheless continued to cherish this dream for their (only) child, pressuring him or her to study hard in hope of "raising a dragon"—a talented, smart, successful offspring.

When it came to their own children, even educators were visibly conflicted about the notion that childhood ought to be a time of leisure and play rather than pressure and toil. The following statement, made by a 39-year-old Shanghai art teacher who is also the mother of a primary school student, demonstrates deep ambivalence even among those in charge of the dissemination of a psychological discourse of childhood:

> Children really work too hard nowadays. Today, in class, a student handed me a particularly good drawing, so I praised him and asked him rather casually: "Does your mother send you to art classes on the weekends?"
>
> "I don't have time for that," he told me. "I already have a full day of lessons on Saturdays and Sundays."
>
> Mind you, these are not drawing or singing lessons or anything like that. We are talking about English, computers, math, physics, and chemistry lessons for six- and seven-year-olds! It's very tiring for a child.... My son only has English lessons during the weekends. That's because he will be tested on it later on and also because it's very important to know English these days. He also plays the piano, but we don't force him to participate in competitions. We don't want to pressure him too much, you see.

Somewhat ironically, Professor Ai, the Shanghai education scholar who studies the introduction of more "age-appropriate, hands-on" teaching methods to primary school math lessons, likewise admitted that as a parent of a fourth-grader, she herself had mixed feelings about the goals of Shanghai's current school reforms:

> My son's school has all sorts of fun, after-school activities, which also contribute to his development. The children there are all

rather lively and bold; they're not afraid to talk to adults and have relatively broad knowledge...but I'm bit concerned about next year. I'm still not sure whether I should let him participate in these sorts of activities anymore. You might say I'm conflicted, and I'm not the only one.... The truth is that we do have reforms, but not all schools actually conform to them. And since everyone has to take an exam at the end, my son might be disadvantaged later on if he doesn't get enough practice at this early stage.

Despite the desire of urban, well-educated parents to associate themselves with a more "civilized" parenting style deemed suitable for a middle-class sensibility, their concerns about the future career chances of their only offspring sometimes led them to disregard the experts' prescriptions that they allow their child to experience a "carefree childhood." Membership in a certain age group may have also played a part in this conflict. A recent report in the Chinese media suggests that well-educated parents born after the introduction of the One-Child family policy in 1979 are often more inclined to allow their children to enjoy "a happy childhood filled with play and fun." These younger parents—most of whom are only-children—grew up with the pressure of being better and smarter than their peers and want to ensure that their own son or daughter experience a different sort of childhood. Notably, many also believe that in doing so, they are conforming to more "modern, scientific" principles of child-rearing (see Guan, 2009).

Many of the Shanghai mothers who took part in my own study belonged to a different generation however. Growing up during the tumultuous decade of the Cultural Revolution (1966–76), these women, now in their late 30s to early 40s, did not have a chance to receive a full course of basic education, not to mention the opportunity to attend university. Sharing a similar generational *habitus* (Bourdieu, 1977; Mannheim, 2005[1927]), members of this so-called "lost generation" in China often report wanting their own children to do better than they had done, and push them to excel at school at all costs (see Anagnost, 2008b; Chee, 2000; Davis and Sensenbrenner, 2000; Fong, 2004b; Milwertz, 1997). My conversations with Shanghai informants in their late thirties to late forties record similar sentiments. They suggest that Chinese mothers of this generation found it particularly difficult to comply with the experts' advice that they ease the pressure on their only child and allow him/her to engage in play rather than constant study.

Many of these informants, though, described their own child-hoods during the Cultural Revolution as a time of relative liberty (see also Naftali, 2010a). Children, they recalled, could "roam about as they please" without having to answer to parents who were away at work or at lengthy political meetings. "At least in our time [during the late 1960 and early 1970s], we let our children run freely," a grandmother I interviewed at a Shanghai pensioner's club told me. "Not like today, when parents won't let their kids be. These days, kids are shut in a big cage at school, and when they come home, they're locked in another cage by their parents."

A lack of formal schooling and poor material conditions during the Cultural Revolution years has shaped the maternal practices of this particular cohort of contemporary Shanghai women in other significant ways. In a recent ethnographic study on urban families in Xiamen, Esther Goh (2011) suggests that in the absence of much to observe from their parents' generation, Chinese men and women who were raised during the Cultural Revolution currently invest "a good deal of time and energy learning from books and taking the advice of experts on how to be good parents" (p. 126). This observation may also apply to the Shanghai mothers included in my own study, several of which reported that their parents could pay very little attention to their schooling and to their emotional needs. These contemporary Shanghai informants were quite keen on consuming psychological advice. Accordingly, they displayed greater involvement in their child's emotional life, attempted to respect his or her feelings and wishes, and believed that their son or daughter had a right to enjoy a "happy childhood". At the same time, these mothers also wanted their only child to enjoy better educational opportunities. Paradoxically then, they often ended up limiting the child's freedom and autonomy, in contrast to the experts' recommendations.

Concluding remarks

In an insightful study on the role of psychology and psychotherapy in the construction of modern-day identities, sociologist Eva Illouz (2008: 20) contends that the popularity of the "therapeutic discourse" among the middle classes in liberal, capitalist societies lies "in its ability to make sense of actors' social experience," including "rapid economic transformation, demographic patterns, downward mobility, and status anxiety." Drawing on this potent observation, this chapter has suggested that the same may be true for urban elite parents in contemporary China, a country which over the past three decades has undergone particularly rapid socioeconomic transformations and where a growing number of individuals are constructing new social and class identities. Indeed, the ability of modern psychological science to provide guidance about uncertain or conflict-ridden areas of social conduct, such as the parent-child relationship (Illouz, 2008: 214), makes it especially attractive for contemporary middle-class Shanghai caregivers, who currently struggle to make sense of new norms and requirements in the familial domain.

Like the middle-class mothers encountered by Lareau (2003), Hays (1996), and Kusserow (2004) in their work on families in North America, well-educated Shanghai parents included in my study embrace the notion that childrearing can no longer be regarded as a spontaneous affair but is best "interpreted through the medium of the therapeutic ethos" (Furedi, 2003: 12). In an attempt to provide their son or daughter with "a happy, healthy childhood" as experts currently recommend, these Shanghai mothers have started to ask themselves: "Am I making any mistakes in my relationship with my child? Will I emotionally damage my child, if I do this or that?" (Elias, 1998: 194). Subscribing, at least in theory, to a modern, liberal logic of parenting, which merges definitions of the person in psychological and in child-right discourses, these Shanghai mothers try to elicit and consider children's feelings, opinions, and thoughts; provide their son or daughter with personal space; and do their best to persuade their child with reason rather than force. In the process, they come to believe—though not always practice—the notion that, by cultivating their son or daughter's "natural need" for freedom, autonomy, and individual happiness, he/she would be able to know and assert his/herself in the future.

For their part, urban Chinese children, particularly those from affluent families of the new middle classes, are now "tutored in the ways of conducting their lives" in order to promote the "necessary conditions for achieving social harmony through mental health" (Rose, 1989: 172; see also Walkerdine, 1984). The current rise of psychological discourses of childhood in post-socialist urban China then may indicate the emergence of a new, neoliberal political program which seeks to govern Chinese society through "the educated and informed choices of 'active' citizens, families, and communities" (Rose, 1996: 20; see also Tomba, 2009b; Greenhalgh and Winckler, 2005; Jing, 2000b; Woronov, 2007).

Yet this chapter has also shown that in China, the popularity of psychological principles which follow the neoliberal logic of reforming individuals so that they are able to govern themselves (Dean, 1999: 210), may not only serve the interests of the Party-state or those of the capitalist market. It may also contribute to a strengthening of rights consciousness among adults and children alike. The notion of rights and the discourse of psychology share important characteristics. They both require respect for a person's autonomy and individual worth on the one hand, and demand a maximization of individual interests on the other (Illouz, 2008). In contemporary urban China, the association between "rights talk" and psychological principles—both of which rest on an individualistic, rational, utilitarian logic of conduct—legitimizes the idea of children as subjects with rights. This is particularly true for a younger generation of teachers and for elite urban parents who place much stock in "modern science."

Even these educators and parents, however, were at times conflicted about the application of the scientific-cum-moral advice of psychological experts when it came to the issue of children's academic work. One obvious source for their hesitation noted in this chapter is the current structure of China's education and evaluation system, which ultimately awards students who work hard and conform to their teachers and textbooks. Another important source of conflict, though, stems from the inherent contradiction between the modern, liberal notion of rights and the Chinese ethos of filial piety. Given that the Chinese family institution was founded on patriarchal and collective principles and on the logic of self-sacrifice and reciprocity, the idea of children's rights, which prescribes the equalization and individualization of old and young alike, inevitably creates confusion, tensions, and conflicts. The next chapter will describe some of these tensions and conflicts in detail, and consider how social and political institutions as well as individual actors in Shanghai attempt to address them while negotiating the notion of rights at home and at school.

4
The Filial Child Revisited: Tradition Holds Its Ground in Modern Shanghai

"When I was young, children had to wait until the adults sat at the table before they could even touch their chopsticks!" Ms Xu, a 55-year-old retiree and a volunteer at a local parents' school, told me. "In the past, we Chinese paid great attention to matters of seniority and propriety.... We used to respect our parents and teachers. Now it's all different. Why, these days, people treat children as if they were adults!"

The complaint was typical of an objection I heard from Shanghai educators, parents, and grandparents when asked about the idea of children's rights and its relevance to contemporary life in China. Even among informants who declared that they adhered to the principles of "modern, scientific" family education and "fully supported" the notion that children are autonomous persons worthy of respect, there was often the sense that the correct boundaries between children and adults were becoming dangerously blurred in contemporary China. Informants worried that the notion of children's rights would damage those boundaries even further.

Arguably, this blurring of age boundaries and the shift in social and familial hierarchies in China is not a recent phenomenon, but could be traced back to the Maoist era (1949–76). During the Cultural Revolution (1966–76) in particular, Chinese schoolchildren and youths would take part in violent struggles against their teachers and in public denunciations of "counter-revolutionary" parents.[1] However, most of my interlocutors (many of whom were too young to have taken active part in Cultural Revolution struggles), saw the introduction of the One-Child family policy in 1979 as a decisive turning point in the relationship between adults and children. The policy, they argued, had produced a generation of self-centered, stubborn "little emperors" who expected their elders to serve them.[2] Some informants believed however that the disappearance of appropriate age distinctions in China was as much a product of the introduction of "foreign" models of childhood, which stress children's individual needs and rights, as it was the result of recent demographic changes. Informants all agreed on one point, however: the indigenous ethos of filial piety, which emphasized children's respect for elders and seniors and reciprocal family relations, still had much to offer, even if some of its elements needed to change to suit the conditions of twenty-first-century China.

This particular finding matches the evidence from a growing number of studies, which reveal that despite the anti-Confucian rhetoric of the Maoist era (1949–76) and the effects of contemporary modernization processes, the norms of filial piety persist in present-day China. Moreover, both young Chinese and their caregivers continue to share an understanding of the importance of this ethos to the integrity of family and social life (Evans, 2008; Cockain, 2011; Fong, 2004a, 2004b, 2007; Kipnis, 2011). The life choices, behavior, and personal narratives of young Chinese in both rural and urban areas may reflect a growing emphasis on individual freedom. However, they also remain entangled with a perception of "the family as a collective of indisputable economic, social, and emotional importance" (Hansen and Pang, 2010: 61). The filial ethos is not imposed on Chinese youngsters by "dominating parents or, for that matter, resisted by cantankerous children but is understood, justified and practiced by both parties as a mutually acceptable way of acting out traditional discourses" (Cockain, 2011: 108–9). Yet these traditional discourses have undergone some significant transformations, as the older persons in the family are now experiencing a decline in their power, influence, and positions (Goh, 2011: 96; see also Fong, 2007).

Drawing on these crucial observations, this chapter explores the changing form of the notion of filial piety in contemporary urban China by juxtaposing it with the new discourse of children's rights. A comparison between the two reveals some important tensions. While the filial ethos assumes a series of obligations which focus on "rules of conduct constrained by status definitions," rights are in contrast more analytically abstract and more inclusive. They define social relations in terms of "entitlements that are universally shared" (Wilson, 1993: 112). Moreover, the child-rights discourse is based on a utilitarian understanding of social relationships and a more rational and quasi-economic approach to family life. It requires adults to re-frame their relations with the young in terms of "reason" and "law" rather than the Confucian precepts of "humaneness," "reciprocity," or "self-sacrifice." When informants attempt to apply these different rationalities in their daily interactions with children, the result is inevitable conflict.

This chapter describes how official, academic, and media publications in China attempt to address this conflict in various creative ways. It further considers how Chinese parents and teachers negotiate the tensions between the modern child-rights discourse and the more traditional ethos of filial piety by selectively employing the principles of the former in some areas, while evoking the idealized figure of the filial child in others. Noting informants' diverse reasons for this apparent dichotomy, I suggest that to some parents and teachers in Shanghai, the traditions of filial piety simply "seem ordained in the order of things" and they "rest in the certainty that these traditions exist without necessarily participating in them" (see Swidler, 1986). Others view the filial ethos as a powerful foil to the perceived fragility of social and family life in contemporary China. Regardless of social class and generational *habitus*, these informants continue to uphold the notion of the respectful, submissive child in some areas. However, they have considerably attenuated this indigenous ethos to fit the modern, individualistic discourse of children's rights.

The attraction of tradition and the perils of freedom

Many of the teachers I spoke to in Shanghai, particularly those born around the time of the introduction of market reforms in 1978, professed strong support of liberal pedagogies that emphasized children's initiative, autonomy, and personal dignity. Teachers' actual practices, both in and outside the class, however, at times contributed to the maintenance of a starkly unequal adult-child relationship.

This was apparent in a couple of regular class practices. Every lesson in the two schools I worked in started and ended in the same manner: the teacher declares the class is about to start (or end); the students rise, bow respectfully, and greet the teacher in unison. During the lesson itself, students called to address a question in class had to provide the answer while standing in their seats. If the teacher regarded the reply as incorrect or irrelevant, the student had to remain standing until the teacher would permit the child to sit again, in some instances after five or even ten minutes. Though not strictly a form of punishment, this sort of normative practice did serve to physically mark (and arguably humiliate) those children whose performance did not please the teacher.

Complementing this ritualized display of obedience, some teachers made a habit of requesting that children perform various services for them, including the passing of personal messages to a teacher on another floor, or in one instance, even asking a child to rub the back of a teacher who complained of back pain. To paraphrase Bourdieu (1977: 95), such practices, while seemingly "demanding the insignificant," nonetheless managed to "exhort the essential" from students and obtained their "respect for form and forms of respect," which constituted children's submission to the unequal order that dominated school life.

Even the physical layout of the primary school classroom continued to reinforce the "naturalness" of the teacher-student uneven power relationship. Despite teachers' talk of treating students as "colleagues" or "friends" rather than subordinates or "passive objects," most of the classrooms I visited still consisted of rows of desks facing the teacher and the blackboard.[3] The arrangement focused attention on the teacher as the primary subject of the learning experience and did little to encourage free-flowing, equal interactions between the children and the (all-knowing) adult teacher (see Anderson-Levitt, 2002).

Teachers' modes of speech further reinforced the notion that students and teachers stood on entirely different grounds. When I asked my school informants whether they thought students "should be allowed to criticize their teachers," some—particularly those in their mid-30s to mid-40s—visibly flinched at my use of the verb "criticize (*piping*)" in conjunction with students' dealings with teachers. Indeed, quite a few middle-aged teachers (and even some middle-aged teacher trainers) told me that it was completely "unacceptable" for a student to "criticize" her teacher, at least not to the teacher's face. "A teacher is, *after all*, a teacher," they explained. Their reply embodied the deeply rooted notion that the teacher-student relationship is, by definition, starkly unequal. As one teacher put it:

> Traditional Chinese thinking dictates that a teacher is the child's senior, and while it is okay for the teacher to criticize (*piping*) students, it is most inappropriate for students to do the same. Some teachers might tell you that they don't mind students' criticism, but in practice they would never accept it; not from a small child, anyway.

Interestingly, this observation again glosses over the events of the Cultural Revolution, during which students were actively encouraged to criticize, if not physically attack, their teachers, and many did in fact do so. The omission may reflect the notion, shared by other school informants, that Cultural Revolution practices were in fact a temporary anomaly in Chinese history.

The notion that a person must respect and adhere to his or her seniors dominated the thinking and behavior of some teachers not only in their dealings with students, but also in their interactions with their own superiors. Teacher-training seminars I attended in Shanghai reflected this thinking clearly. Consisting of lectures, lesson demonstrations, and round-table discussions, the seminars were designed to introduce the principles of a "learner-centered education" while illustrating the use of enquiry-based (*tan jiu*) and hands-on, active learning (*zuo zhong xue*) techniques in the classroom. Yet in each of the seminars, the majority of participants— several dozen primary school teachers from different schools across the city—seemed to prefer the role of passive listeners to that of active learners. Cast in the position of students, Shanghai teachers were often reluctant to raise questions, challenge their trainers in any way, or even point to possible difficulties in implementing new teaching methods in the classroom. Participants' submissive approach did not seem to stem from a lack of interest, however. Indeed, I frequently heard teachers whispering disapproving comments to each other after exiting the room or during breaks. Yet they seldom voiced their criticisms and misgivings in public.[4] When I shared this impression with Professor Ai, the education scholar involved in introducing innovative math teaching methods, she displayed her exasperation:

> That is how it usually is in these seminars. Many teachers are just used to carrying out whatever assignment they are given without asking questions. They are products of the old system and are not used to challenging their superiors in any way. The exception may be the younger teachers. Some of them are rather bold...but most teachers just sit there and listen, and when they get back to the classroom, they don't necessarily implement what they've heard. They just continue teaching the old way.

Shanghai primary school teachers, especially those in their mid-30s to mid-40s, often held complex and even contradictory views of the desired teacher-student relationship. While outwardly acknowledging the principle of "treating students as subjects with rights," which the city's educational reforms advance, teachers' words and behavior divulged a deep sense of ambiguity and even uneasiness about the notion that students were in fact "persons" in the full sense of the word—that is, possessing individual needs and feelings, as well as valuable thoughts and ideas that deserved to be heard in the classroom. Teachers' misgivings were reinforced by the notion that the present generation of only-children already lacked respect for their elders and seniors.

Spoiled by parents and grandparents at home, Shanghai's singletons "did whatever they liked" at school and were often self-centered to begin with, argued older teachers. "Indulging children's every whim" and granting them "too much freedom in the classroom," they reasoned, would only aggravate the situation and may result in unruly, chaotic behavior both inside and outside the classroom. Noting that "Western countries" emphasize freedom and individuality, Teacher Ye described what she saw as the dangers of liberalism:

> If children have *too much* freedom, this can often lead to criminal acts or all sorts of behavioral problems. In China, we handle this issue pretty well. Our students are rather restrained (*yueshu*) in

their behavior and have good moral values. Some people say that being restrained is not that good, but I disagree, because when you hear about what is happening in other countries, where youth crime rates are so high, you realize that in China, the social situation is much more stable. Several of my former schoolmates went abroad because they wanted their children to study in a better environment, but they told me they were quite disappointed. Compared to China, primary school education [in the West] is much too relaxed (*tai song le*), so they would rather have their children finish school here.

Teacher Lu, 37, agreed. "Children in China may be more quiet (*anjing*) and well-behaved (*laoshi*) [than Western children], but is that such a bad thing?" she asked. As reflected by these statements, teachers' ambivalence about the implementation of liberal education in the classroom was to some degree fuelled by a sense of national pride as well. Ms Zha, a Chinese- and class teacher who had been working at Whitewater Primary School since the mid-1980s, observed that: "Until recently, Chinese education used to emphasize children's ability to withstand hardship. Since our students' ability to think for themselves is thought to be low, however, our leaders *now* believe that we must adopt Western methods to improve the quality of our education system. Deng Xiaoping's theory emphasizes borrowing from the outside, even if that means bringing negative things, like AIDS or divorce, into China."

Despite the apparent consensus over the "low quality" of Chinese students compared to their colleagues in economically developed countries then, middle-aged teachers at both schools often expressed concern over what they saw as the incorporation of "too many foreign elements" into China's contemporary education system. Bakken (1999: 148–9) notes that teachers he met in China during the 1980s and the early 1990s strongly defended the use of strict educational methods on the grounds of their "Chineseness," viewing these methods as alternatives to the system practiced in "capitalist countries." In my own conversations with Shanghai teachers conducted in the mid-2000s, informants, particularly those born and raised prior to the introduction of market reforms, expressed similar views. Ms Rui, a math and class teacher at the Affiliated Primary School, argued that education which focuses on students' needs and rights "originated outside China," and as such, "has no basis in the actual experience of Chinese teachers." Later in the conversation, she reiterated this point by claiming that "China should not fully adopt Western educational methods."

"We need to recognize that our methods also have their strengths," she argued, "although we are a modern people (*xiandai ren*) now, we can't discard all of our traditional ways."

One of the long-standing methods that she and others seemed especially reluctant to part from was learning by rote (*beisong*), a technique which had repeatedly come under attack by education reformers throughout the history of modern China. Some of the contemporary literature on the Education for Quality reforms similarly castigates learning by rote as a faulty method that encourages conformity of thought and stifles students' creativity and individuality. Yet some Shanghai teachers (notably even the younger ones) were keen on maintaining rote-learning on the grounds that entry into university was determined by a standardized exam which rewarded those with an ability to memorize, a point also noted in Woronov's (2007) and (2008) studies. Other school informants stressed that "learning by rote had been in use in China for thousands of years" and "had proven its worth as an effective learning tool," not only in the study of Chinese language, but in other subjects as well.

Concerns about the foreign origins of China's recent school reforms were closely linked to a sense of unease regarding the potentially negative effects of liberal reforms on the contemporary generation of urban Chinese children. As noted by many of my interlocutors, today's urban children are much more knowledgeable about the world compared to their predecessors, since they have been increasingly exposed to diverse sources of information through various media, including television and the Internet. While some of the youngest teachers, those in their early twenties, viewed this as a mainly positive development, others—especially those who were born and at least partly educated prior to the 1980s—seemed alarmed about the fact that "today's children know more than adults do."

"Today's children understand much more than we ever did, because they have more information and are also exposed to the influences of the outside world," said Ms Ye, who served as assistant to the vice-principal and Chinese teacher at Whitewater Primary School. "I've been a teacher for seventeen years, so I have a lot of experience, but some of the things students say in class these days really leave me dumbfounded. Sometimes they talk about things I have never even heard of!"

Other school informants shared her feelings. Anxious about the fact that children's field of vision had suddenly expanded, older Shanghai educators were concerned about the attempt of recent reform plans to "lift students up while putting teachers down," as one teacher phrased it.

To summarize, though some educators, particularly those in their early twenties, thought that Chinese teachers "had much to learn from their Western colleagues" who were thought to be less "harsh and controlling of children's every move," older teachers were warier of the possible effects of introducing a more liberal, livelier atmosphere into schools and classrooms. Many believed that "treating students as subjects" and encouraging children to exercise their right to self-ownership were preconditions to the production of a modern, advanced citizenry, and a stronger, economically prosperous nation, as the government discourse suggested. At the same time, however, these older teachers also expressed anxiety about the possible implications of introducing new concepts of childhood and personhood, not only for the school, but for society as a whole.

Respecting children's rights or upholding filial piety?

Parents were as concerned about the potential consequences of implementing the discourse of rights within the home as teachers were concerned about providing too much freedom for children in the classroom. Ms Hui told me that she wished for a "democratic" relationship with her eight-year-old son, in which he would treat her as "an older sister" rather than as an awe-inspiring parent. But it became clear that she also wanted her child to show appropriate respect for his elders. When her son was a little younger, she recalled:

> He was a bit selfish and, like other children, often thought only of himself. For example, whenever we invited his grandparents for dinner, he would always choose the best piece of every dish.

We told him he should let his grandparents have it first, but he wouldn't listen. He would just put the food in his mouth and tell us: "If I let them have it, there would be none for me!"

This was unacceptable. My husband and I believe that children should respect their elders. We gradually taught him some table manners, and now he is much better in this regard. When we sit down to eat, he always offers the best portions either to us or to his grandparents.

Parents then may have been willing to embrace the notion of egalitarian family relations in theory, but many continued to uphold the values of filial piety in their daily practices.⁵ Other women too spoke of their concern about the implications of maintaining an equal relationship with their offspring.

Ms An, a Shanghai native, was a former factory worker who was sent to the countryside during the Cultural Revolution, stopping her education before she entered high school. Sitting in the kitchen of a mutual friend, she described the kind of relationship she hoped to have with her daughter:

I want her to respect me, of course. These days, some parents will tell you that they have a "friendly" relationship with their children. But I don't see the point in that.... What does it mean to treat your child as a friend anyway? In a friend-like relationship, each person thinks about himself before all else.... I want my daughter to do what I say because I am older than she is and because I take care of all her needs.

Ms Liang, a homemaker with a high-school diploma, similarly emphasized that she expected her child to show her and her husband "filial respect," for instance by taking care of them when they reached old age. Significantly, even better educated women who stated that a child "is an individual worthy of respect" expressed a sense of unease about the application of this principle in some situations.

Ms Feng, a 29-year-old math teacher and herself a mother, was the first informant at Whitewater Primary School who agreed to take part in my study. Enthusiastic and talkative, she came across as a genuine supporter of the city's recent school reforms, including the idea that teachers should respect children's rights and treat students as equal partners and not as subordinates. "What about at home?" I asked her during a break between classes. "Would this principle apply to the way parents should treat their children as well?"

"The education you give a child at home should certainly be democratic (*minzhu*)," Ms Feng replied. "A child has his own ideas, and parents shouldn't decide about each and every matter. They should consider problems from his point of view as well." Then, after a short pause, she added:

> Of course, the relationship between parents and children cannot be *entirely* equal. After all, parents *are* parents, right? They are the child's seniors (*zhangbei*) and you have to respect them for everything they have done for you. You see, in China we distinguish between the young and the old (*you zhang you zhi fen de*). When you meet your elders, for example, you need to greet them respectfully. And children must yield to their seniors. They can't "climb over their parents' heads" (*padao baba mama tou shangqu*)!

This statement reflects the belief, evident among many of my Shanghai informants, that "parents have sacrificed themselves to raise you, so you should be grateful and show them respect in return." Moreover, many teachers reiterated that respect for one's elders and seniors, a central tenet of the ethos of filial piety, has been and should remain, an "important part of China's culture."

That message was also evident in teachers' handbooks. In a 2000 teachers' manual on nurturing the "psychological quality" of fourth-grade students, lesson plans were designed to encourage students to express their independent views or challenge teachers and correct them whenever they make a mistake. However, class activities were also meant to teach children through games and discussion to "respect, praise, and extol" their teachers who are their "their elders and seniors" (*Xiaoxuesheng xinli suzhi peiyang: si nianji jiaoshi yongshu*, 2000).[6]

Similar paradoxes are also apparent in the Chinese government's 1999 official Decision on Promoting Education for Quality reforms in the nation's schools. Teachers should "get along well with students on an equal basis, respect the personality of students,...and protect the students' legitimate rights and interests," declares the document, but they should also ensure that students "acquire a strong sense of discipline." Educators must "stimulate the students' independent thinking and creativity" and improve children's "ability to express themselves," but they should also do their best to "standardize [children's] behavior (*xingwei guifan*)" in order to "cultivate their morality" (Communist Party of China, 2000: 231–2).

The emphasis on instilling in children both "rights-awareness" and a morality grounded in respect toward elders and seniors forms part of a broader campaign to rehabilitate Confucian values in Chinese social and public life. Since the early 1990s, the dissemination of Confucian works has begun in numerous schools, colleges, and universities (including a number of Shanghai middle schools). Statues of Confucius are now found in Chinese schools and colleges, and since 1989, large ceremonies to celebrate Confucius's birthday have been held across the country (Shanghai Daily, 2005; *Xinhua* News Agency, 2004b).

The CCP has sanctioned and even encouraged these and similar public activities. In 1994, President Jiang Zemin praised Confucius's contributions to Chinese society on the occasion of his 2,550th birthday (China Daily, 2000). The message seemed to have seeped to the lower rungs of the government bureaucracy. A decade later, an official of the Shandong Provincial government reportedly declared: "Confucian ideology is important to administrators...for if an administration does not care for the interests of the masses, it is sure to be short-lived" (*Xinhua* News Agency, 2004b). The promotion of the principle of "constructing a socialist, harmonious society" under Hu Jintao and Wen Jiabao further reflects this recent "Confucian revival" in CCP ideology and rhetoric.

In the Shanghai schools in which I worked, educators took pains to translate this "traditional Confucian" ethic into class practices designed to teach children not only about their new rights under the law, but also how to show their parents gratitude and respect. Children were encouraged to do small chores around the house, or perform caring gestures such as washing their parents' feet. The latter activity, explained Ms Qu, Party Secretary at Whitewater Primary School, was being promoted in both class and Young Pioneers' activities as part of a television campaign titled The Loving Heart Passes On [*Ai xin chuandi*].

"The Loving Heart Passes On"

The campaign Ms Qu described was hard to miss—even among the multitude of television commercials selling cosmetic products, nutritional supplements, and household appliances on Chinese television. The "Loving Heart Passes On" public service announcement (*gongyi guangao*) first aired on China's state-run television network (CCTV) in 2001, and was still showing on CCTV at the time I conducted my fieldwork.

The ad began with a caption that read: "Love for the elderly starts from the heart." The viewer is then transported to what appears to be a relatively affluent urban Chinese home. A young mother kneels by her son's bed and washes his feet while telling him a bedtime story. When she is finished, she asks the boy to wait in his room and promises to tell him the story again in a little while. A minute later, we see her carrying a second water bucket to another room while tiredly wiping her brow.

Instead of waiting, the little boy impatiently slips out of his room to look for his mother. Peeping behind the living room door, he sees her washing her own mother's feet. A wheelchair by her side, the elderly woman affectionately caresses her daughter's hair and asks her if she "wouldn't like to rest for a bit after working so hard all day long." Looking up with a smile, the young woman assures her mother that she is "not at all tired" and, in any case, "washing feet is good for one's health." Looking up, the old woman's sighs with pleasure, and the boy quickly turns away before the two women see him.

Having washed the grandmother's feet, the boy's mother returns to her son's room but finds it empty and goes to look for him. In a moment appropriately marked by a crescendo in the traditional Chinese tune playing in the background, we then see the little boy, who appears to be no more than four or five years old, struggling to balance a washing basin full of water. "Mama, I want to wash your feet," he tells the young woman, whose puzzled expression is quickly replaced by a grateful smile. Finally, in a scene recalling the opening image, we see the mother and child back in the boy's room. Only this time, it is the boy who is kneeling next to the bed, washing his mother's feet.

In a television interview, Xu Jian, the female producer of "The Loving Heart Passes On" clip (*Shi hua shi shuo*, 2004), explained what compelled her to create the public service announcement:

These days, people think that it is perfectly natural for a mother to wash her son's feet, but the opposite doesn't seem so natural anymore [...] Society is changing very fast these days. Everyone is so busy with their work, their studies and their social life that they barely have time for their families [...] But doesn't this turn us into "business colleagues" (*tongshi*) instead of relatives? [...] Family is the basic unit of society. If there are warm feelings (*qinqing*), morality (*daode*), and humanness (*renxing*) in the family, there will be warm feelings, morality, and humanness throughout society.

The last phrase would certainly ring familiar to many Chinese viewers. It alludes to the Confucian notion that the correct handling of family relations (that is, the relation between father and son; husband and wife, and elder brother and younger brother) would ultimately lead to a proper handling of the ruler-subject relationship and to harmonious social connections overall. The "Loving Heart Passes On" clip clearly plays on this traditional theme by stressing the importance of caring for one's elders, and by contrasting it with a modern ethic of care based on a rational interests and business-like negotiations. Notably, there is an underlying, gendered message as well. The voice-over at the end of the clip informs us that "parents are the child's best teachers" ("*fumu shi haizi zui hao de laoshi*"). The ad itself however conveys the notion that the responsibility for instructing children how to respect their elders lies with mothers rather than fathers; there is no father figure in this picture of intergenerational harmony. Female viewers are taught that by diligently fulfilling their domestic duties in the way that the young woman is shown in the ad, they will ensure that "social harmony" will prevail in the family and in society as a whole.

When I asked my Shanghai interlocutors whether they had seen this ad and what they made of it, I discovered that mothers were indeed familiar with the campaign. "It's a very good clip and quite moving too" remarked Ms Tao, an office worker with a high-school diploma and mother of an 11-year-old son.

"This ad shows you how important it is to teach children how to respect their elders (*xiaojing*), not just through words but also through your own personal example," another well-educated mother commented.

Despite their positive response however, none of the women I talked to practiced feet washing at home. "Our parents don't need us to wash their feet, they can manage it on their own," remarked some. For the same reason, no mother expected her school-aged child to wash her feet either. Furthermore, noted several women, "Children are so busy with schoolwork these days, that they barely have time for anything else...we wouldn't want to burden them with making them take care of us."

Ms Gui, the academic married to a wealthy entrepreneur, went even further. Contrary to the traditional dictates of filial piety, she emphasized, neither she nor her husband expected their two sons to take care of them in old age. "All we want is for them to become independent, self-sustaining adults," she reiterated during our conversation.

What these statements reveal is an ambiguous attitude toward the traditional tenets of filial piety. As some informants noted, the filial ethos did not sit well with the liberal ideas prescribed by the discourse of children's rights. At the same time however, there was a clear reluctance to part with the tradition altogether. In her study of three-generation households in urban Xiamen, Esther Goh similarly finds that parents "were keen to teach their children to respect their elders according to the principle of *zhang you you xu* (respect and observe the hierarchy of order from old to young)" (2011: 96). However, she also notes that most parents and grandparents who took part in the study refrained from taking concrete disciplinary action in light of these principles. As a result, children frequently ignored and undermined their elders. In a study on parent-child communication problems in urban China, Vanessa Fong (2007: 89–90, 110) likewise found that a majority of city parents wanted their children to internalize the values of independence and self-reliance which they link to a modern, neoliberal market system. However, parents also attach great importance to the value of "obedience" (*tinghua*) to elders and superiors, associated with the Confucian ideology of filial piety.

It is a paradox that I would come across time and again during my own research in Shanghai homes. Well-educated caregivers were generally supportive of the idea that youngsters should be treated as subjects with rights, and accordingly rejected the traditional notion that children should fully submit to their elders and seniors, as dictated by the ethos of filial piety. Yet when it came to the issue of children's schoolwork, even well-educated, elite caregivers who were keen on adopting a modern, middle-class *habitus* were less inclined to respect children's rights and wishes. Many of the mothers I talked to insisted, for instance, that their school-aged child work hard at his/her studies, even if that meant foregoing children's individual wishes, or the sort of "happy, healthy" childhood currently recommended by child experts and liberal educators.

Chinese parents' stress on children's academic achievements is a well-documented phenomenon. Studies by Charles Stafford (1995), Ruth Chao (1994), and Andrew Kipnis (2008, 2011) have shown that Chinese parents around the world often expect a child to work hard at his/her schoolwork from a relatively early age. Parents feel that they have a moral duty to train the child to succeed in school while children in turn must repay their parents for their care and investment by obtaining good grades and later a successful career. In her 2011 study, Goh notes that unlike other aspects of parent-child relationships in contemporary urban Xiamen, children's academic work was often "considered non-negotiable with little room for compromise" (Goh, 2011: 196).

Similar notions may have led the Shanghai mothers who took part in the present study to uphold the ethos of filial piety at the expense of children's rights when it came to the issue of schoolwork. While some mothers no longer subscribed to the strictly hierarchical parent-child relationship recommended by filial piety, they nonetheless felt that applying the idea of children's rights to the realm of schoolwork would not only compromise their only-child's career chances and future social status, but may also undermine the basic structure of the family. Shaken by the One-Child family policy, and by the introduction of the individualistic, business-like logic of market transactions, the urban Chinese family, many felt, was already much too fragile. To these Shanghai caregivers and educators, adherence to a considerably attenuated logic of filial piety, which nonetheless stresses familial duties and relatively well-defined boundaries between old and young, is perceived as a possible bulwark against the unnerving pace of social change in twenty-first-century urban China.

Concluding remarks

The modern, global discourse of children's rights seeks to empower children—arguably the weakest members of societies—and to protect them from psychological and physical harm instigated by adults, including their own parents. But it fosters a particular mode of thinking about the relationship between parent and child, "as quasi-contractual, limited, and directed toward the promotion of an abstract public good" (Schoeman, 1980: 8). Such an emphasis assumes that the familial bond is a one-way relationship aimed almost solely at promoting the best interest of the child, an assumption which stands in sharp contrast to the common conceptualization of the family worldwide as a web of "nonabstract moral relationships, in which talk about rights of others, respect for others, and even welfare of others is to a certain extent irrelevant" (Schoeman, 1980: 8; see also Archard, 2004; Stephens, 1995b).

The findings of the present chapter show that this conflict is especially salient in contemporary urban China. In a recent study on the changing moral life of the person in China, Yan Yunxiang (2011: 54) observes that "while more and more Chinese individuals embrace the new ethics of individual rights, others lament the decline of collective ethics of responsibilities." He further notes that, since the 1990s, the sense of cultural belonging has grown ever stronger" in China as "nationalism and consumerism emerge together as the main threads to construct the world of meaning for many Chinese."

Yan's observation may explain why some Shanghai parents and teachers view children's rights with such ambiguity. As we saw, the discourse of children's rights is gaining ground among a younger generation of teachers and among elite, educated parents, especially those who wish to associate themselves with a modern, middle-class *habitus.* Yet, the rapid pace of social, economic, and demographic transformations, and rising concerns about the integrity of Chinese cultural and national identity in an age of increased global integration, also leads to confusion, tensions, and conflict. Responses to this conflict are far from uniform. Some elite parents and young educators in Shanghai seek to move away from "an ethic of care realized by fulfilling differential obligations depending on status" and instead emphasize "care achieved by honoring equally held rights" (see Wilson, 1993: 113). In contrast, middle-aged teachers, who are products of both the collectivist *habitus* of the Maoist period (1949–76), and of the individualistic and outward-oriented *habitus* of the Reform period (1978–), often cleave to a more hierarchical logic of conduct while yearning for clearer boundaries between old and young. Although supportive of the need to prepare children for success in a global capitalist job market, they are also outwardly nostalgic about an idealized time in which "teachers were teachers" and "students were students" as one teacher phrased it.

Like teachers, mothers' attitudes toward the notion of children's rights are best understood as a product of a traditional ethos of filial piety, Maoist-era collectivist agendas, as well as a new, neoliberal ethos of childhood and subjectivity. While proud of their child's newfound ability to assert his or her individual right to privacy, to protection from violence, or the voicing of personal opinions, some Shanghai mothers nonetheless continued to place a premium on children's display of reverence for elders and seniors, particularly through arduous academic labor. To elite Shanghai caregivers in the mid-2000s, the indigenous ethos of filial piety constitute "a tenet of basic human decency" (Fong, 2004a: 634) and an inevitable part of social existence. Diverse, rather than unified, partial rather than all-embracing, this ethos, and the modes of child-rearing it produces, do not always inspire enthusiastic assent (Swidler, 1986: 279) on the part of individual teachers and caregivers. To many, they nonetheless continue to constitute the most natural way of raising and educating the young in contemporary urban China.

Conclusion

This book began with a short account describing the alarm and dismay felt by a Chinese educator at the sight of a woman beating her child in public. The denunciation of this mother's actions over the pages of a CCP news publication, I suggested, indicates a pivotal shift in Chinese conceptions of childhood, power, and subjectivity in the post-socialist era. Rather than appendages to their families, to society, or the nation, as has been the case for much of Chinese history, children in China are now increasingly recast in the role of "small subjects," worthy of rights and respect. Exploring the origins and dynamics of this shift, this book has argued that it is a product not only of the changing value of urban youngsters in the era of economic reforms and the One-Child Policy, but also, and no less significantly, of the increasing influence of a modern, liberal discourse on children's rights in post-1989, urban China.

Drawing its logic and rhetoric from the global discourse of children's rights, China's child-rights discourse invokes psychological theories of child development and emphasizes individual rather than collective wants and needs. It presents children as autonomous subjects entitled to self-ownership and able to express their own views and wishes. Though subject to capture by the Chinese Party-state's on-going project of "raising the quality of the population" and building a strong, prosperous nation through the production of enterprising citizens and consumers, the emergent discourse on children's rights carries important implications for adult-child relations in China.

In Shanghai, the proliferation of "rights talk" in media publications, academic literature, pedagogic materials, government policies, and legal codes of the past two decades or so has affected family and school life in several important ways. Though bound by the requirement to prepare young students for the crucial National College Entrance Examination (the *gao kao*), primary school teachers in Shanghai, especially those born or raised after 1978, are increasingly willing to treat children as subjects rather than objects of the learning process, and to allow students a greater scope of freedom, both in a physical and a psychological sense. Shanghai caregivers, particularly those who uphold modern, "scientific" child-rearing methods, are also keener on adopting a psychologized, rights-based conception of the self.

Like middle-class parents elsewhere in the capitalist, industrial world, well-educated Shanghai parents of means exhibit greater respect for children's personal opinions, private possessions, and individual space. They are also increasingly doubtful about the use of physical force in the disciplining of the young. Indeed, to some of these elite Shanghai caregivers, the child-rights discourse functions as a type of class marker. With its uniquely modern view of childhood as a separate and sentimentalized period of life, and of children as independent persons capable of entering into rational contracts with those around them, the discourse of children's rights embodies a highly-desirable global, middle-class *habitus*. The spread of the child-rights discourse in contemporary urban China is therefore closely linked to, and largely sustained by, the rise of new social formations in the post-socialist era.

The emergent taboo against the use of violent, repressive power between parents and children, teachers and students in contemporary urban China, this book notes, is also accompanied by a demand, or even enforcement, of a higher degree of self-control from children and adults alike. These developments closely match Norbert Elias's observations about the nature of social relations in modern, industrial societies (1998). They also match the Foucauldian theory of the emergence of a modern, bio-political rationality of power—one that is more subtle and that works through the freedom of individuals. Indeed, some scholars (e.g., Greenhalgh, 2011; Rofel, 2007; Yan Hairong, 2003) have gone as far as to argue that China is currently experiencing a decisive shift from an authoritarian, sovereign mode of governance toward a neoliberal, bio-political strain of rule.

This book has argued that this may not be true, even for those Chinese educators and caregivers who generally subscribe to the individualistic logic of rights. Rather, within contemporary Chinese discursive formulations of childrearing and education, we find several strains of thinking which tensely coexist with, and at times contradict the neoliberal notion of children as autonomous persons with rights. These divergent constructions of children and childhood have various implications for family and school life in China. In this concluding chapter, I address these implications, while pointing to future lines of research on the construction of the child-rights discourse in twenty-first-century China.

Rights, intimacy, and belonging

Participants in discussions over the issue of human rights in non-Western, developing countries tend to frame their position using the dichotomies of "local/traditional" and "global/modern" forms of government and modes of life, while frequently basing their argument on a fantasy about the modern/liberal/capitalist West (Kennedy, 2004: 21). In discussing China's child-rights discourse, we likewise saw that various advocates of children's entitlements—from government and communist party officials, to media writers, academics, and educators—commonly endorse the promulgation of youngsters' rights as an embodiment of legal, political, and/or social modernization. Indeed, to liberal intellectuals in China, as well as to young teachers and elite caregivers, the idea of children's rights, with its aura of universality, rationality, and civility, constitutes a crucial part of belonging to the modern, global world. Yet, the association with global modernity also makes the child-rights discourse a particularly controversial topic in China.

As we saw, Shanghai educators and caregivers, particularly those whose system of dispositions and embodied habits, or *habitus*, has been shaped prior to the introduction of market reforms in 1978, often express concern that implementing the notion of child-rights at home and at school would result in a loss of "national culture" and national identity and, at a more personal level, a loss of intimacy, a sense of security, and a sense of belonging. In a study on the moral basis of the contemporary child-rights movement, legal philosopher Ferdinand Schoeman reflects that people everywhere often derive meaning in their lives not from the maximization of individual interests or the display of respect for the boundaries of others, but from establishing their "roots in others" (1983: 279).

The findings of the present study suggest that this observation may be true for China's child-rights discourse. It explains why some Shanghai teachers and caregivers declare support for children's rights but stick to "traditional" prescriptions for maintaining family and social order, for instance by demanding that young children show respect for age and seniority whether at the dinner table or in the classroom. Anxious about the effects of market reforms and of the One-Child Policy on the stability of family and social life, urbanites in China may revert to a more familiar ethos which seeks to define the adult-child relationship in a much clearer and more hierarchical fashion. Popular adherence to the notion of filial piety, even if at the rhetorical level only, is also understandable considering the crisis of faith experienced by many Chinese citizens following the demise of collectivist ideology over the past three decades or so.

Notably, it is a sentiment that the CCP leadership is willing to exploit. Amid increased civil unrest, particularly among disgruntled workers and farmers, the Chinese leadership has, over the past two decades or so, begun to search for a new basis of legitimacy to sustain its rule. As evident in the patriotic rhetoric of contemporary school reform plans and the primary school curriculum, nationalism constitutes one source of loyalty to the state (Unger, 1996: xi; see also Zhao, 2004; Woronov, 2007). "Traditional" family values may be another.

The current emphasis on filial piety as a condition to maintaining harmonious social relations reveals that the post-socialist Party-state in China has been staking its authority on being "the guardian of national pride" (Unger, 1996: xi), and on its ability to provide economic growth while maintaining social order and harmony within the family and in society at large. The Chinese government promotes a neoliberal deregulation of the economy and the labor market; it is willing to endorse a new emphasis on the individual and his/her personal desires in the realms of everyday culture and consumerism. However, the government also attempts to restrain this individualization process "by linking it with officially celebrated values such as the nation and the family" (Beck and Beck-Gernsheim, 2010: xix) and on the "glorious Chinese tradition" of filial piety.

Commenting on the re-emergence of "tradition" in reform-era China, Bakken (1999) suggests that we view this phenomenon not as the remains of a pre-modern past but in terms of the modern mechanisms of social control. Tradition, he notes, always has "a 'binding,' normative character which holds society in a given form over time." In contemporary China, the force of tradition is directed against the disorder brought forth by neoliberal modernity. In the realms of childrearing and education, however, this is a problematic strategy since the sort of "traditional" pedagogy that the CCP seeks to employ rests on a logic that is quite different from that of modern, neoliberal governmentality or the notion of children as autonomous persons with rights. The "traditional" logic corresponds to authoritarian modes of education which emphasize order, discipline, and conformity, rather than individual interests and desires. It seeks to "produce a citizenry that will follow the models the government puts forth unthinkingly" (Kipnis, 2011: 73) rather than self-governing, innovative citizens and workers.

This traditional pedagogy, however, also stresses the importance of mutual care rather than the satisfaction of selfish individual interests within the familial realm. As such, it carries much attraction for individuals in contemporary China for whom the family remains a crucial source of social, emotional, and psychological security, even as they increasingly pursue individual interests (Hansen and Pang, 2010: 47). Contemporary Chinese may pay much more attention to the "individual psyche" but this process leaves many people may feeling not only liberated but also increasingly alienated (Kipnis, 2012: 7). In Shanghai, caregivers and teachers are deeply concerned about the increasing fragility of social and familial relations in an era of rapid marketization. They therefore continue to uphold an idealized familial and social ethos which promotes "warm feelings (*qinqing*)," "morality (*daode*)," and "humanness (*renxing*)" in familial and social relations instead of the contract-based, business-like interactions prescribed by the liberal rights-discourse or the neoliberal market economy.

As the present study has further shown however, in the hands of individual caregivers and teachers, this indigenous, "traditional" logic of governing family and school life has been modified and in some respects reconciled with the modern logic of rights. Familial and social harmony is now to be attained not through adherence to strict notions of hierarchy and subordination to elders and seniors but through the creation of more equal adult-child relationships based on mutual respect and reciprocal duties as well as individual rights. What we are witnessing in contemporary China then, is not a "single blend" of governance (Kipnis, 2011: 77; see also Nonini, 2008), but rather conflicting modes of thinking about children, rights, and subjectivities. And while it may be tempting to neatly associate one mode of thinking with particular social actors and/or institutions, the data provided in the present study suggests that we would be rash to do so.

Authoritarian modes of governing children in China (grounded in either socialist and/or Confucian ethics) hold an attraction for some government and CCP officials, academics, media writers, educators, and caregivers. At the same time though, the modern, liberal discourse of children's rights may be hailed by other writers, educators, and caregivers, and even within the government and Party establishment. Moreover, some writers and informants believe that it is possible to fuse the idea of children's rights with some of the elements of the filial piety ethos, and that these two modes of governance can and should complement each other. We may therefore conclude that the emergent notion of children's rights in post-1989 China, and its increasing popularity among some sectors of Chinese society signify an important shift in public and private conceptions of childhood, family, and education. It may also carry significant implications for Chinese notions of power and citizenship.

The political implications of China's child-rights discourse

Noting the deepening sense of self and the growing emphasis on the individual in China, especially in the context of the rising middle classes, Kleinman and his colleagues have suggested that this moral and psychological shift may hold larger political significance and ultimately involve "the reshaping of governance" in post-socialist China (2011: 30). The present study likewise argues that the deepening rights consciousness among contemporary urban teachers, caregivers, and children themselves may carry long-term implications not only for the relationship between children and adults, but also between the state and its citizenry in post-socialist urban China.

Admittedly, the child-rights consciousness is particularly prevalent among members of the emerging middle classes who are still a minority in China. Moreover, China's new middle classes have so far acted as a force for social stability rather than one for political change (see for example, Cai, 2005; Tsai, 2005; Guo Yingjie, 2008; Tomba, 2009a; Chen and Dickson, 2010; Li Cheng, 2010; Yang Jing, 2010). However, the rising middle classes play an exemplary role in China's contemporary public and official discourse, and their behavioral norms are setting the standards for a "civilized" mode of conduct for other social groups, such as migrants arriving in large cities or the urban working class (Tomba, 2009a: 10). Therefore, the concept of children's rights, and the logic of governance it implies, may not necessarily stay within the realm of this small (albeit growing) social group, but may spread into other sectors of Chinese society.

The present association of the child-rights discourse with a particular social group in China nonetheless raises the question of whether the notion of rights is equally applicable to every child or whether certain categories of young people are deemed more capable of exercising—and therefore more deserving of possessing—rights and privileges. The present study has focused on the relatively well-off, educated, predominately Han population of Shanghai, admittedly one of China's wealthiest, most cosmopolitan cities. Yet even within the privileged space of Shanghai, gender, and to a greater extent, class, play an important role in determining the rights of a child and his or her ability to enjoy them. Moreover, while the past several decades have seen significant development in Chinese notions of citizenship and rights, this process has been accompanied by the development of categories such as "quality" (*suzhi*) that "work not to broaden citizenship and promote equality but, rather, to potentially perpetuate categories of exclusive citizenship and inequality" (Sigley, 2009: 539; see also Murphy, 2004; Yan Hairong, 2003).

Indeed, the present study has documented how, to some native-born Shanghai educators and parents, children of rural migrants or those residing in China's hinterland (the latter constituting a fair share of the nation's children) are in fact of "lower quality" compared to Shanghai-born children, partly because their parents treat them "no better than animals." Such elitist notions, also recorded in Woronov's (2008) and Yi's (2008, 2011) studies of migrant schools in Beijing and Xiamen, could be seen as a manifestation of an "internal Orientalism" which deems that the masses in China are incapable of handling freedom and "are not mature enough for human rights and democracy" due to their "lack of civilization" (Svensson, 2000: 205; see also Anagnost, 1995, 1997a).

The exclusion of various social categories by the cultural and political elites has a long history in the development of modern Chinese notions of rights and citizenship (Goldman and Perry, 2002). However, the economic reforms launched in 1978 have in some respects deepened both the perceived and objective gaps between different layers of society in China. Some of the country's rural children, and in particular girls who reside in China's poorest regions, are still unable to enjoy a full course of basic education (Kipnis, 2001; Adams and Hannum, 2008; Hannum et al., 2011), let alone the right to privacy or to express their own views.

Moreover, while the reforms and the shift to a market economy have loosened government control over freedom of movement to urban areas, children of rural migrants are frequently no better off than those in the countryside. By law, city schools should admit children of migrant workers; in reality these children are often turned away from urban public schools unless they can pay hefty tuition fees. As a result, they are forced to attend sub-standard, self-run institutions that are often poorly equipped and seriously under-staffed (Woronov, 2008; Kahn and Yardley, 2004). If it is true then that the extension of the right to education and to social services to each and every child in modern nation states amounts to "an extension of the status of citizenship to children" as T.H. Marshall has claimed (cited in Rose, 1989: 122), then we must conclude that, in contemporary China, many children continue to occupy the position of "second-class" or even "non"-citizens.

The unequal treatment of certain categories of children is closely related to another central problem in the modern Chinese concept of rights: the tendency of governments and political activists alike to view rights as revocable privileges conferred by the state, rather than natural prerogatives possessed by each individual (Goldman and Perry, 2002: 6; Bruun and Jacobsen, 2000; Beck and Beck-Gernsheim, 2010). Compared to the Maoist era, it is certainly true that adult Chinese citizens now enjoy more latitude to speak their minds in private and in public. Yet those who seek to petition the government are frequently harassed and even arrested, and many are "too keenly aware of the lack of strong legal institutions to envision themselves as citizens with guaranteed legal rights" (Ching Kwan Lee, 2007: 116). State interventions in issues related to the care and development of children could similarly be dismissed as mere rhetoric. The introduction of child-rights legislation can be seen as a ploy to legitimize the Chinese government's coercive population policy, as an attempt to "cast itself as a modernistic and compassionate regime" and strengthen its political standing (Jing, 2000b: 4, 14; see also Greenhalgh and Winckler, 2005).

This claim has some merit. However, it is precisely because of persistent state encroachments on the personal interests of adult Chinese citizens that we should not underestimate the significance of the emergent notion that even the very young are entitled to voice their opinions and to protect their personal interests from the intrusion of others with the aid of the law. The recognition of an individual's right to privacy—in both a physical and a symbolic sense—is likewise not just part of the economics of private property in post-socialist China, but a political issue which signifies a transformation in the relationship between the state and its citizenry (see Feuchtwang, 2002: 226).

In a recent volume on China's contemporary privacy standards, legal scholar Wang Hao of Beijing's Renmin University laments the lack of a working definition of privacy in China which prevents the general population from understanding "what the concept of privacy is" (2011: v). As this study documents, however, this is slowly beginning to change. More and more young Chinese are learning about their new rights under the law at school and from the media, and some are quick to quote this law when they feel their personal interests are being violated.

Would the present generation of primary school children in China, who are becoming relatively more assertive at home and school, go on to demand increasing freedom of speech and more civic and political rights as adults? Would these youngsters grow up to become a new type of daring, assertive citizen in years to come? Future studies, which would explore perceptions of rights and citizenship among Chinese children of different age groups, genders, and ethnicities, and among vulnerable children, including those who reside in rural areas, children of migrant workers, and disabled children, would help shed light on these crucial questions. Clearly though, to Chinese citizens, the notion of children's rights, associated with an idealized Western "Other" and refracted through the ethos of filial piety and the imperatives of a non-democratic state, still carries a real transformative power.

Notes

Introduction

1 Ian Hacking (1999) suggests that the movement against child abuse started around 1961–2 by a group of American pediatricians who drew the attention of the public to children who seemed to suffer from repeated injuries. However, as Eva Illouz (2008) persuasively argues, the reason pediatricians could shake public opinion so swiftly was because this category of crime suited already established views of the child's psyche and of the long-lasting effects of injuries experienced during childhood.

2 These include the International Covenant on Civil and Political Rights; the International Covenant on Economic, Social, and Cultural Rights; the Convention on the Elimination of All Forms of Racial Discrimination; the Convention Against Torture and Other Cruel, Inhuman or Degrading Treatment or Punishment; the Convention on the Elimination of All forms of Discrimination Against Women, and as discusses here, the Convention on the Rights of the Child (Kent, 1999).

3 Both are pseudonyms. The names of schools and of all informants cited in the study have been altered to protect their identities.

4 "Key Schools" or "Key Point Schools" (*zhongdian xuexiao*) are elite educational institutes, designated as such in the early 1950s due to the shortage of education funding. During the Cultural Revolution (1966–76), the "key school" system was abolished, but re-appeared in China in the late 1970s and the early 1980s. Schools that had received the "key" designation (often based on records of past educational accomplishment) were given priority in the assignment of teachers, equipment, and funds and were allowed to recruit the best students. From the mid-1980s onward, local governments around the country (Shanghai included) began to eliminate the system due to its controversial, elitist nature. In reality, however, the former key schools, most of which are located in urban areas, retained their facilities and teachers and continued to concentrate the best talent in every way (Pepper, 1996: 511; and see also Pepper, 1990).

5 Since the late 1970s and early 1980s, there has been an increase in teacher attrition in China, with many of the departing teachers being the best qualified. As appealing possibilities open up in other sectors of the economy and their social and economic status remains relatively low, it is not surprising perhaps that many teachers have left the profession "to seek brighter futures elsewhere" (Paine, 1992: 186).

6 Teacher-training institutes in China generally enrol middle-school graduates and offer either 3- or 4-year programs. These include compulsory

courses, optional courses, teaching practice, and extracurricular activities. Compulsory courses consist of Ideological and Political Education, Chinese (including Methodology of Chinese Teaching in Primary Schools), Mathematics (including Methodology of Mathematics Teaching in Primary Schools), Physics, Chemistry, Biology, History, Geography, Psychology, Pedagogy for Primary School, Basic Audio-visual Education, Physical Education, Music, Fine Arts, Laboring Skills, and Basics of Computer Application. Optional courses are said to vary with "regional education needs" and to include subjects that "help broaden and deepen the students' knowledge and foster their interests and aptitudes." In some regions, vocational and technical subjects are offered to meet the requirements of local economic development (China Education and Research Network, 2001).

7   In contrast, teachers in the countryside often have no training at all. Rural schools in China generally have a higher student-teacher ratio, and the teachers have lower qualifications than those in urban areas. In recent decades, the implementation of compulsory education by extending mass education through grade nine has further exacerbated these problems (see United Nations Development Program in China, 2001; Paine, 1992).

8   At the time I conducted my research, a breach of the population policy normally incurred a penalty of at least 50,000 Yuan (US$6,200), "a trifling amount for China's new rich," according to the *People's Daily* (2007a) article which quotes this number.

Chapter 1   Recasting Children as Autonomous Persons: Children as Future Citizens and Workers

1   The law was again amended in 2001, but there were no significant changes in the clauses pertaining to children.

2   By 2012, 193 Parties, including every member of the United Nations except Somalia, South Sudan, and the United States, had ratified the UN Convention of the Rights of the Child. Governments of countries that have ratified the Convention are bound to it by international law, and required to report to, and appear before, the United Nations Committee on the Rights of the Child periodically to be examined on their progress with regards to the advancement of the implementation of the Convention and the status of child rights in their country.

3   The involvement of the Chinese delegation to the UN was, at least in one instance, limiting in nature. The Chinese delegates who had actively participated in the drafting of Article 14 of the Convention, which sought to grant children freedom of thought, conscience, and religion, reportedly sought to restrict children's ability to freely choose their religion if that choice went against the will of their families (Johnson, 1992: 102).

4   According to a study carried out by the China Youth University of Political Sciences, the country had about 2–3 million child laborers

(aged under 16) at the end of the 1990s. As of 2007, employment of children is reportedly still widespread in some manufacturing companies, especially in South China (China Daily, 2007).

5 Since the 1990s, local regulations on the protection of minors which draw on the language and principles of the national 1992 Law have been adopted by provincial governments across China.

6 Both goals have been placed at the top of the political agenda during the 2005 National People's Congress and the 6th plenary session of the CCP Central Committee of the CCP (Beijing Review, 2005; People's Daily, 2006b; *Xinhua* News Agency, 2004a).

7 Indeed, women made up the majority of teachers at both Whitewater and the Affiliated Primary School.

8 Surveys conducted in China in the mid- and late-1990s similarly suggest that children from a very young age were active participants in and influenced family purchases and leisure activities (see for example, Davis and Sensenbrenner, 2000, Jing, 2000b).

9 In her study of child-rearing values among Chinese parents in Dalian, Vanessa Fong (2007: 91) records a similar gender bias in regard to girls. However, she finds that boys were also encouraged to exercise "obedience" since too defiant an attitude was perceived as an obstacle on the road to academic and career success.

10 In the two Shanghai primary schools I studied, children took turns cleaning their homeroom at the end of the school day.

11 Her observation received some support from the results of a Literacy, Numeracy and Life Skills test administered in 1995 by the Chinese State Education Commission together with UNICEF and UNESCO. While Chinese children performed well on the first two parts of the test, which examined reading and computing abilities, they apparently fared less well on questions such as: "While cooking rice in a pot, the steam lifts the cover causing the water to spill over. What do you do?" Many children reportedly replied that they would "use force to press the lid down" or "call an adult for help," while more than a third of the 100,000 school-children who participated in the test said they simply "had no idea what to do" (Yang and Wang, 1995).

12 This teacher's statement supports Bakken's observation that, in China, "processes of imitation have come to represent...a kind of habitus," and "even modernity takes place in a climate of imitation" (1999: 139).

Chapter 2   Children's Right to Self-Ownership: Space, Privacy, and Punishment

1 The endeavors of the Maoist to take over the care of children were only partially effective, however. Studies show that a clear majority of urban children under the age of seven were still cared for by parents, friends, and relatives or, in many cases, grandmothers (Kessen, 1975; Wolf, 1985). This may have been due to resistance on the part of parents to

collective childcare institutions, which were often viewed as a threat to the family unit (see Honig and Hershatter, 1988). Contradictory official messages may have also played a role however. For instance, despite sustained efforts to convince Chinese women that devoting "too much time to their families" was "bourgeois and selfish" (Jacka, 1992: 126), official women and youth journals, and images in propaganda posters from the 1950s to the 1970s continued to depict women as possessing "natural responsibilities to the domestic sphere," including the responsibility for childcare (Evans, 2008: 84).

2 Commenting on shifts in rural residential patterns of the Reform era, Yan Yunxiang (2003: 137–8) describes a similar trend of remodeling contemporary rural houses by allocating multiple bedrooms to individual members of the family.

3 An academic survey conducted by (Tang and Dong, 2006) among more than 300 high-school students in Shanghai likewise records high rates of support for the idea that parents should knock before entering their teenage child's room if the door is closed, and also for the notion that "parents have no right to examine teenage kids' rooms, backpacks or purses without their knowing." Notably, the same study found that the parents of these older students' were less supportive of such statements however (p. 291).

4 The study was conducted by the government organization "China Human Rights Development Foundation," which has also set up a special fund for education against violence in the family.

5 Similar, if slightly higher, rates of domestic violence against Chinese children have been recorded in Kim *et al.* (2000), who also find a resemblance between Chinese and Korean rates of corporal punishment. Notably, these rates are also similar to those recorded in the US and the UK (see for example, Straus and Stewart, 1999; Nobes and Smith, 1997). A 2010 study, led by Desmond Runyan documented that in Brazil, Chile, Egypt, India, the Philippines and the United States, corporal punishment was used in at least 55% of the families, and in some communities, including the US, reached almost 80% among preschoolers. Runyan and colleagues also found that Corporal punishment was more widely used by mothers with fewer years of education; rates of corporal punishment vary widely among communities within the same country; and harsh punishment by parents may be more common in low- and middle-income countries.

6 Notably, the UNCRC does not *specifically* prohibit parental corporal punishment (Kaufman and Rizzini, 2009: 426). China moreover is not alone in omitting this particular prohibition: the legal systems of countries such as the UK and the US lack it as well. However, in 2004, the Council of Europe adopted a ban on parental corporal punishment. The decision means that states that have ratified the European Convention are not required to ban parental corporal punishment, but if they choose to do so, they are not violating the rights of parents (Kaufman and Rizzini, 2009: 425).

7   Indeed, a recent study conducted in 11 primary schools in Gansu Province shows that corporal punishment is still prevalent in this rural, northwestern province. 13% of all children included in the sample reported being hit by the teacher and over 57% of students who reported that they violated school discipline also relayed that they were hit by the teacher (Sargent, 2009: 656). Katz *et al.* (2011) record similar findings.

8   It could be argued that the presence of a foreign, outside observer in the classroom may have prevented teachers from engaging in such practices in the first place.

9   Martin Schoenhals (1993: 163) similarly notes that the use of physical punishment, particularly with preadolescent children, "is accepted by many [urban Chinese] parents", even those who consider themselves "progressive."

10 In an insightful ethnographic study of urban families in Xiamen, Esther Goh (2011) similarly documents one instance in which a mother questioned her method of inflicting physical pain as a way to ensure compliance after her child commented: "you are not a good mother because you beat me" (p. 86). Katz *et al.* (2011), who conducted interviews in a poor, rural country in northern China, likewise report that "some children said they had learned from their teachers that parental beating and scolding of children was child abuse." Regrettably, Katz and his colleagues do not discuss the implications of this particular finding in more detail.

Chapter 3   Constituting Rights as Needs: Psychology and the Rise of Middle-Class Childhood

1   Field (1995) and Cho (1995) note a similar trend in contemporary Japan and South Korea. In both countries, the intensive disciplining of children at school—through long hours of study, constant testing, the use of corporal punishment, and the monitoring of conduct—has reportedly caused an increase in children's suicides, alongside the appearance of so-called "adult stress-related diseases" such as baldness and ulcers. These developments, Field (1995: 51–2) suggests, have led to a so-called "disappearance of childhood in Japan," driven by "some of the same global forces that are responsible for the disappearance of childhood in the U.S."

2   In Chinese, the term *"siyou caichan"* ("private property") is normally used to designate all kinds of inanimate assets, including for instance, buildings and land.

3   In 2008, the Chinese government published an eight-year national plan to install "mental health counseling offices" in urban as well as rural schools across the country (*Xinhua* News Agency, 2008).

4   Arguably, such statements could also be regarded as a tactic of psychology experts in China, who seek to justify and legitimize their profes-

sional activities in the eyes of the government by employing the trope of "harmonious society."

5　The disappearance of revolutionary-era ascetic themes in children's moral education books is likely linked to a significant transformation in China's food culture during the reform era. From the 1990s onward, urban areas have seen an explosion of fresh food products in markets. An increasing number of supermarkets offering imported foods, as well as a rapid growth of the restaurant culture, are "attracting people who were once accustomed to eating from their work-unit canteen or at home every night" (see Farquhar Judith, 2002: 49–50).

6　For more detailed, in-depth analyses of the use of role models in old-style Moral Education textbooks in China, see Bakken (1999) and Woronov (2009).

7　Her words echo those of Xu Kuangdi, Shanghai's mayor in the years 1995–2001 and former CCP Central Committee member, who declared in 2001 that societies which place an emphasis "on nurturing children's health and all-round development show that they have truly reached a high degree of civility (*wenming*)" (Xu Kuangdi, 2001).

8　A detailed discussion of the nature of these Western influences on contemporary Chinese education can be found in Cleverley (1985) and Pepper (1996).

9　For further discussion of Chinese primary schools exercises such as these, See Borevskaya, 2001: 46; Woronov, 2009: 578–9.

10　Due to the small sample size, these findings cannot be considered representative, yet they correspond with the results of large-scale surveys conducted in China in the past decade or so. A survey on book reading habits conducted in 1998 among 400 households in Shanghai, Tianjin, and Shenzhen revealed, for instance, that white-collar administrative workers and white-collar professionals with secondary or post-secondary education were much more likely to read books on children's education, compared to unskilled or semi-skilled service workers, or self-employed workers of low levels of education, rural origins, and migrant backgrounds (Wang Shaoguang *et al.*, 2006).

11　Woronov (2008) documents similar practices among the middle-class Beijing parents she interviewed.

12　Studies on the consumption patterns of urban Chinese parents reveal that while city parents do tend to indulge their single child, toys rank relatively low in priority after items such as music and English language classes, computers, Western fast foods, and clothes (Croll, 2006: 180; Chan and McNeal, 2004: 140–3; see also Davis and Sensenbrenner, 2000). According to Croll, Chinese parents tend to regard toys primarily "as sources of enjoyment and recreation for children *up to age 7 years*, but from 7 to 8 years of age, play gives way to learning and only toys and games that are perceived to be educational aids tend to find favour with parents" (2006: 180, emphasis added).

13　Woronov (2008) documents a similar practice among the Beijing parents included in her study.

14 According to statistics from China's MOE, about 9.15 million students applied to take the NCEE in June 2012. With only 6.85 million university and college places, admission is far from guaranteed. Even for those who actually make it to university, the competition continues to be tough even after graduation. According to the Ministry of Human Resources and Social Security, about 25 million Chinese in urban areas currently need jobs, while the employment market creates about 12 million new jobs in urban areas every year (*Xinhua* News Agency, 2012).

Chapter 4   The Filial Child Revisited: Tradition Holds Its Ground in Modern Shanghai

1 Such a view appears, for instance, in Schoenhals (1993: 163). For a slightly more complex view on the effects of the Cultural Revolution on parent–child relations in China, see Lupher (1995), and Fong (2007: 91).

2 Goh's ethnographic work among three-generation households in urban Xiamen similarly records that some of the parents who took part in the study were "resigned to the fact" that the position of grandparents in the family has declined compared with that of only-children, and recognized this decline "as an inevitable consequence of the one-child policy" (2011: 96).

3 In many cases, this arrangement did not change even during group work segments. Instead, teachers often told students to turn around in their seats in order to form a group with those seating behind them.

4 Based on her 1982–4 fieldwork at a pre-service teacher training college, Lynn Paine (1992: 190) similarly notes the centrality of texts and textual knowledge in the instruction of teachers-to-be in China. Teaching at the college level, she observed, "puts the faculty member in the role of master, and the students in the role of disciples, and makes instruction a unilateral process as professors expound on texts," and students "reproduced these interpretations in examinations." As the present study finds, two decades later, the situation was largely unchanged.

5 Grandmothers I spoke to related similar stories about a young grandchild who was disrespectful at first, but then was taught "the correct manner" to treat his elders.

6 For further discussion of some of the inherent contradictions in the official discourse of "Education for Quality" see also Woronov (2009).

References

Adams, Jennifer and Emily Hannum (2008) "Girls in Gansu, China: Expectations and Aspirations for Secondary Schooling". Gansu Survey of Children and Families Papers. University of Pennsylvania. Electronic document, http://repository.upenn.edu/gansu papers/4

Adams, Paul, Leila Berg, Nan Berger, Michael Duane, A.S. Neill, and Robert Ollendorff (1971) *Children's Rights: Toward the Liberation of the Child*. New York: Praeger.

AFP (2004) "Nearly One-Quarter of Shanghai's Kids Contemplate Suicide". Electronic document, http://story.news.yahoo.com/news?tmpl=story&cid= 1508&e=2&u=/afp/health_china_suicide, accessed October 13, 2004.

All-China Women's Federation (ACWF) (2006) "Law of the PRC on the Protection of Minors". Electronic document, http://www.womenofchina.cn/ Policies_Laws/Laws_Regulations/1479.jsp, accessed June 1, 2006.

Alston, Philip (1994) "The Best Interests Principle: Towards a Reconciliation of Culture and Human Rights". *In* Philip Alston, ed. *The Best Interests of the Child: Reconciling Culture and Human Rights*, pp. 1–25. Oxford and New York: Oxford University Press.

Anagnost, Ann (1995) "A Surfeit of Bodies: Population and the Rationality of the State in Post-Mao China". *In* Faye D. Ginsburg and Rayna Rapp, eds. *Conceiving the New World Order: The Global Politics of Reproduction*, pp. 22–41. Berkeley: University of California Press.

— (1997a) "Children and National Transcendence in China". *In* Kenneth G. Lieberthal, Shuen-fu Lin, and Ernest P. Young, eds. *Constructing China: The Interaction of Culture and Economics*, pp. 195–222. Michigan Monographs in Chinese Studies, 78. Ann Arbor: Center for Chinese Studies, University of Michigan.

— (1997b) *National Past-Times: Narrative, Writing, and History in Modern China*. Durham: Duke University Press.

— (2004) "The Corporeal Politics of Quality [*Suzhi*]", *Public Culture*, 16: 189–208.

— (2008a) "From 'Class' to 'Social Strata': Grasping the Social Totality in Reform Era China", *Third World Quarterly*, 29(3): 497–519.

— (2008b) "Imagining Global Futures in China: The Child as a Sign of Value". *In* J. Cole and D. Durham, eds. *Figuring the Future: Globalization and the Temporalities of Children and Youth*, pp. 49–73. Santa Fe: School for Advanced Research Press.

Anderson-Levitt, Kathryn M. (2002) *Teaching Cultures: Knowledge for Teaching First Grade in France and the United States*. Cresskill, NJ: Hampton Press.

Appadurai, Arjun (1990) "Disjuncture and Difference in the Global Cultural Economy". *In* Mike Featherstone, ed. *Global Culture: Nationalism,*

Globalization and Modernity: A Theory, Culture, and Society Special Issue, pp. 295–310. London: Sage Publications.

Archard, David (2004) *Children: Rights and Childhood*. 2nd edition. London; New York: Routledge.

Archard, David and Colin M. Macleod, eds (2002) *The Moral and Political Status of Children*. Oxford; New York: Oxford University Press.

Ariès, Philippe (1962) *Centuries of Childhood: A Social History of Family Life*. Robert Baldick, transl. New York: Vintage Books.

Baba mama wang [Mom and dad's network] (2004) "*Zhongguo fumu chang fan de shi da cuowu* [The ten biggest mistakes Chinese parents often make]". Electronic document, http://www.88mm.cn/Article/ShowArticle.asp?ArticleID=2814, accessed March 8, 2005.

Bai, Limin (2005a) "Children at Play: A Childhood Beyond the Confucian Shadow", *Childhood*, 12(1): 9–32.

— (2005b) *Shaping the Ideal Child: Children and Their Primers in Late Imperial China*. Hong Kong: The Chinese University Press.

Bakken, Børge (1999) *The Exemplary Society: Human Improvement, Social Control, and the Dangers of Modernity in China*. Oxford: Oxford University Press.

Bastid, Marianne (1987) "Servitude or Liberation? The Introduction of Foreign Educational Practices and Systems to China from 1840 to the Present". *In* Ruth Hayhoe and Marianne Bastid, eds. *China's Education and the Industrialized World*, pp. 3–20. Armonk, NY: M.E. Sharpe.

Beck, Ulrich and Elisabeth Beck-Gernsheim (2010) "Forward: Varieties of Individualization". *In* Mette Halskov Hansen and Rune Svarverud, eds. *iChina: The Rise of the Individual in Modern Chinese Society*, pp. xiii–xx. Copenhagen: NIAS – Nordic Institute of Asian Studies.

Beijing Review (2005) *Project of a Harmonious Society*, March 17, 2005: 18–19.

Benn, Stanley I. (1984) "Privacy, Freedom and Respect for Persons". *In* Ferdinand D. Schoeman, ed. *The Philosophical Dimensions of Privacy*, pp. 223–244. Cambridge: Cambridge University Press.

Boling, Patricia (1996) *Privacy and the Politics of Intimate Life*. Ithaca: Cornell University Press.

Borevskaya, Nina Y. (2001) "Searching for Individuality: Educational Pursuits in China and Russia". *In* Glen Peterson, Ruth Hayhoe, and Yongling Lu, eds. *Education, Culture, and Identity in Twentieth-Century China*, pp. 31–53. Ann Arbor: The University of Michigan Press.

Bourdieu, Pierre (1977) *Outline of a Theory of Practice*. Richard Nice, transl. Cambridge, UK: Cambridge University Press.

— (1984) *Distinction: A Social Critique of the Judgment of Taste*. Richard Nice, transl. Cambridge, MT: Harvard University Press.

Boyden, Jo (2001) "Childhood and the Policy Makers: A Comparative Perspective on the Globalization of Childhood". *In* Allison James and Alan Prout, eds. *Constructing and Reconstructing Childhood: Contemporary Issues in the Sociological Study of Childhood*, 2nd edition, pp. 190–229. London: RoutledgeFalmer.

Bray, Francesca (1997) *Technology and Gender: Fabrics of Power in Late Imperial China*. Berkeley: University of California Press.

Brownell, Susan and Jeffrey N. Wasserstrom, eds (2002) *Chinese Femininities/ Chinese Masculinities: A Reader*. Berkeley: University of California Press.

Bruun, Ole and Michael Jacobsen (2000) "Introduction". *In* Michael Jacobsen and Ole Bruun, eds. *Human Rights and Asian Values: Contesting National Identities and Cultural Representations in Asia*, pp. 1–20. Richmond: Curzon.

Burman, Erica (1996) "Local, Global or Globalized? Child Development and International Child Rights Legislation", *Childhood: A Global Journal of Child Research*, 3: 45–66.

— (2005) "Discourses of the Child". *In* Chris Jencks, ed. *Childhood*, pp. 26–41. London: Routledge.

Cai, Yongshun (2005) "China's Moderate Middle-Class: The Case of Homeowners Resistance", *Asian Survey*, 45(5): 777–779.

CASS (Chinese Academy of Social Sciences) (2007) "Scholars Discuss Psychology and Harmonious Society", CASS News, July 23, 2007. Electronic document, http://english.cas.cn/english/news/detailnewsb. asp?InfoNo=26656, accessed October 20, 2008.

CAST (China Association for Science and Technology) (2007) "Psychological Science Should Serve the Construction of A Harmonious Society, CAST Annual Meeting, Wuhan, September 8–14, 2007", CAST News, September 8, 2007. Electronic document, http://english.cast.org.cn/n1181872/ n1182018/n1182077/47809.html, accessed March 1, 2010.

Cha, Ariana Eunjung (2007) "In China, Stern Treatment for Young Internet 'Addicts'", *Washington Post*, February 22: A01. Electronic document, www.washingtonpost.com/wp-dyn/content/article/2007/02/ 21/AR2007022102094_pf.html, accessed October 28, 2008.

Chai, Mi (2004) "Drawing a New Roadmap", *Beijing Review*, April 1, pp. 20–27.

Champagne, Susan (1992) "Reproducing the Intelligent Child: Intelligence and the Child Rearing Discourse in the People's Republic of China". Ph.D. Diss., Stanford University.

Chan, Anita (1985) *Children of Mao: Personality Development and Political Activism in the Red Guard Generation*. London: Macmillan.

Chan, Kara and James U. McNeal (2004) *Advertising to Children in China*. Hong Kong: The Chinese University Press.

Chan, Ying-Keung (2000) "Privacy in the Family: Its Hierarchical and Asymmetrical Nature", *Journal of Comparative Family Studies*, pp. 1–17.

Chang, Doris F., Tong Huiqi, Shi Qijia, and Zeng Qifeng (2005) "Letting a Hundred Flowers Bloom: Counseling and Psychotherapy in the People's Republic of China", *Journal of Mental Health Counseling*, 27(2): 104–116.

Chao, Ruth K. (1994) "Beyond Parental Control and Authoritarian Parenting Style: Understanding Chinese Parenting through the Cultural Notion of Training", *Child Development*, 65(4): 1111–1119.

Chee, Bernadine W.L. (2000) "Eating Snacks and Biting Pressure: Only Children in Beijing". *In* Jun Jing, ed. *Feeding China's Little Emperors: Food, Children, and Social Change*, pp. 48–70. Stanford: Stanford University Press.

Chen, Jie and Bruce J. Dickson (2010) *Allies of the State: China's Private Entrepreneurs and Democratic Change.* Cambridge: Harvard University Press.

Chen, Peiling (2004) *"Peiyang haizi duli chengzhang de jiazhi* [Cultivating the value of children's independent growth]", Sina.com. Electronic document, http://baby.sina.com.cn/edu/2004-11-08/55_11143.shtml, accessed December 19, 2004.

Cheng, Xianshu and Ren Guoqiang (2004) *"Shanghai xiugai weichengnian baohu fa* [Shanghai amends the law on the protection of minors]", *Xinwen wanbao* [*Xinwen* evening news], August 27, 2004. Electronic document, http://news.sina.com.cn/c/2004-08-27/12123512109s.shtml, accessed August 27, 2004.

China Daily (2000) "Confucian Teachings Stand Test of Time", December 11, 2000. Electronic document, http://www.china.org.cn/english/2000/Dec/5153.htm, accessed January 12, 2005.

— (2004a) "Kids: Less Study, More Time for Life". May 26, 2004. Electronic document, http://www.china.org.cn/english/culture/96504.htm, accessed June 12, 2004.

— (2004b) "60% of Chinese Children Suffer Corporal Punishment". December 7, 2004. Electronic document, http://www.chinadaily.com.cn/english/doc/2004-12/07/content_397964.htm, accessed December 7, 2004.

— (2005) "Children Lost in Cyberspace". January 7, 2005. Electronic document, http://english.people.com.cn/200501/07/eng20050107_169914.html, accessed January 7, 2005.

— (2007) "Government Mulls New Rules to Protect Children's Rights". May 25, 2007. Electronic document, http://english.people.com.cn/200705/25/eng20070525_377891.html, accessed May 25, 2007.

— (2010) "Mental Health Hotlines are Coming". February 20, 2010. Electronic document, http://english.cast.org.cn/n1181872/n1182018/n1182078/11756466.html, accessed March 10, 2010.

— (2011) "12-Year-Old's Poetic Bid Ends Homework Toil". January 28, 2011. Electronic document, http://www.chinadaily.com.cn/china/2011-01/28/content_11934134.htm, accessed January 30, 2011.

China Education and Research Network (2001) "Teacher Education in China". Electronic document, http://www.edu.cn/introduction5_1399/20060323/t20060323_4028.shtml, accessed April 3, 2005.

Ching, Frank (2004) "Creating a More Caring China", *The Japan Times*, August 7.

Ching, Kwan Lee (2007) *Against the Law: Labor Protests in China's Rustbelt and Sunbelt.* Berkeley: University of California Press.

Cho, Hae-joang (1995) "Children in the Examination War in South Korea: A Cultural Analysis". *In* Sharon Stephens, ed. *Children and the Politics of Culture*, pp. 141–168. Princeton, NJ: Princeton University Press.

Chow, Rey (1995) *Primitive Passions: Visuality, Sexuality, Ethnography, and Contemporary Chinese Cinema.* Number of. New York: Columbia University Press.

Cleverley, John F. (1985) *The Schooling of China: Tradition and Modernity in Chinese Education.* Sydney: G. Allen & Unwin.

Cockain, Alex (2011) "Students' Ambivalence Toward Their Experiences in Secondary Education: Views from a Group of Young Chinese Studying on an International Foundation Program in Beijing", *The China Journal*, 65: 101–118.

Communist Party of China (2000) "The Decision of the CPC Central Committee and the State Council on Deepening Education Reform and Promoting Quality Education in an All-around Way (13 June 1999)". *In* Robert J. Perrins, ed. *China Facts and Figures Annual Handbook*, 25, pp. 230–241. Gulf Breeze, FL: Academic International Press.

Cook, Camille W. (1989) "Chinese Family Law: A Potential Statutory Revolution". *In* Ralph H. Folsom and John H. Minan, eds. *Law in the People's Republic of China: Commentary, Readings, and Materials*, pp. 390–397. Dordrecht; Boston: M. Nijhoff Publishers.

Croll, Elisabeth (2006) *China's New Consumers: Social Development and Domestic Demand*. London and New York: Routledge.

Cui, Liying and Huang Yichun (2002) *Xinli suzhi jiaoyu lun* [Theories of psycho-logical education for quality]. Guangzhou: Guangdong jiaoyu chubanshe.

Cui, Xianglu, ed. (1999) *Suzhi jiaoyu: Zhongxiaoxue jiaoyu gaige de zhuxuanlu* [Education for quality: Main themes of the primary and middle school education reforms]. Jinan: Shandong jiaoyu chubanshe.

Cui, Yutao (2005) "*Zhi you zuo xia lai jiaotan cai jiao goutong?* [Does communication merely mean sitting down to talk?]", *Fumu bi du* [Parenting science], 304: 40.

Dardess, John (1991) "Childhood in Premodern China". *In* Joseph M. Hawes and N. Ray Hiner, eds. *Children in Historical and Comparative Perspectives: An International Handbook and Research Guide*, pp. 71–94. New York: Greenwood Press.

Davis, Deborah (1993) "Urban Households: Supplicants to a Socialist State". *In* Deborah Davis and Stevan Harrell, eds. *Chinese Families in the Post-Mao Era*, pp. 50–76. Berkeley: University of California Press.

— (2000) "Introduction: A Revolution in Consumption". *In* Deborah Davis, ed. *The Consumer Revolution in Urban China*, pp. 1–22. Berkeley: University of California Press.

Davis, Deborah and Julia S. Sensenbrenner (2000) "Commercializing Childhood: Parental Purchases for Shanghai's Only Child". *In* Deborah S. Davis, ed. *The Consumer Revolution in Urban China*, pp. 54–79. Berkeley: University of California Press.

Davis, Deborah and Stevan Harrell (1993) "Introduction: The Impact of Post-Mao Reforms on Family Life". *In* Deborah Davis and Stevan Harrell, eds. *Chinese Families in the Post-Mao Era*, pp. 1–22. Berkeley: University of California Press.

Davis-Friedmann, Deborah (1991) *Long Lives: Chinese Elderly and the Communist Revolution*, expanded edition. Stanford: Stanford University Press.

Daws, Andy and Ed Cairns (1998) "The Machel Study: Dilemmas of Cultural Sensitivity and Universal Rights of Children", *Peace and Conflict*, 4(4): 335–348.

Dean, Mitchell (1999) *Governmentality: Power and Rule in Modern Society*. Thousand Oaks, Calif.: Sage Publications.

Deleuze, Gilles and Felix Guattari (1983)[1977] *Anti-Oedipus: Capitalism and Schizophrenia*. Robert Hurley, Mark Seem, and Helen R. Lane, transl. Minneapolis: University of Minnesota Press.

Diamant, Neil (2000) *Revolutionizing the Family: Politics, Love, and Divorce in Urban and Rural China, 1949–1968*. Berkeley: University of California Press.

Diamant, Neil J., Stanley B. Lubman, and Kevin J. O'Brien (2005) "Law and Society in the People's Republic of China". *In* Neil J. Diamant, Stanley B. Lubman, and Kevin J. O'Brien, eds. *Engaging the Law in China: State, Society, and Possibilities for Justice*, pp. 3–30. Stanford: Stanford University Press.

Donald, Stephanie Hemelryk (1999) "Children as Political Messengers: Art, Childhood, and Continuity". *In* Harriet Evans and Stephanie Hemelryk Donald, eds. *Picturing Power in the People's Republic of China: Posters of the Cultural Revolution*, pp. 79–150. Lanham, Maryland: Rowman & Littlefield.

— (2005) *Little Friends: Children's Film and Media Culture in China*. Lanham, MD: Rowman & Littlefield.

Donald, Stephanie Hemelryk and Yi Zheng (2008) "Richer than Before: The Cultivation of Middle Class Taste: Education Choices in Urban China". *In* David S. Goodman, ed. *The New Rich in China: Future Rulers, Present Lives*, pp. 71–82. London: Routledge.

— (2009) "Introduction: Post-Mao, Post-Bourdieu: Class Culture in Contemporary China", *PORTAL Journal of Multidisciplinary International Studies*, 6(2): 1–11.

Donzelot, Jacques (1997)[1979] *The Policing of Families*. Robert Hurley, transl. Baltimore: Johns Hopkins University Press.

Duara, Prasenjit (1988) *Culture, Power and the State: Rural North China, 1900–1942*. Stanford: Stanford University Press.

Dutton, Michael R. (1998) *Streetlife China*. Cambridge: Cambridge University Press.

Eastday.com (November 6, 2001) "Shanghai Residents Favor Family Education". Electronic document, http://www.china.org.cn/english/LIfe/14464.htm, accessed November 22, 2005.

Elias, Norbert (1998) "The Civilizing of Parents". *In* Johan Goudsblom and Stephen Mennell, eds. *The Norbert Elias Reader: A Biographical Selection*, pp. 189–211. Oxford: Blackwell.

Engels, Friedrich (1978)[1884] "The Origin of the Family, Private Property, and the State". *In* Robert C. Tucker, ed. *The Marx-Engels Reader*, 2nd edition, pp. 734–759. New York and London: W.W. Norton.

Er, Bao (2008) *China's Child Contracts: A Philosophy of Child Rights in Twenty-First Century China*. Blaxland, Australia: The Blue Mountains Legal Research Centre.

Erwin, Kathlyn (2000) "Heart-to-Heart, Phone-to-Phone: Family Values, Sexuality, and the Politics of Shanghai's Advice Hotlines". *In* Deborah S. Davis, ed. *The Consumer Revolution in Urban China*, pp. 145–170. Berkeley: University of California Press.

Evans, Harriet (1997) *Women and Sexuality in China: Female Sexuality and Gender since 1949*. New York: Continuum.

— (2008) *The Subject of Gender: Daughters and Mothers in Urban China*. Lanham, MD: Rowman & Littlefield.

Farquhar, Judith (2001) "For Your Reading Pleasure: Self-Health [*Ziwo baojian*] Information in 1990s Beijing", *Positions: East Asia Cultures Critique*, 9(1): 105–130.

— (2002) *Appetites: Food and Sex in Postsocialist China*. Durham, NC: Duke University Press.

Farquhar, Mary Ann (1999) *Children's Literature in China: From Lu Xun to Mao Zedong*. Armonk, NY: M.E. Sharpe.

Fass, Paula S. (2011) "A Historical Context for the United Nations Convention on the Rights of the Child", *The Annals of the American Academy of Political and Social Science*, 633: 17–29.

Fernsebner, Susan R. (2003) "A People's Playthings: Toys, Childhood, and Chinese Identity, 1909–1933", *Postcolonial Studies*, 6(3): 269–293.

Feuchtwang, Stephan (2002) "Reflections on Privacy in China". *In* Bonnie S. McDougall and Anders Hansson, eds. *Chinese Concepts of Privacy*, pp. 211–230. Leiden, The Netherlands: Brill.

Field, Norma (1995) "The Child as Laborer and Consumer: The Disappearance of Childhood in Contemporary Japan". *In* Sharon Stephens, ed. *Children and the Politics of Culture*, pp. 51–78. Princeton, NJ: Princeton University Press.

Flekkoy, Malfrid Grude and Natalie Hevener Kaufman (1997) *The Participation Rights of the Child: Rights and Responsibilities in Family and Society*. London: Jessica Kingsley Publishers.

Fong, Vanessa L. (2004a) "Filial Nationalism among Chinese Teenagers with Global Identities", *American Ethnologist*, 31(4): 631–648.

— (2004b) *Only Hope: Coming of Age under China's One-Child Policy*. Stanford: Stanford University Press.

— (2007) "Parent-Child Communication Problems and the Perceived Inadequacies of Chinese Only Children", *Ethos*, 35(1): 85–127.

Foucault, Michel (1991)[1978] "Governmentality". *In* Graham Burchell, Colin Gordon, and Peter Miller, eds. *The Foucault Effect: Studies in Governmentality*, pp. 87–104. Chicago: University of Chicago Press.

Freeman, Michael (2000) "The Future of Children's Rights", *Children and Society*, 14: 277–293.

Fu Daoqun, ed. (2002) *Xin kecheng yu jiating jiaoyu* [The new curriculum and family education]. Beijing: Jiaoyu kexue chubanshe.

Fu Daoqun and Xu Changjiang, eds (2001) *Xin kecheng yu jiaoshi juese zhuanbian* [The new curriculum and the transformation of the teacher's role]. Beijing: Jiaoyu kexue chubanshe.

Fumu bi du [Parenting science] (2002) *Fumu bi du* website. Electronic document, http://baby.sina.com.cn/pc/2002-11-25/101/3.html, accessed March 23, 2006.

— (2004) "*Hao haizi shi kuachulai de ma*? [Should you praise a good child?]", November, pp. 20–3.

— (2005) "*Baba mama de 'jingdian yan lianpu'* [Parents' 'classical roles']", May, pp. 4–6.

Furedi, Frank (2003) *Therapy Culture: Cultivating Vulnerability in an Uncertain Age*. London: Routledge.

Gamble, Jos (2003) *Shanghai in Transition: Changing Perspectives and Social Contours of a Chinese Metropolis*. London: RoutledgeCurzon.

Glosser, Susan L. (2003) *Chinese Visions of Family & State, 1915–1953*. Berkeley: University of California Press.

Goh, Esther C.L. (2011) *China's One-Child Policy and Multiple Caregiving: Raising Little Suns in Xiamen*. New York, NY: Routledge.

Goldman, Merle (2005) *From Comrade to Citizen: The Struggle for Political Rights in China*. Cambridge, MA: Harvard University Press.

Goldman, Merle and Elizabeth J. Perry (2002) "Introduction: Political Citizenship in Modern China". *In* Merle Goldman and Elizabeth J. Perry, eds. *Changing Meanings of Citizenship in Modern China*, pp. 1–22. Cambridge, Massachusetts: Harvard University Press.

Gottschang, Suzanne Z. (2000) "A Baby-Friendly Hospital and the Science of Infant Feeding". *In* Jun Jing, ed. *Feeding China's Little Emperors: Food, Children, and Social Change*, pp. 160–184. Stanford: Stanford University Press.

Greenhalgh, Susan (2011) "Governing Chinese Life, from Sovereignty to Biopolitical Governance". *In* Everett Zhang, Arthur Kleinman, and Tu Weiming, eds. *Governance of Life in Chinese Moral Experience: The Quest for an Adequate Life*, pp. 146–162. London: Routledge.

Greenhalgh, Susan and Edwin A. Winckler (2005) *Governing China's Population: From Leninist to Neoliberal Biopolitics*. Stanford: Stanford University Press.

Gu, Xiaobo (2002) "*Guanzhu ertong de xinli jiankang* [Paying attention to children's psychological health]". *In* The Ministry of Education, The All-China Women and Children's Federation, and The Communist Youth League, eds. *Geng xin jiating jiaoyu guannian baogaoji* [A report on new views of family education], pp. 184–195. Beijing: Zhongguo fazhi chubanshe.

Guan, Xiaomeng (2009) "'Spoiled Generation' Paves Way for New Age Parenting", *China Daily*, July 14. Electronic document, http://www.chinadaily.com.cn/china/2009-07/14/content_8427903.htm, accessed July 19, 2009.

Guangdong sheng kepu xinxi zhongxin [Guangdong Province Popular Science Information Department] (2008) *Xinli jiankang yu hexie shehui* [Mental Health and Harmonious Society]. Electronic document, http://ycqkj.gov.cn/book.asp?t_id=604, accessed May 1, 2010.

Guo, Yingjie (2008) "Class, Stratum and Group: The Politics of Description and Prescription". *In* David S.G. Goodman, ed. *The New Rich in China: Future Rulers, Present Lives*, pp. 38–52. London and New York: Routledge.

Guo, Yuhua (2000) "Family Relations: The Generation Gap at the Table". *In* Jun Jing, ed. *Feeding China's Little Emperors: Food, Children, and Social Change*, pp. 94–113. Stanford: Stanford University Press.

Guo, Zi (2004) "Education Aimed at Building the Whole Person", *China Daily*, October 26, p. 6.

Habermas, Jürgen (1991) *The Structural Transformation of the Public Sphere: An Inquiry into a Category of Bourgeois Society*. Cambridge, MA: MIT Press.

Hacking, Ian (1999) *The Social Construction of What?* Cambridge, MA: Harvard University Press.

Hannum, Emily, An Xuehui, and Cherng Hua-Yu S. (2011) "Examinations and Educational Opportunity in China: Mobility and Bottlenecks for the Rural Poor", *Oxford Review of Education*, 37(2): 267–305.

Hansen, Mette Halskov and Cuiming Pang (2010) "Idealizing Individual Choice: Work, Love and Family in the Eyes of Young, Rural Chinese". *In* Mette Halskov Hansen and Rune Svarverud, eds. *iChina: The Rise of the Individual in Modern Chinese Society*, pp. 39–64. Copenhagen: NIAS – Nordic Institute of Asian Studies.

Hanson, Karl and Olga Nieuwenhuys (2012) "Living Rights, Social Justice, Translations". *In* Karl Hanson and Olga Nieuwenhuys, eds. *Reconceptualizing Children's Rights in International Development: Living Rights, Social Justice, Translations*, pp. 3–26. Cambridge: Cambridge University Press.

Haraway, Donna J. (1991) *Simians, Cyborgs, and Women: The Reinvention of Nature*. New York: Routledge.

Hays, Sharon (1996) *The Cultural Contradictions of Motherhood*. New Haven and London: Yale University Press.

He, Dongliang (2007) *"Xinlixue shiye xia de hexie shehui* [Harmonious society from the perspective of psychology]", *Changshu sheke wang, Changshushi zhexue shehui kexuejie lianhehui* [Changshu's Social Science Network, Changshu City's Social Sciences Association], November 5, 2007. Electronic document, http://www.cssa.gov.cn/skl/disp/skl/skl_message.asp?id=499, accessed June 10, 2009.

Henze, Jurgen (1992) "The Formal Education System and Modernization: An Analysis of Developments since 1978". *In* Ruth Hayhoe, ed. *Education and Modernization: The Chinese Experience*, pp. 103–140. Oxford: Pergamon Press.

Hershatter, Gail (2004) "Making the Visible Invisible: The Fate of 'the Private' in Revolutionary China". *In* Joan W. Scott and Debra Keats, eds. *Going Public: Feminism and the Shifting Boundaries of the Private Sphere*, pp. 309–329. Urbana and Champaign: University of Illinois Press.

Hesketh, Therese, Zhang Shu Hong, and Margaret A. Lynch (2000) "Child Abuse in China: The Views and Experiences of Child Health Professionals", *Child Abuse & Neglect*, 24(6): 867–872.

Heywood, Colin (2001) *A History of Childhood: Children and Childhood in the West from Medieval to Modern Times*. Oxford, UK: Polity Press.

Hirschfeld, Lawrence (2002) "Why Don't Anthropologists Like Children?" *American Anthropologist*, 104(2): 611–627.

Hoffman, Lisa M. (2010) *Patriotic Professionalism in Urban China: Fostering Talent*. Philadelphia: Temple University Press.

Honig, Emily and Gail Hershatter (1988) *Personal Voices: Chinese Women in the 1980s*. Stanford: Stanford University Press.

Hsiung, Ping-chen (2005) *A Tender Voyage: Children and Childhood in Late Imperial China*. Stanford: Stanford University Press.

Hu, Shen, ed. (2000) *Suzhi lun: Chensi zhuti zishen zhi mi* [On quality: Contemplating the concept of self and the subject]. Beijing: Huayi chubanshe.

Huang, Shuguang, Wang Lunxin, and Yuan Wenhui (2001) *"Zhongguo jichu jiaoyu gaige de wenhua shiming* [The cultural mission of reforming China's basic education]*"*, *Shiji zhi jiao zhongguo jichu jiaoyu gaige yanjiu congshu* [Studies on the reform of China's basic education at the turn of the century]. Beijing: Jiaoyu kexue chubanshe.

Hultqvist, Kenneth (1998) "A History of the Present of Children's Welfare in Sweden: From Fröbel to Present-Day Decentralization Projects". *In* Thomas S. Popkewitz and Marie Brennan, eds. *Foucault's Challenge: Discourse, Knowledge, and Power in Education*, pp. 91–116. New York: Teachers College Press.

Illouz, Eva (2008) *Saving the Modern Soul: Therapy, Emotions, and the Culture of Self-Help*. Berkeley: University of California Press.

Information Office of the State Council of the PRC (1996) "The Situation of Children in China". Electronic document, http://news.xinhuanet.com/employment/2002-11/18/content_633190.htm, accessed May 2, 2005.

Jacka, Tamara (1992) "The Public/Private Dichotomy and the Gender Division of Rural Labour". *In* Andrew Watson, ed. *Economic Reform and Social Change in China*, pp. 117–143. London and New York: Routledge.

James, Allison (2009) "Agency". *In* Jens Qvortrup, William A. Corsaro, and Michael-Sebastian Honig, eds. *The Palgrave Handbook of Childhood Studies*, pp. 34–45. Basingstoke: Palgrave Macmillan.

— (2011) "To Be (Come) or Not to Be (Come): Understanding Children's Citizenship", *The Annals of the American Academy of Political and Social Science*, 633: 167–179.

James, Allison and Alan Prout (1997)[1990] "A New Paradigm for the Sociology of Childhood? Provenance, Promises and Problems". *In* Allison James and Alan Prout, eds. *Constructing and Reconstructing Childhood: Contemporary Issues in the Sociological Study of Childhood*, revised edition, pp. 7–33. London: Falmer Press.

James, Allison, Chris Jenks, and Alan Prout (1998) *Theorizing Childhood*. Cambridge, UK: Polity Press.

Jiefang ribao [Liberation daily] (2004) *"Shanghai: Erqi kegai zhuyao mubiao* [Shanghai: The main goals of the Second Phase Curriculum Reform]*"*. Electronic document, http://education.163.com/edu2004/editor_2004/zhongkao/041117/041117_164999.html, accessed November 17, 2004.

Jing, Jun, ed. (2000a) *Feeding China's Little Emperors: Food, Children, and Social Change*. Stanford: Stanford University Press.

— (2000b) "Food, Children, and Social Change in Contemporary China". *In* Jun Jing, ed. *Feeding China's Little Emperors: Food, Children and Social Change*, pp. 1–26. Stanford: Stanford University Press.

Johnson, David (1992) *Ideologies of Children's Rights*, Michael Freeman and Phillip Veerman, eds, pp. 95–114. New York: Springer.

Jones, Andrew F. (2002) "The Child as History in Republican China: A Discourse on Development", *Positions: East Asia Cultures Critique*, 10(3): 695–727.

Kahn, Joseph and Jim Yardley (2004) "Amid China's Boom, No Helping Hand for Young Qingming", *The New York Times*, August 1.

Katz, Ilan, Shang Xiaoyuan, and Zhang Yahua (2011) "Missing Elements of a Child Protection System in China: The Case of LX", *Social Policy and Society*, 10(1): 93–102.

Kaufman, Natalie H. and Irene Rizzini (2009) "Closing the Gaps between Rights and the Realities of Children's Lives". *In* Jens Qvortrup, William A. Corsaro, and Michael-Sebastian Honig, eds. *The Palgrave Handbook of Childhood Studies*, pp. 422–434. Basingstoke: Palgrave Macmillan.

Keith, Ronald C. (1997) "Legislating Women and Children's 'Rights and Interests' in the PRC", *The China Quarterly*, 149: 29–55.

Kennedy, David (2004) *The Dark Sides of Virtue: Reassessing International Humanitarianism*. Princeton, NJ: Princeton University Press.

Kent, Ann (1999) *China, the United Nations, and Human Rights: The Limits of Compliance*. Philadelphia: University of Pennsylvania Press.

Kessen, William, ed. (1975) *Childhood in China*. New Haven: Yale University Press.

Kim, Dae-Ho, Kim Kwang-Iel, Park Yong-Chon, Zhang Liang Dong, Lu Ming Kang, and Li Donggen (2000) "Children's Experience of Violence in China and Korea: A Transcultural Study", *Child Abuse & Neglect*, 24(9): 1163–1174.

King, Ambrose Y.C. (2002) "The Emergence of Alternative Modernity in East Asia". *In* Dominic Sachsenmaier and Jens Riedel, eds, with Shmuel N. Eisenstadt, *Reflections on Multiple Modernities: European, Chinese and Other Interpretations*, pp. 139–152. Leiden: Brill.

Kinney, Anne Behnke (1995a) *Chinese Views of Childhood*, Anne Behnke Kinney, ed. Honolulu: University of Hawai'i Press.

— (1995b) "Introduction". *In* Anne Behnke Kinney, ed. *Chinese Views of Childhood*, pp. 1–14. Honolulu: University of Hawai'i Press.

Kipnis, Andrew B. (2001) "The Disturbing Educational Discipline of 'Peasants'", *The China Journal*, 46: 1–24.

— (2006) "*Suzhi*: A Keyword Approach", *China Quarterly*, 186: 295–313.

— (2007) "Neoliberalism Reified: *Suzhi* Discourse and Tropes of Neoliberalism in the People's Republic of China", *Journal of the Royal Anthropological Institute*, 13: 383–400.

— (2008) "Education and the Governing of Child-Centered Relatedness". *In* Susan Brandtstädter and Gonçalo D. Santos, eds. *Chinese Kinship: Contemporary Anthropological Perspectives*, pp. 204–222. London: Routledge.

— (2011) *Governing Educational Desire in China*. Chicago: University of Chicago Press.

— (2012) "Introduction: Chinese Modernity and the Individual Psyche". *In* Andrew B. Kipnis, ed. *Chinese Modernity and the Individual Psyche (Culture, Mind and Society)*, pp. 1–18. New York: Palgrave Macmillan.

Kleinman, Arthur, Yan Yunxiang, Jun Jing, Lee Sing, Everett Zhang, Pan Tianshu, Wu Fei, and Guo Jinua (2011) "Introduction: Remaking the

Moral Person in a New China". *In* Arthur Kleinman *et al.*, eds. *Deep China: The Moral Life of the Person: What Anthropology and Psychiatry Tell Us About China Today*, pp. 1–35. Berkeley: University of California Press.

Kuan, Teresa (2011) "'The Heart Says One Thing but the Hand Does Another': A Story about Emotion-Work, Ambivalence and Popular Advice for Parents", *The China Journal*, 65: 77–100.

Kusserow, Adrie (2004) *American Individualisms: Child Rearing and Social Class in Three Neighborhoods*. New York: Palgrave Macmillan.

Landsberger, Stefan (2001) "Learning by What Example? Educational Propaganda in Twenty-First-Century China", *Critical Asian Studies*, 33(4): 541–571.

Lareau, Annette (2003) *Unequal Childhoods: Class, Race, and Family Life.* Berkeley: University of California Press.

Lee, Leo Ou-fan (1991) "Modernity and Its Discontents: The Cultural Agenda of the May Fourth Movement". *In* Kenneth Lieberthal, ed. *Perspectives on Modern China: Four Anniversaries*. Armonk, NY: M.E. Sharpe.

Lee, Sing (2011) "Depression: Coming of Age in China". *In* Arthur Kleinman *et al.*, eds. *Deep China: The Moral Life of the Person: What Anthropology and Psychiatry Tell Us About China Today*, pp. 177–212. Berkeley: University of California Press.

Leung, Angela K.C. (1995) "Relief Institutions for Children in Nineteenth-Century China". *In* Anne Behnke Kinney, ed. *Chinese Views of Childhood*, pp. 251–278. Honolulu: University of Hawai'i Press.

Levinson, Bradley (1999) "Resituating the Place of Educational Discourse in Anthropology", *American Anthropologist*, 101(3): 594–604.

Li, Cheng (2010) "Introduction: The Rise of the Middle Class in the Middle Kingdom". *In* Cheng Li, ed. *China's Emerging Middle Class: Beyond Economic Transformation*, pp. 3–31. Washington DC: Brookings Institution Press.

Li, Chongli (2003) "*Jiaoyu jiaoxue bixu yi xuesheng wei zhongxin* [Education and teaching must be student-centered]", *Qinghai jiaoyu* [Qinghai education], 7–8: 11–12.

Li, Yixian (1992) "*Jianli wenming fuzi guanxi* [Build a civilized parent-child relationship]", *Renmin ribao* [People's Daily], December 30, p. 3.

Lim, Louisa (2011) "And You Thought the Tiger Mother Was Tough", NPR, December 14, 2011. Electronic document, http://www.npr.org/2011/12/14/143659027/and-you-thought-the-tiger-mother-was-tough, accessed December 26, 2011.

Liu, Fan (1982) "Developmental Psychology in China", *International Journal of Behavioral Development*, 5: 391–411.

Liu, Ying (1992) "*Xianxue huanlai jiaoxun: tigao fumu suzhi* [A lesson learnt in blood: Improve the quality of parents]", *Renmin ribao* [People's Daily], December 14, p. 3.

Lozada, Eriberto P., Jr. (2000) "Globalized Childhood?: Kentucky Fried Chicken in Beijing". *In* Jun Jing, ed. *Feeding China's Little Emperors: Food, Children, and Social Change*, pp. 114–134. Stanford: Stanford University Press.

Lu, Hanlong (2000) "To be Relatively Comfortable in an Egalitarian Society". *In* Deborah S. Davis, ed. *The Consumer Revolution in Urban China*, pp. 124–144. Berkeley: University of California Press.

Lupher, Mark (1995) "Revolutionary Little Red Devils: The Social Psychology of Rebel Youth, 1966–1967". *In* Anne Behnke Kinney, ed. *Chinese Views of Childhood*, pp. 321–343. Honolulu: University of Hawai'i Press.

Ma, Baolan and Guo Xiaoping (1995) *An Evaluation Study of Parent Schools in China. Action Research in Family and Early Childhood.* Paris: The Young Child and the Family Environment Project, UNESCO.

Mannheim, Karl (2005)[1927] "The Problem of Generations". *In* Chris Jenks, ed. *Childhood: Critical Concepts in Sociology*, pp. 273–285, Vol. 3. New York: Routledge.

McDougall, Bonnie S. (2002) "Particulars and Universals: Studies on Chinese Privacy". *In* Bonnie S. McDougall and Anders Hansson, eds. *Chinese Concepts of Privacy*, pp. 3–24. Leiden, The Netherlands: Brill.

— (2005) "Discourse on Privacy by Women Writers in Late Twentieth-Century China", *China Information*, 19: 97–119.

McDougall, Bonnie S. and Anders Hansson, eds. (2002) *Chinese Concepts of Privacy.* Leiden: Brill.

McNeal, James U. and Yeh Chyon-Hwa (1997) "Development of Consumer Behavior Patterns among Chinese Children", *Journal of Consumer Marketing*, 14(1): 45–57.

Milwertz, Cecilia Nathensen (1997) *Accepting Population Control: Urban Chinese Women and the One-Child Family Policy.* Richmond, Surrey, UK: Curzon Press.

Ministry of Education (2006) "*Zhonghua Renmin Gongheguo yiwu jiaoyu fa* [Compulsory Education Law of the People's Republic of China]". Electronic document, http://www.moe.edu.cn/edoas/website18/info20369.htm, accessed August 30, 2006.

Moore, Barrington (1984) *Privacy: Studies in Social and Cultural History.* Armonk, NY: M.E. Sharpe.

Murphy, Rachel (2004) "Turning Peasants into Modern Chinese Citizens: 'Population Quality' Discourse, Demographic Transition and Primary Education", *The China Quarterly*, 177: 1–20.

Naftali, Orna (2008) "Treating Students as Subjects: Globalization, Childhood, and Education in Contemporary China". *In* Julia Resnik, ed. *The Production of Educational Knowledge in the Global Era*, pp. 251–274. Rotterdam: Sense Publishers.

— (2009) "Empowering the Child: Children's Rights, Citizenship and the State in Contemporary China", *The China Journal*, 61: 79–104.

— (2010a) "Caged Golden Canaries: Childhood, Privacy, and Subjectivity in Contemporary Urban China", *Childhood: A Journal of Global Child Research*, 17(3): 297–311.

— (2010b) "Recovering Childhood: Play, Pedagogy, and the Rise of Psychological Knowledge in Contemporary Urban China", *Modern China*, 36(6): 589–616.

Neill, Alexander Sutherland (1960) *Summerhill: A Radical Approach to Child Rearing*. New York: Hart Publishing Company.

Nobes, Gavin and Marjorie Smith (1997) "Physical Punishment of Children in Two-Parent Families", *Clinical Child Psychology and Psychiatry*, 2(2): 271–281.

Nonini, Donald M. (2008) "Is China Becoming Neoliberal?" *Critique of Anthropology*, 28(2): 145–176.

Nylan, Michael (2003) "Childhood, Formal Education, and Ideology in China". In Willem Koops and Michael Zuckerman, eds. *Beyond the Century of the Child: Cultural History and Developmental Psychology*, pp. 136–158. Philadelphia: University of Pennsylvania Press.

O'Brien, Kevin J. and Li Lianjiang (2006) *Rightful Resistance in Rural China*. New York: Cambridge University Press.

Ong, Aihwa (1996) "Anthropology, China and Modernities: The Geopolitics of Cultural Knowledge". *In* Henrietta L. Moore, ed. *The Future of Anthropological Knowledge*, pp. 60–92. London: Routledge.

— (2006) *Neoliberalism as Exception: Mutations in Citizenship and Sovereignty*. Durham and London: Duke University Press.

— (2008) "Self-Fashioning Shanghainese: Dancing Across Spheres of Value". *In* Zhang Li and Aihwa Ong, eds. *Privatizing China: Socialism from Afar*, pp. 182–196. Ithaca: Cornell University Press.

Ong, Aihwa and Zhang Li (2008) "Introduction: Privatizing China: Powers of the Self, Socialism from Afar". *In* Zhang Li and Aihwa Ong, eds. *Privatizing China: Socialism from Afar*, pp. 1–20. Ithaca: Cornell University Press.

Paine, Lynn (1992) "Teaching and Modernization in Contemporary China". *In* Ruth Hayhoe, ed. *Education and Modernization: The Chinese Experience*, pp. 183–210. Comparative and International Education, 11. Oxford: Pergamon Press.

Panter-Brick, Catherine (2002) "Street Children, Human Rights, and Public Health: A Critique and Future Directions", *Annual Review of Anthropology*, 31: 147–171.

Pease, Catherine E. (1995) "Remembering the Taste of Melons: Modern Chinese Stories of Childhood". *In* Anne Behnke Kinney, ed. *Chinese Views of Childhood*, pp. 279–320. Honolulu: University of Hawai'i Press.

Pei, Minxin (2010) "Rights and Resistance: The Changing Contexts of the Dissident Movement". *In* Elizabeth Perry and Mark Selden, eds. *Chinese Society: Change, Conflict and Resistance*, 3rd edition, pp. 31–56. London: Routledge.

People's Daily (2004a) "New Concept Focuses on Balanced Progress", March 4, 2004. Electronic document, http://english.people.com.cn/200403/04/eng20040304_136487.shtml, accessed April 5, 2006.

— (2004b) "Balanced Development: No Easy Challenge but Necessary", March 5, 2004. Electronic document, http://english.people.com.cn/200403/05/eng20040305_136646.shtml, accessed March 5, 2004.

— (2005) "China Works to Create Well-Rounded College Students", June 7, 2005. Electronic document, http://english.people.com.cn/200506/07/eng20050607_188929.html, accessed June 7, 2005.

— (2006a) "Schools Told: Give Students Test Scores in Private", August 29, 2006. Electronic document, http://english.people.com.cn/200608/29/eng20060829_297769.html, accessed September 2, 2006.

— (2006b) "CPC Key Plenum Elevates Social Harmony to More Prominent Position", October 12, 2006. Electronic document, http://english.people.com.cn/200610/12/eng20061012_311239.html, accessed October 12, 2006.

— (2007a) "The Rich 'Have to Follow' Family Planning", January 24, 2007. Electronic document, http://english.people.com.cn/200701/24/eng20070124_344188.html, accessed January 24, 2007.

— (2007b) "China's Children Too Busy for Playtime", May 13, 2007. Electronic document, http://english.people.com.cn/200705/13/eng20070513_374164.html, accessed May 13, 2007.

Pepper, Suzanne (1990) *China's Education Reform in the 1980s: Policies, Issues, and Historical Perspectives*. Berkeley: Institute of East Asian Studies University of California at Berkeley Center for Chinese Studies.

— (1996) *Radicalism and Education Reform in 20th-Century China: The Search for an Ideal Development Model*. Cambridge, England: Cambridge University Press.

Pinde yu shehui, yi nianji [Morality and Society, Grade 1] (2002) *Shiyong ben* [experimental edition]. Shanghai: Shanghai keji jiaoyu chubanshe.

Pinde yu shehui, wu nianji [Morality and Society, Grade 5] (2007) *Shanghaishu zhongxiaoxue (you'er yuan) kechang gaige weiyuanhui* [Committee for the Reform of Shanghai's School (Kindergarten) Curriculum]. *Shiyong ben* [experimental edition]. Shanghai: Shanghai jiaoyu chubanshe.

Potter, Sulamith Heins and Jack M. Potter (1990) *China's Peasants: The Anthropology of a Revolution*. Cambridge, England: Cambridge University Press.

PRC National People's Congress (2001) "Decision of the Standing Committee of the National People's Congress on the amendment to the Marriage Law of the People's Republic of China (Order of the President No. 51)". Electronic document, http://english.gov.cn/laws/2005-09/25/content_70022.htm, accessed October 21, 2013.

Qi, Wanxue and Tang Hanwei (2004) "The Social and Cultural Background of Contemporary Moral Education in China", *Journal of Moral Education*, 33(4): 465–480.

Qiao, D.P. and Chan, Y.C. (2005) "Child Abuse in China: A Yet-to-be-Acknowledged 'Social Problem' in the Chinese Mainland", *Child & Family Social Work*, 10(1): 21–27.

Read, Benjamin L. (2008) "Assessing Variation in Civil Society Organizations: China's Homeowner Associations in Comparative Perspective", *Comparative Political Studies*, 41(9): 1240–1265.

Reuters (2005) "Study Shows Worrying Trend of Child Abuse in China". Electronic document, http://www.alertnet.org/thenews/newsdesk/PEK242681.htm, accessed May 18, 2005.

Reynolds, James (2008) "Chinese Youth 'Face Suicide Risk'", BBC News, September 10, 2008. Electronic document, http://news.bbc.co.uk/go/pr/fr/-/2/hi/asia-pacific/7608575.stm/, accessed September 10, 2008.

Rofel, Lisa (1999) *Other Modernities: Gendered Yearnings in China after Socialism.* Berkeley: University of California Press.

— (2007) *Desiring China: Experiments in Neoliberalism, Sexuality, and Public Culture.* Durham: Duke University Press.

Rose, Nikolas (1989) *Governing the Soul: The Shaping of the Private Self.* London: Routledge.

— (1996) *Inventing Our Selves: Psychology, Power, and Personhood.* Cambridge, UK: Cambridge University Press.

Rosen, Stanley (2004) "The Victory of Materialism: Aspirations to Join China's Urban Moneyed Classes and the Commercialization of Education", *China Journal*, 51(January): 27–51.

— (2009) "Contemporary Chinese Youth and the State", *The Journal of Asian Studies*, 68: 359–369.

Rousseau, Jean Jacques (1964[1762]) "Émile". *In* R.L. Archer, ed. *Jean Jacques Rousseau: His Educational Theories Selected from Emile, Julie and Other Writings*, pp. 76–262. Woodbury, NY: Barron's Educational Series.

Runyan, Desmond *et al.* (2010) "International Variations in Harsh Child Discipline", *Pediatrics*, 126(3): e1–e11.

Saari, Jon L. (1990) "Legacies of Childhood: Growing Up Chinese in a Time of Crisis, 1890–1920", *Harvard East Asian Monographs*, 136. Cambridge, Mass.: Harvard University Press.

Sargent, Tanja Carmel (2009) "Revolutionizing Ritual Interaction in the Classroom: Constructing the Chinese Renaissance of the Twenty-First Century", *Modern China*, 35: 632–661.

Schell, Orville and David Shambaugh, eds. (1999) *The China Reader: The Reform Era.* New York: Vintage Books.

Scheper-Hughes, Nancy (1987) *Child Survival: Anthropological Perspectives on the Treatment and Maltreatment of Children.* Dordrecht: D. Reidel.

Schoeman, Ferdinand (1980) "Rights of Children, Rights of Parents, and the Moral Basis of the Family", *Ethics*, 91(1): 6–19.

— (1983) "Childhood Competence and Autonomy", *The Journal of Legal Studies*, 12(2): 267–287.

Schoenhals, Martin (1993) "The Paradox of Power in a People's Republic of China Middle School", *Studies in Contemporary China.* Armonk, NY: M.E. Sharpe Inc.

Schwarcz, Vera (1986) *The Chinese Enlightenment: Intellectuals and the Legacy of the May Fourth Movement of 1919.* Berkeley: University of California Press.

Schwartzman, Helen B. (2001) "Introduction: Questions and Challenges for a 21st-Century Anthropology of Children". *In* Helen B. Schwartzman, ed. *Children and Anthropology: Perspectives for the 21st Century*, pp. 1–14. Westport, CT: Bergin and Garvey.

Shanghai Daily (2005) "Shanghai Classrooms Offer Confucius Reading Course", October 19, 2005. Electronic document, http://www.china. org.cn/english/culture/145925.htm, accessed December 11, 2005.

Shanghai People's Congress Standing Committee [*Shanghai shi renmin daibiao dahui changwu weiyuanhui*] (2004) *Shanghai shi weichengnian ren baohu tiaoli*

[Shanghai Municipal Regulations on the Protection of Minors]. Electronic document, http://www.shmec.gov.cn/xxgk/PubInfo/rows_content.php? article_code=201042005001, accessed December 1, 2005.

Shanghai Star (2004) "Legislation Targets Risky Behaviour by Children". Electronic document, http://www.chinadaily.com.cn/english/doc/2004-12/05/content_397385.htm, accessed December 5, 2004.

Sheng, Yu, Wang Deyi, and Wu Changzen (1989) "Chinese Law and Status of Children", *Law in the People's Republic of China: Commentary, Readings, and Materials*, pp. 426–441. Dordrecht; Boston: M. Nijhoff Publishers.

Shehui, wu nianji diyi xueqi [Society, Grade 5, Semester 1] (2001) *Shanghai shi zhongxiaoxue kecheng jiaocai gaige weiyuanhui* [Reform commission of primary and secondary school curriculum materials, Shanghai]. *Shiyong ben* [experimental edition]. Shanghai: Shanghai shiji chuban jituan, Shanghai jiaoyu chubanshe.

Shi hua shi shuo [Tell it like it is] (2001) *Jiating xieyi* [Family contract]. Liang Jianzeng, prod. 45 minutes. CCTV1. China.

— (2004) *Shou, zu, qing* [Hands, feet, emotions]. Liang Jianzeng, prod. 45 minutes. CCTV1. China.

Shu, Qixing (2007) *"Diaocha xianshi geren yinsi he xiaoyuan baoli show weichengnianren guanzhu* [Study reveals that minors are most concerned about personal privacy and school violence]", *Zhongguo qingnian bao* [China Youth Daily], December 14, 2007. Electronic document, http://news.xinhuanet.com/edu/2007-12/14/content_7246355.htm, accessed March 26, 2010.

Sigley, Gary (2009) *"Suzhi*, the Body, and the Fortunes of Technoscientific Reasoning in Contemporary China", *Positions*, 17(3): 537–566.

Sixiang pinde, yi nianji [Ideology and Moral Character, Grade 1] (1993) Vol. 2. Experimental edition. Shanghai: Shanghai jiaoyu chubanshe.

Stafford, Charles (1995) *The Roads of Chinese Childhood: Learning and Identification in Angang*. Cambridge: Cambridge University Press.

Stephens, Sharon, ed. (1995a) *Children and the Politics of Culture*. Princeton, NJ: Princeton University Press.

— (1995b) "Introduction: Children and the Politics of Culture in 'Late Capitalism'". *In* Sharon Stephens, ed. *Children and the Politics of Culture*, pp. 3–48. Princeton, NJ: Princeton University Press.

Straus, Murray A. and Julie H. Stewart (1999) "Corporal Punishment by American Parents: National Data on Prevalence, Chronicity, Severity, and Duration, in Relation to Child, and Family Characteristics", *Clinical Child and Family Psychology Review*, 2(2): 55–70.

Sun, Lichun (2001) *Suzhi jiaoyu xin lun* [New theories of education for quality]. Jinan: Shandong jiaoyu chuban she.

Sun, Wanning (2002) *Leaving China: Media, Migration, and Transnational Imagination*. Lanham: Rowman & Littlefield.

Svensson, Marina (2000) "The Chinese Debate on Asian Values and Human Rights". *In* Michael Jacobsen and Ole Bruun, eds. *Human Rights and Asian Values: Contesting National Identities and Cultural Representations in Asia*, pp. 199–226. Richmond: Curzon.

— (2002) *Debating Human Rights in China: A Conceptual and Political History*. Lanham, MD: Rowman & Littlefield.

Swidler, Ann (1986) "Culture in Action: Symbols and Strategies", *American Sociological Review*, 51: 273–286.

Tang, Hong (2005) "*Jiating huiyi* [Family meeting]", *Fumu bi du* [Parenting science], 304: 25–27.

Tang, Jing (2003) "*Haizi shi yi ben shu* [A child is like a book]", *Zhongguo jiaoyu xinwen wang* [China's Educational News Network]. Electronic document, http://www.jyb.com.cn/gb/jybzt/2002zt/jtjy/19.htm, accessed March 15, 2005.

Tang, Shengming and Dong Xiaoping (2006) "Parents' and Children's Perceptions of Privacy Rights in China: A Cohort Comparison", *Journal of Family Issues*, 27: 285–300.

Tang, Zhisong (2001) "*Tanjiu shi jiaoxue de jiben yuanze* [Basic principles of enquiry-method education]", *Zhongguo jiaoyuxue kan* [Journal of the Chinese Society of Education], 5: 13–16.

Tardif, Twilla and Miao Xiaochun (2000) "Developmental Psychology in China", *International Journal of Behavioral Development*, 24(1): 68–72.

Thøgersen, Stig (2002) *A County of Culture: Twentieth-Century China Seen from the Village Schools of Zouping, Shandong*. Ann Arbor: University of Michigan Press.

Tian, Doudou (2005) "*Tao Hongkai: yu 'wangyin' zhengduo haizi* [Tao Hongkai helps children with 'internet addiction']", *Renmin ribao* [People's Daily], May 23, p. 11.

Tomba, Luigi (2009a) "Middle Classes in China: Force for Political Change or Guarantee of Stability?" *PORTAL Journal of Multidisciplinary International Studies*, 6(2): 1–12.

— (2009b) "Of Quality, Harmony, and Community: Civilization and the Middle Class in Urban China", *Positions: East Asia Cultures Critique*, 17(3): 592–616.

Tsai, Kellee S. (2005) "Capitalists Without a Class: Political Diversity among Private Entrepreneurs in China", *Comparative Political Studies*, 38: 1130–1158.

Unger, Jonathan (1996) "Introduction". *In* Jonathan Unger and Geremie Barmé, eds. *Chinese Nationalism*, pp. xi–xviii. Armonk, NY: M.E. Sharpe.

UNICEF (2007) "Convention on the Rights of the Child". Electronic document, http://www.unicef.org/crc/, accessed February 16, 2007.

— (2010) *Child Disciplinary Practices at Home: Evidence from a Range of Low- and Middle-Income Countries*. NY: UNICEF.

United Nations Committee on the Rights of the Child (2005a) China's Second Periodic Report to the UN Committee on the Rights of the Child, June 27, 2003 (English Translation). Electronic document, http://www.ohchr.org/english/bodies/crc/crcs40.htm, accessed January 11, 2006.

— (2005b) Consideration of China's Second Periodic Report (Summary Record of the Fortieth Session, 1062nd Meeting of the Committee on the Rights of the Child, Held on 20 September 2005). Electronic document, http://www.ohchr.org/english/bodies/crc/crcs40.htm, accessed January 11, 2007 General Comment No. 8: The right of the child to protection from corporal punishment and other cruel or degrading forms of punishment. Committee on The Rights of the Child forty-second session, Geneva, 15 May–2 June 2006.

United Nations Development Program in China (2001) Thematic Areas: Basic Education. Electronic document, http://www.unchina.org/theme/html/edu.shtml, accessed April 23, 2002.

Walkerdine, Valerie (1984) "Developmental Psychology and the Child-Centered Pedagogy: The Insertion of Piaget into Early Education". *In* Julian Henriques, Wendy Hollway, Cathy Urwin, Couze Venn, and Valerie Walkerdine, eds. *Changing the Subject: Psychology, Social Regulation and Subjectivity*, pp. 153–202. London: Methuen.

— (2005) "Developmental Psychology and the Study of Childhood". *In* Chris Jenks, ed. *Childhood: Critical Concepts in Sociology*, Vol. 3, pp. 13–25. New York: Routledge.

Waltner, Ann (1995) "Infanticide and Dowry in Ming and Early Qing China". *In* Anne Behnke Kinney, ed. *Chinese Views of Childhood*, pp. 193–217. Honolulu: University of Hawai'i Press.

Wang, Hao (2011) *Protecting Privacy in China: A Research on China's Privacy Standards and the Possibility of Establishing the Right to Privacy and the Information Privacy Protection Legislation in Modern China*. Heidelberg: Springer.

Wang, Jing (2005) "Bourgeois Bohemians in China? Neo-Tribes and the Urban Imaginary", *The China Quarterly*, 183: 532–548.

Wang, Leslie (2010) "Importing Western Childhoods into a Chinese State-Run Orphanage", *Qualitative Sociology*, 33: 137–159.

Wang, Lingyu (2002) "*Gei haizi yisheng de caifu* [Provide the child with life-long assets]". *In* The Ministry of Education, The All-China Women and Children's Federation, and The Communist Youth League, eds. *Geng xin jiating jiaoyu guannian baogaoji* [A report on new views of family education], pp. 9–20. Beijing: Zhongguo fazhi chubanshe.

Wang, Peng (2002) "*Zai jiating jiaoyu zhong zouchu ertong guan de wuqu* [Avoiding erroneous views of the child in family education]". *In* The Ministry of Education, The All-China Women and Children's Federation, and The Communist Youth League, eds. *Geng xin jiating jiaoyu guannian baogaoji* [A report on new views of family education], pp. 104–113. Beijing: Zhongguo fazhi chubanshe.

Wang, Shaoguang *et al.* (2006) "The Uneven Distribution of Cultural Capital: Book Reading in Urban China", *Modern China*, 32(3): 315–348.

Wang, Shuguang (2004) "*Haizi jiankang chengzhang de jiating fenwei* [A family atmosphere that enables the healthy growth of the child]". Electronic document, http://www.chinafamilyeducation.com/200411/gz2004-11.htm, accessed November 20, 2004.

Watson, James L., ed. (1997) *Golden Arches East: McDonald's in East Asia*. Stanford: Stanford University Press.

Wei, Zongxuan, ed. (2000) *Xiaoxue suzhi jiaoyu* [Education for quality in primary schools]. Changsha: Hunan renmin chubanshe.

Westin, Alan (1984) "The Origins of Modern Claims to Privacy". *In* Ferdinand D. Schoeman, ed. *The Philosophical Dimensions of Privacy*, pp. 56–74. Cambridge: Cambridge University Press.

Wicks, Ann Barrott and Ellen B. Avril (2002) "Introduction: Children in Chinese Art". *In* Ann Barrott Wicks, ed. *Children in Chinese Art*, pp. 1–30. Honolulu: University of Hawai'i Press.

Wilson, Richard W. (1993) "Change and Continuity in Chinese Cultural Identity: The Filial Ideal and the Transformation of an Ethic". *In* Lowell Dittmer and Samuel S. Kim, eds. *China's Quest for National Identity*, pp. 104–124. Ithaca: Cornell University Press.

Wolf, Margery (1985) *Revolution Postponed: Women in Contemporary China*. Stanford: Stanford University Press.

Woodhead, Martin (1997) "Psychology and the Cultural Construction of Children's Needs". *In* Allison James and Alan Prout, eds. *Constructing and Reconstructing Childhood: Contemporary Issues in the Sociological Study of Childhood*, pp. 63–84. London: Falmer.

Woronov, Terry E. (2007) "Chinese Children, American Education: Globalizing Childrearing in Contemporary China". *In* Jennifer Cole and Deborah Durham, eds. *Generations and Globalization: Youth, Age, and Family in the New World Economy*, pp. 29–51. Bloomington, IN: Indiana University Press.

— (2008) "Raising Quality, Fostering 'Creativity': Ideologies and Practices of Education Reform in Beijing", *Anthropology & Education Quarterly*, 38(4): 401–422.

— (2009) "Governing China's Children: Governmentality and 'Education for Quality'", *Positions*, 17(3): 567–589.

Wu, David Y.H. (1996) "Parental Control: Psychocultural Interpretations of Chinese Patterns of Socialization". *In* Sing Lau, ed. *Growing Up the Chinese Way: Chinese Child and Adolescent Development*, pp. 1–26. Hong Kong: The Chinese University Press.

Wu, Xingqing and Zhao Jiangqing (2003) "*Qie weile ertong: 20 shiji 90 niandai yilai Shanghai ertong shiye de fazhan licheng* [For the children: The process of advancing the cause of Shanghai children since the 1990s]". Electronic document, http://www.stats-sh.gov.cn/2003fnet/jcbg/kygg5.htm, accessed December 1, 2004.

Xiaoxuesheng xinli suzhi peiyang: Si nianji jiaoshi yongshu [Nurturing the psychological quality of primary school students: Fourth grade teacher's manual] (2000) Beijing: Primary and Middle School Psychological Health Education Study Group, and the Psychological Quality Education Research Center, Kaiming chubanshe.

Xiaoxuesheng xinli suzhi peiyang: Yi nianji jiaoshi yongshu [Nurturing the psychological quality of primary school students: First grade teacher's manual] (2001). Beijing: Primary and Middle School Psychological Health Education Study Group, and the Psychological Quality Education Research Center, Kaiming chubanshe.

Xiao, Yang (1955) "*Haizi bu shi fumu de sichan* [Children are not the private property of parents]", *Renmin ribao* [People's Daily], May 11, p. 3.

Xinhua News Agency (2001) "Schools for Parents Popular in Beijing", March 19, 2001. Electronic document, http://www.china.org.cn/english/SOe/9322.htm, accessed November 22, 2005.

— (2003) "'Mother's Helpers' Emerge", December 23, 2003. Electronic document, http://www.china.org.cn/english/China/83232.htm, accessed November 22, 2005.

— (2004a) "NPC Deputies, CPPCC Members on Scientific Concept of Development", March 9, 2004. Electronic document, http://www.china.org.cn/english/10th/89706.htm, accessed March 9, 2004.

— (2004b) "Confucius Reenters Mainstream Culture", June 8, 2004. Electronic document, http://www.china.org.cn/english/culture/97647.htm, accessed March 23, 2006.

— (2008) "Psychological Education to Cover Schools", February 6, 2008. Electronic document, http://www.china.org.cn/2008-02/06/content_1242267.htm, accessed October 10, 2008.

— (2011) "'Wolf Dad' Stirs Debate Over 'Stick Parenting'", *China Daily*, November 19, 2011. Electronic document, http://www.chinadaily.com.cn/photo/2011-11/19/content_14125255.htm, accessed October 21, 2013.

— (2012) "Job Market Grim for New Graduates", June 7, 2012. Electronic document, http://www.china.org.cn/china/2012-06/07/content_25593348.htm, accessed October 19, 2012.

Xiong, Chaoshu (2003) "*Lixing duidai haizi: Duo yixie pinghe, shao yixie keke; duo yixie yindao, shao yixie yali* [Treat the child reasonably: With more moderation, less harshness; more guidance, less pressure]", *Zhongguo jiaoyu bao* [Chinese Education], March 30, 2003. Electronic document, http://www.jyb.com.cn/gb/jybzt/2002zt/jtjy/23.htm, accessed September 4, 2005.

Xu, Kuangdi (2001) "*Nuli shixian Shanghai funü ertong gongzuo de xin kuayue* [Make all effort to implement the new plan of Shanghai's Working Committee on Children and Women]". Electronic document, http://www.stats-sh.gov.cn/2003fnet/gzzl/gzzl11.htm, accessed December 1, 2004.

Xu, Minqiang (2004) "*Peiyang haizi de xinli suzhi* [Foster children's psychological quality]", *Renmin ribao* [People's Daily], August 13, p. 12.

Xu, Shan (2004) "*Qing fangshou, gei haizi fuze de rensheng taidu* [Let go, so that your child can have a responsible attitude in life]", *Weile haizi* [For the children], 12B: 13.

Yan, Hairong (2003) "Neoliberal Governmentality and Neohumanism: Organizing *Suzhi*/Value Flow through Labor Recruitment Networks", *Cultural Anthropology*, 18(4): 493–523.

Yan, Wenhua and Li Chengyan (2001) *Peiyang jiankang kuaile de haizi* [Raising a happy, healthy child]. Shanghai: Shaonian ertong chubanshe.

Yan, Yunxiang (1997) "McDonald's in Beijing: The Localization of Americana". *In* James L. Watson, ed. *Golden Arches East: McDonald's in East Asia*, pp. 39–76. Stanford: Stanford University Press.

— (2003) *Private Life under Socialism: Love, Intimacy, and Family Change in a Chinese Village, 1949–1999*. Stanford: Stanford University Press.

— (2009) "The Individualization of Chinese Society", *London School of Economics Monographs on Social Anthropology*. Oxford; New York: Berg.

— (2011) "The Changing Moral Landscape". *In* Arthur Kleinman *et al.*, eds. *Deep China: The Moral Life of the Person: What Anthropology and Psychiatry Tell Us about China Today*, pp. 36–77. Berkeley: University of California Press.

Yang, C.K. (1959) *The Chinese Family in the Communist Revolution*. Cambridge, MA: MIT Press.

Yang, Jing (2010) "Stumbling on the Rocky Road: Understanding China's Middle Class", *International Journal of China Studies*, 1(2): 435–458.

Yang, Lifei (2004) "Students Get to Sleep Later: Primary Classes Shortened, Lunch Break Extended", *Shanghai Daily*, August 28–29, p. 2.

Yang, Liu and Wang Sihai (1995) "*Moli jiaoyu: Shizai bixing* [Education for toughening oneself: A practical necessity]", *Sichuan Ribao* [Sichuan daily], October 11, 1995, p. 6.

Yang, Mayfair Mei-hui (1994) *Gifts, Favors, and Banquets: The Art of Social Relationships in China*. Ithaca, NY: Cornell University Press.

— (2002) "The Resilience of Guanxi and Its New Deployments: A Critique of Some New Guanxi Scholarship", *The China Quarterly*, 170: 459–476.

— (2004) "Spatial Struggles: Postcolonial Complex, State Disenchantment, and Popular Reappropriation of Space in Rural Southeast China", *The Journal of Asian Studies*, 63(3): 719–755.

— (2011) "Postcoloniality and Religiosity in Modern China: The Disenchantments of Sovereignty", *Theory, Culture & Society*, 28(2): 3–45.

Ye, Weili and Ma, Xiaodong (2005) *Growing Up in the People's Republic: Conversations Between Two Daughters of China's Revolution*. New York: Palgrave Macmillan.

Yi, Lin (2008) *Cultural Exclusion in China: State Education, Social Mobility and Cultural Difference*. London: Routledge.

— (2011) "Turning Rurality into Modernity: *Suzhi* Education in a Suburban Public School of Migrant Children in Xiamen", *The China Quarterly*, pp. 313–330.

Zarrow, Peter (2002) "The Origins of Modern Chinese Concepts of Privacy: Notes on Social Structure and Moral Discourse". *In* Bonnie S. McDougall and Anders Hansson, eds. *Chinese Concepts of Privacy*, pp. 121–146. Leiden, The Netherlands: Brill.

Zelizer, Viviana A. (1985) *Pricing the Priceless Child: The Changing Social Value of Children*. New York: Basic Books.

Zeng, Qi, ed. (2004) *Xin kecheng yu jiaoshi xinli tiaoshi* [The new curriculum and the emotional adjustment of teachers]. Beijing: Jiaoyu Kexue chubanshe.

Zhang, Everett (2011) "Introduction: Governmentality in China". *In* Everett Zhang, Arthur Kleinman, and Tu Weiming, eds. *Governance of Life in Chinese Moral Experience: The Quest for an Adequate Life*, pp. 1–30. London and New York: Routledge.

Zhang, Hua (1997) "*Suzhi Jiaoyu benzhi tanlun* [Exploring the essence of education for quality]", *Zhongguo jiaoyuxue kan* [Journal of the Chinese Society of Education], 3: 23–25.

— (2002) "*Jiaoyu yu ren de zhutixing fazhan: Xin zhuti jiaoyu lungang* [Education and the development of subjectivity: An outline of education for a new subjectivity]", *Jiaoyu lilun yu shiji* [Theory and practice of education], 22(7): 1–6.

Zhang, Jun (2004) "Law on Minors' Rights Debated: Comments to Be Sought from School Students, Teachers", *Shanghai Daily*, August 27, p. 3.

Zhang, Li (2008) "Private Homes, Distinct Life Styles: Performing a New Middle Class". *In* Li Zhang and Aihwa Ong, eds. *Privatizing China: Socialism from Afar*, pp. 23–40. Ithaca: Cornell University Press.

Zhang, Rong (2004) "*Shanghai ertong tiqian 'dabiao': 'Liu yi' tebie baodao guanzhu weichengnian ren* [Shanghai children "make the grade": Special Children's Day report on minors]", *Xinwen wanbao* [*Xinwen* evening news], May 25, 2004. Electronic document, http://old.jfdaily.com/gb/node2/node17/node38/node33760/node33773/userobject1ai503564.html, accessed June 1, 2004.

Zhang, Suying (1995) "*Bu yi dangzhog xun zi* [Don't admonish children in public]", *Sichuan ribao* [Sichuan daily], October 11, p. 6.

Zhang, Yan-hua and Zhou Rong (2008) "System Construction on Psychological Harmony Education of College Students", *US-China Education Review*, 5(3): 49–53.

Zhao, Shiping (2002) "*Jiating ruhe fazhan haizi de dulixing* [How can families develop the child's independence]". *In* The Ministry of Education, The All-China Women and Children's Federation, and The Communist Youth League, eds. *Geng xin jiating jiaoyu guannian baogaoji* [A report on new views of family education], pp. 175–183. Beijing: Zhongguo fazhi chubanshe.

Zhao, Suisheng (2004) *A Nation-state by Construction: Dynamics of Modern Chinese Nationalism*. Stanford: Stanford University Press.

Zhao, Yanyan (2002) "*Jiating: Haizi chengzhang de yaolan* [Family: A child's cradle of development]". *In* The Ministry of Education, The All-China Women and Children's Federation, and The Communist Youth League, eds. *Geng xin jiating jiaoyu guannian baogaoji* [A report on new views of family education], pp. 165–174. Beijing: Zhongguo fazhi chubanshe.

Zhongguo funü wang [Chinese Women Network] (2007) *Quanguo Fulian deng ba bu weilian hefa "Quanguo jiating jiaoyu gongzuo 'shiyiwu' guihua"* [The All-China Women's Federation and Eight Ministries and Commissions Jointly Announce "The Eleventh 5-Year-Plan on National Family Education"] May 22, 2007. Electronic document, http://www.china.com.cn/health/zhuanti/kletj/2007-05/22/content_8290124.htm, accessed June 1, 2007.

Zhong, Qiquan, Cui Yunhuo, and Zhang Hua, eds. (2001) *Weile Zhonghua minzu de fuxing, weile mei wei xuesheng de fazhan: Jichu jiaoyu kecheng gaige gangyao shixing* [For the revival of the Chinese people and the development of every student: An attempt to outline basic education curriculum reforms]. Shanghai: Huadong Shifan Daxue Chubanshe.

Zhou, Feng (1998) *Suzhi jiaoyu: Lilun, caozuo, jingyan* [Education for quality: Theory, operation, and experience]. Huizhou: Guangdong renmin chuban she.

Zhou, Shizhang (2005) *"Dui Shanghai zhongxiaoxue erqi kegai de renshi yu sikao* [Reflections on Shanghai's second phase curriculum reform]". Electronic document, http://www.21shte.net/teachforum/hezuomeiti/pdjy-1.htm, accessed March 23, 2005.

Index

Printed and bound by CPI Group (UK) Ltd, Croydon, CR0 4YY

HYDE'S HONOUR

After four years, Patrick Cullen Williams finally recovered his father's Texas silver mine. He expected trouble, but felt safe in the knowledge that Hyde would help him out. However, trouble is brewing with their neighbours, Don Pedro de la Valle and his impetuous son, Marco. Filled with hatred for Hyde, Marco is determined to get his hands on the mine, even to the extent of using Comanches who have their own score to settle with both Williams and Hyde . . .

GILLIAN F. TAYLOR

HYDE'S HONOUR

Complete and Unabridged

LINFORD
Leicester

First published in Great Britain in 2001 by
Robert Hale Limited
London

First Linford Edition
published 2003
by arrangement with
Robert Hale Limited
London

British Library CIP Data

Taylor, Gillian F.
    Hyde's honour.—Large print ed.—
    Linford western library
    1. Western stories
    2. Large type books
    I. Title
    823.9'14 [F]

    ISBN 0–7089–9440–7

WES
147156 2

Published by
F. A. Thorpe (Publishing)
Anstey, Leicestershire
Set by Words & Graphics Ltd.
Anstey, Leicestershire
Printed and bound in Great Britain by
T. J. International Ltd., Padstow, Cornwall

This book is printed on acid-free paper

1

There was wailing and mourning in the Comanche village deep in the south-west of Texas. Many of the young men had ridden out with Black Dog, all armed with the repeating rifles given to them by a white man and all keen to take coups and prove their bravery. But Black Dog's medicine had been bad and only five men had returned from the twenty-five who had left to seek glory. Comanche women cut their fine deer-skin clothes to rags and slashed open their arms, howling and weeping for their loss. The men mourned more quietly; one or two cut off some of their hair, and they offered the first morsel of food at each meal to the spirits of the dead. The leader of the band sent a crier through the camp announcing that the band was moving to a new site, leaving the bad memories behind.

When the tipis and belongings were packed, the last of the new repeating rifles were left behind, abandoned as bad luck.

One of the remaining young men rode apart from the others. His grey stallion was as fine as any other horse in the band even though the rider had a weak and twisted leg. He had never had a warrior's skills but instead had befriended a medicine man and learnt his powers. Sloping Leg used those powers and the force of his personality to control others, just as his brother, Black Dog, had used his courage and strength. Since Black Dog's death, Sloping Leg had been praying to his spirits, asking for the powers to avenge his brother. Other young men in mourning were starting to listen to him but they were reluctant to take action. Sloping Leg needed their help to kill the white men who had killed his brother. Attacks on homesteads and ranches would cause too much trouble with the Army and the Texas Rangers;

the other men didn't want that. Sloping Leg wanted to find the men who had been on the stagecoach that Black Dog had attacked. Then he could get the support he needed for his own revenge. He sang aloud to his spirits as he rode to the next camping-place, waiting impatiently for their help to come.

★   ★   ★

Pat Cullen Williams kissed the folded paper he was holding. Then he jumped off the sidewalk in front of the land agent's office and hurried along the El Paso street. He moved swiftly enough in spite of his slight paunch, ably skipping over a pile of horse dung on the plain dirt street. It only took a few moments for him to reach the saloon where his partner was waiting. Williams pushed open the batwing doors, grateful to leave the August heat behind as he entered the cooler adobe building. He paused there to let his eyes adjust to the dimmer light inside. A grin spread

3

across his good-natured face as he saw a Mexican boy trying to sell a serape to Hyde.

'Is very good, *señor*,' the boy pleaded, holding out the brightly striped poncho. 'My mother, she work for weeks to make it. Only five dollars to you.'

Williams tried to picture Hyde swapping his neat black jacket for a Mexican serape, and nearly laughed aloud. The Southerner was altogether too dignified to go native.

'I don't want it,' Hyde drawled, turning his head sufficiently to stare at the child with his cool, grey eyes. The only touch of colour in his black and grey clothing was a yellow neckerchief and the ivory grips of his twin Army Colts.

'Please, *señor*, look at the fine weaving.' The boy expertly threw the cloth half across the table and half across Hyde's lap, gesturing to the bold stripes.

'I done told you, I don't want it.'

4

With a single gesture, Hyde tossed the serape on to the floor.

The boy gave a cry of dismay and hurried to pick it up. Sawdust from the floor clung to the wool, though plenty flew about as the boy vigorously shook the serape to try and clean it. A few specks landed on Hyde's clothes and floated dangerously close to his pale beer.

Williams hurried forward to intervene. 'Here, *chico*,' he tossed a dime to the boy. 'Better luck someplace else, eh?'

The boy nodded, grinning, as he caught the coin. '*Gracias, señor.*'

Hyde wasted no more time on the boy. 'Did you get the deed?' he asked, his usually languid South Carolina drawl sharpened by anxiety.

'Sure did.' Williams handed it over and stopped for a moment to watch Hyde swiftly reading it.

They seemed unlikely partners, with little in common. Pat Williams had an open, good-natured face, with a sparkle in his blue eyes that suggested he was about to tell a funny story. He wore a slightly crumpled blue shirt, brown suit trousers, a brown Derby and low-heeled boots suited to town life. A short-barrelled copy of a Navy Colt sat in a battered gunbelt fastened with a Confederate States Army plate but he gave the misleading impression of wearing it mostly for show. When he did draw the gun, Williams handled it with a quiet confidence at odds with his unassuming exterior.

Hyde had seen Pat Williams fight and kill and knew about the gritty determination that few others saw. He was some five years older than his partner, now just over thirty, and was the taller of the two. His face was reserved and watchful, like a hunter's, and he looked plenty capable of using the matched Colts he wore. From his neatly brushed clothes to his recently trimmed dark hair, Hyde was a man who took pride in himself. It was those touches, as much as his slow drawl and self-assurance, that betrayed his past as a wealthy plantation son. However leisured his past might have been, he was now a tanned, lean man who relied on no one else for anything.

He read the paper while Williams went to the bar. The precious paper was Williams's formally registered claim for the silver-mine that his father had discovered just before the Civil War. The map for the mine had been lost when his father was killed in action and Williams had spent the four years since the War searching for his family's inheritance. Three weeks ago he had finally recovered the stolen map and found his mine. Hyde had helped him out then and intended staying on, offering his gun skill for a share in the silver. Hyde read the deed eagerly, and only looked up as Williams returned with a bottle of good whiskey and two shot-glasses.

'I bet you're surely glad to have it all legal at last,' he drawled.

'Even when word gets out, no claim-jumper's going to take it away from me,' Williams said, retrieving his paper and putting the glasses down.

'There's some folks just bound to be jealous, but nothing we can't handle.'

'All we got to do now is find that prospector Spragg told us about, and we're ready,' Williams said cheerfully, pouring two typically generous measures.

'That and make us some peace with the Comanches,' Hyde reminded him.

'We whupped Black Dog and broke his medicine power on our way here,' Williams pointed out. 'I bet the other braves'll be willing to take a few gifts and leave us alone.'

'It's our lives you're betting with, Cull . . . Williams,' Hyde drawled, correcting himself half-way through. Williams had been using his middle name when searching for the map and Hyde was still learning to call him by his proper name. He gave a mock scowl. 'Damned if I don't call you something else altogether.'

'You can call me 'Boss',' Williams teased. He lifted his glass. 'Drink up and cheer up! To the Two Moccasins Mine!'

'To the mine.'

★   ★   ★

Working a mine was harder, noisier and messier than either Williams or Hyde had realized. The man who had stolen the map had got it almost ready to start producing. One look at the stamp mill, the Washoe pans and the furnace had convinced Pat Williams of the need to hire someone who knew what he was doing. He took on two experienced miners, and a Mexican youth named Balzar to look after the horses and do the cooking.

'Got a purty l'il claim, sure enough,' remarked Hank O'Malley as he inspected the set-up with them.

Two Moccasins Mine was a couple of days' ride from El Paso, deep in the

Hueco Mountains of south-west Texas. It was in a narrow canyon, once overgrown with buckeye, hackberry and cottonwoods, much of which had been slashed back in the working areas. The silver-mine itself was dug into a cliff on the south side of the canyon. The entrance had once been a natural cavern but it had been worked out and widened, first by the Spanish, and lately by Williams's predecessor. Two burros hauled the cars of rough rock to the stamp mill built upstream along the broad creek that wandered along the canyon floor. The bubbling water had been damned there to power the mill, then was diverted along a wooden flume with a series of riffles built along the bottom.

At present, the flume was being worked by the other miner, McKindrick. He was a black haired Scot who habitually wore a collarless shirt and a faded kilt of red and green tartan that revealed his knotty calves and scarred knees. As usual, he had missed a patch when he last shaved and a tuft of wiry black bristles showed at the corner of his jaw as he leaned over to pour crushed rock into the flume. The lighter pieces of rock were carried along in the rushing water while little piles of heavier material built up behind the riffles. Hyde reached into the enticingly cold water and stirred up the collected dirt, watching as it was whirled along the wooden flume to the next riffle.

'Leave that be, damn you,' cursed O'Malley.

Hyde turned swiftly, glaring at the shabbily dressed miner.

'You ever worked a mine afore?' O'Malley demanded scornfully.

Hyde shook his head, still half angry at being told off.

'Didn't reckon as a fine gennlemen like you would know no better,' O'Malley remarked, wiping his face with the polka-dotted kerchief he usually wore around his grubby neck. While Hyde was well groomed and clean shaven, the miner had uncut, almost matted hair and whiskers to match. He wore ageing bib overalls over his undershirt and a slouch hat that might once have been either grey or brown, but which was now neither. The only well-kept things about him were his stout work-boots and the Tranter revolver he kept by his bedroll.

'The rock with the ore's heavier than the waste stuff,' O'Malley lectured. 'Them riffles're in the flume to catch the heavy stuff so's we kin git the silver from it. You go on stirring up the rich rock so's it floats on down an' it'll git thrown out with the tailings.' He pointed to the small pile of waste material already dumped on the far side of the canyon.

Hyde grunted something that might have been an apology. Williams's blue eyes gleamed with amusement at seeing his partner discomfited, but he knew better than to tease the Southerner any further. They followed O'Malley as he led them to the rough lumber-mill building lower down the creek. The single room was almost filled with the iron pans of the Washoe Pan processor and the solid bulk of the furnace in the corner. Williams and Hyde both stared at the great processing machine in wonder.

O'Malley patted the side of the Washoe Pan affectionately. 'This doo-hickey here's sure some better than the ol' *arresta*,' he said. 'Gets the whole amalgamation done in jest a few hours instead of weeks.'

'How's it work?' Williams asked.

'Mix the crushed ore an' water to slime,' O'Malley instructed. 'Then add salt, copper sulphate, quicksilver and mebbe a coupla other things to be sure.'

'Like what?' Williams interrupted, keen to learn.

O'Malley winked. 'You want to run this yoreself? Reckoned not,' he went on, barely pausing for an answer. 'Man's gotta know what he's doin' to run the pans an' all.'

'This is steam-powered too, isn't it?' Hyde asked, examining the boiler.

'Sure it is,' O'Malley answered. 'Steam heats the mix and makes them paddles move, keeps stirring the mix better'n any mule. The steam's what makes the process faster'n the Mex method. And it don't take no skill to keep the boiler steamin',' he added, with a sly look at Hyde. 'Even a feller with a head full of grammar kin put coal on a fire.'

Williams saw the glitter in Hyde's grey eyes and spoke up.

'The four of us will take spells at digging, sorting the ore, stoking the fires and suchlike jobs.' He headed to the furnace. 'The silver amalgamates to the quicksilver, doesn't it?'

O'Malley nodded. 'We'll roast the mix in here an' drive off the quicksilver; most o' that we kin reclaim. Then we jest smelt the silver down ter bullion and sell it.'

'And I thought mining silver was something like panning for gold,' Williams said thoughtfully as he looked around again at the machinery.

'Some fellers jest sell the ore,' O'Malley reminded him. 'But I reckon this's a sound vein you got here. Might's well do the whole job. And them finished blocks o' silver's a mighty purty sight,' he added with a sentimental sigh. 'Mighty purty.'

'I'm surely looking forward to seeing one,' Hyde declared.

★   ★   ★

He had to wait longer than he'd thought. Williams, Hyde, O'Malley and McKindrick worked for over a week on digging, crushing and sorting the ore before O'Malley announced that they had almost enough to make the first batch of processing worthwhile. By then it was the end of another hot day of labouring and Balzar had got supper ready. The weary men returned to the shack that served as cookhouse and bunkhouse, settling themselves on the boxes and stumps that passed as seats. Balzar was at the cook-fire, ladling something spicy-smelling from the cauldron on to tin plates as he sang softly to himself in Spanish. His elaborate silver spurs glittered in the evening sun and jingled cheerfully as he moved, prompting his happy smile. The gangly Mexican youth was eager to please, and loved looking after the horses and burros, but had a childlike mind in spite of being almost twenty.

Hyde had paused to wash in the creek and was the last to arrive for supper. He settled himself gingerly on the uneven log that was the only place left and stretched out his legs with a sigh. Another day of digging ore in the mine had left him stiff and cramped in the shoulders and neck. Hyde inspected his hands; the skin was scuffed and torn and he had a blister forming on his right palm.

'If the Comanches attack, we're going to have trouble holding them off,' he said. 'I can't use my guns properly with my hands like this.'

'I never yet saw a born gennleman

16

who could do a day's work without whining about it,' O'Malley remarked to no one in particular as he bent down to fuss his brindled coyote-dog. He rarely missed a chance to rile Hyde, especially since discovering that the Southerner had once owned slaves.

'I can do a day's work,' Hyde snapped. 'But I've been slaving harder this last week than any of my field hands ever worked.'

'You ain't a slave though. You kin quit any time you like,' O'Malley answered. 'I'm fair 'mazed you stuck it out this long, ain't you, Tara?' he asked the dog.

'I had grit enough to stick out four years of war,' Hyde snarled.

'Sure, an' I jest bet you took along yer darky servant to clean yer boots and bile up hot water fer to shave in,' O'Malley mocked.

His guess was spot on, as Hyde's expression made clear.

'I had a bunch of duties my men didn't,' Hyde answered hotly. 'An officer's got to write reports, make inspections, roll calls. I had less free time than my men.'

'And you figgered iffen you was fightin' ter keep yer slaves, them slaves might's well take the risks and go ter war too,' O'Malley answered.

'That's enough,' Williams interrupted. He was glad that Hyde left his Colts in the bunkhouse when digging, or gun-play might have erupted before now. 'Supper's ready,' he went on, forcing a cheerful tone to his voice. 'I'm plumb ready for mine.'

The talking ceased as Balzar handed round the hot platefuls. Hyde took the plate and poked at the brown mass with his fork. It seemed to be some combination of stewed beef with chilli and refried beans. The hot smell of the spices made his nose itch.

'Can't that fool boy cook anything but this!' Hyde exclaimed, suddenly revolted by the Mexican food. 'He's cooked the same damned mess every day for a week now.'

'After two years of nothing but salt

hoss, corn pones and baled hay in the War, I swore I'd never grumble about food again,' Williams said, picking up a forkful.

'You weren't no cavalry officer,' O'Malley said. 'You didn't git ter steal chickens outta folks' gardens.'

Hyde hurled the full plate towards the fire and jumped to his feet.

'Goddamn you and Goddamn all this!' he exclaimed. He strode into the shack and buckled on his gunbelt, settling the Army Colts carefully in their holsters without even thinking about it, and picked up his horse's tack. Without another word he stalked to the corral and saddled his liver chestnut horse. A couple of minutes later he was riding back down the canyon, past the other men as they ate supper. Balzar was scraping the spilled food back on to the plate, tears gleaming in his dark eyes as he cleared up the rejected offering.

'*Lo siento, señor*,' Balzar called unhappily.

Hyde ignored him, bitterly quenching the surge of guilt he felt at upsetting the harmless young man. Once past the shack, he sent his horse on at a fast lope.

The liver chestnut was pleased to be running after a week with little exercise. It raced eagerly over the dry landscape, bounding sure-footedly along the winding trail. Hyde easily sat his horse's high-spirited bucks, sending it on until both were calmer and ready to slow. He didn't turn back, but rode for the best part of an hour until he reached Hueco, the small town that was the nearest settlement to the mine.

Night was falling as he rode up the single street and tethered the liver chestnut outside the adobe saloon. There were only three men inside the sawdust-scented building, and one of them was the barman. He got up from the game of monte he was playing and wandered behind the crude bar.

'What you want, friend?' he enquired good-naturedly.

'Whiskey.'

Hyde swallowed the shot of brown liquid in one. He found the simple saloon, with its mostly home-made furnishings, almost as depressing as the mine. 'I want a meal,' he said.

The barkeep shook his head. 'Lunch-times only.'

Hyde slapped two coins on the lumber counter that served as a bar. 'I'll pay two dollars for a plate of ham and eggs.'

'Ham and eggs?' the barman repeated, astonished at the amount offered for a twenty-five cent meal.

'Yes. No damned Mex food,' Hyde insisted.

The barman grinned suddenly, under-standing Hyde's wish for plain, unspiced food.

'For two dollars I'll throw in a tin of peaches after,' he promised.

Hyde nodded once. 'Thanks.'

It was full dark when he got back to Two Moccasins Mine. Hyde watered his horse at the creek, then turned it loose in the corral further upstream and strolled back to the bunkhouse. The quiet sounds of the desert night were drowned by McKindrick's rich, Scottish snores as Hyde entered. He was making his way carefully to his own bedroll when one of the other men sat up with a soft rustling from his light quilt. Hyde didn't need the faint starlight coming in through the open door to know it was Pat Williams.

'Feeling better?' Williams asked quietly.

'A mite,' Hyde replied equally softly.

'I didn't know how tough the mining is when I got you involved,' Williams said. 'And I sure didn't realize how mean O'Malley is. I told him to quit plaguing you and he said he'd up and quit iffen I didn't want him around.'

'You need him,' Hyde said. 'You surely need two men around who know what they're doing and it isn't either of us.'

'I promised you five hundred dollars to help me get poppa's map back. I can go to the bank in El Paso and pay you

the rest off tomorrow iffen you want,'
Williams offered. He had already paid
Hyde half the amount promised but
wanted to keep the rest as capital until
he had some silver in the bank.

That money was more cash than
Hyde had seen at any one time since
the War. He swallowed.

'Why, I don't want to quit on you. I
reckon I got gumption enough to see this
through. I'll not let him rile me so bad.'

Williams chuckled softly. 'What you
really got is gun skill. I guess I forgot
that's what you do. While O'Malley's
taking charge of the processing tomorrow, we'll ride out and look for the
Comanches. See iffen we can make
some peace with them.'

Hyde sat on his bedroll and started
prising off his long riding boots.
'Sounds like a swell idea.'

'Yeah, that's what I thought,' Williams
answered with complete immodesty. In
spite of his aching muscles, Hyde
smiled to himself. Williams was a good
companion to have around.

2

Pat Williams started singing from sheer pleasure as they rode out across country the next morning, much to Hyde's surprise. The two men had met only a few weeks earlier, travelling out from Fort Stockton on the coach together, and they didn't know much about each other yet. For his part, Williams was glad to have quit his old job as a travelling salesman. He had grown up on the Texas frontier and felt at home out in this open land. He rode easily in his deep saddle, his hands light on the horse's reins as he sang in a pleasant tenor.

'Are you usually this cheerful when you're going to meet up with wild Indians?' Hyde drawled.

Williams chuckled. 'Only when I've got me a silvermine. As soon as we get the first bullion melted down, I'll write

Momma and let her know I've got pappy's mine. Louisa won't need to go on teaching no more.'

'That's your sister?'

'The eldest. She went right on teaching school after I got back from the War so I could put my money to searching for the mine.' Williams paused to hum another line of his tune. 'If Wybourn hadn't had the map, I reckon I'd have quit searching. Louisa's been courting three years now but she couldn't quit teaching to get married while the family needed her money.' A smile broke over his round face. 'I got pappy's mine, Louisa can get hitched any time she likes. I haven't felt this free in a real long time.'

Hyde grunted in answer. Williams glanced at him and felt a mild stab of guilt. He tactfully changed the subject.

'Making a peace with the Comanches has got to be easier than digging ore out of the mine.'

'Have you had dealings with them before?' Hyde asked, remembering the

Indian lore that Williams had shown during the journey to El Paso.

'Other than shooting at them from the stage? I've visited Indian camps a few times before. The young bucks are regular hotheads, but they're neighbourly folk mostly.'

'Do you speak Comanche?' Hyde asked the question that had been bothering him.

'Not a word,' Williams said cheerfully. He paused a moment to let Hyde worry before explaining that many Comanches spoke Spanish. 'You don't speak Spanish, do you?' he asked.

Hyde shook his head. 'Just French.'

'French?' Williams repeated, startled.

Hyde flashed his sudden, sharklike grin. 'With a terrible accent,' he admitted. 'What are you planning to give the Comanche?' he asked. 'Horses?'

Williams started laughing. 'Horses? To Comanches? Why don't we give them some pemmican too?'

Hyde took the teasing better than he

would from anyone else. 'Comanches are horse Indians, right?' he asked.

'Sure they are.' Williams chuckled. 'You'll see that yourself.'

⋆　⋆　⋆

The Comanche village was spread out in a wide valley. As Hyde and Williams crested a narrow ridge of land, they saw thirty or more tipis grouped together, each with a horse tethered outside. At the head of the valley roamed a herd of some two hundred horses, watched over by boys.

'Comanches are horse Indians, you see,' Williams remarked.

'Why, how do they get so many horses?' Hyde asked, inwardly impressed, although his face was as calm as ever.

'Catch them, breed them, steal them,' Williams answered. He nudged his horse into a walk. 'Comanches barter and give away horses all the time.' He flashed a smile at his partner. 'Come on, let's go talk to some real wild Indians.'

Hyde set his horse in motion and followed.

Pat Williams led them into the middle of the Comanche village. The tipis were gathered in loose circles around one large, painted, lodge which Williams knew would belong to the head of the band. Scrawny dogs ran barking alongside their horses as they rode in, making Hyde's liver chestnut lay back its ears. The Comanche women were all at work on the summer bounty of meat, fruit and hides. Long slices of jerky were drying on wooden frames in the hot sun like so much ragged laundry. Two women were pounding a deer-hide while another scraped a skin with a stone tool. An older woman sat in the door of her lodge, pausing from her sewing to watch the white men ride past. There seemed to be fewer men about, and most of them vanished into their tipis as the strangers approached.

Williams sensed his partner's growing nervousness. 'They're getting fixed up to meet company,' he explained quietly. 'Comanches sure are vain.'

'I see.' Hyde looked at the squat, heavy-set Indians and wondered what they had to be vain about.

Moments later, the relative peace was shattered. Half a dozen youngsters came bursting through a stand of timber, racing their excited ponies right past the visitors. They whooped and screamed, flailing at their mounts with quirts as they raced past almost under the noses of the white men. Hyde cursed, his face tense as he tried to calm his excited horse.

'Just youngsters,' Williams called, his eyes twinkling. 'Showing off for the girls.' Hyde could hear a woman chuckling and strove to ignore it.

'Comanches like nothing better than a good laugh at someone else,' Williams added.

The remark didn't seem to fit with the stories of stoic Indians that Hyde had read, but the middle-aged man who met them at the centre of the village was no disappointment. Walking Bear wore a dark-blue breechcloth and fine buckskin leggings that were dyed dark green. Leggings and moccasins were finished with long fringes decorated with silver, fur and shells. His long braids were wrapped with spotted jaguar fur and a single yellow feather stuck out from the scalp-lock at the back of his head, to match the streak of yellow paint along the parting. His broad, dark-copper face was painted with dark blue and yellow circles and green dots were painted along his powerful arms. The chief was short and paunchy but he stood erect with a natural dignity.

Williams spoke in slow Spanish. 'Buenos dias, jefe.'

Walking Bear answered slowly in the same language. He invited the white men to dismount and ordered his senior wife to bring food for the visitors. Williams translated quietly for his partner's benefit, adding more advice.

'We'll eat first, and smoke, before talking about what we're here for. Walking Bear's accepted us as his guests so don't worry about someone making a sudden attack.' Hyde reluctantly surrendered his horse to a young woman, who nodded approvingly at it as she tethered it near the big tipi. Other men joined the group, mostly middle-aged and all dressed in their best. The white men were shown into the tipi, which had its lower edges hitched up a foot or so to let a pleasant breeze blow through. Inside, Williams and Hyde copied the example of the Comanche men, sitting on the piles of furs and buffalo robes that served as beds and seats in one.

The meal was a thin stew of boiled meat, some starchy tubers and offerings of hackberries and cherries. It was eaten with fingers and knives then a shallow dish of water was passed around for washing greasy hands. When the women had retreated, Walking Bear solemnly filled a long-stemmed pipe.

He puffed at it, then it was passed around the circle from right to left. Both white men smoked although Williams felt his eyes watering and struggled to hold back a cough. When the polite preliminaries were finished, he started to explain the reason for his visit. He spoke slowly in Spanish, allowing time for his words to be translated. He told the Comanches that he wished only to dig up the silver and to hunt a little game now and again. He wasn't going to hunt the dwindling buffalo, or wild horses, or run cattle over the Comanche's ranges. Williams was a good speaker and sincere in what he was telling the Indians. He asked only to be let alone and offered gifts as a demonstration of his goodwill. The packets of tobacco, matches, coffee, needles and salt he had brought were handed to Walking Bear, who examined them briefly before putting them aside to be shared out later.

Walking Bear and his council listened without interrupting. When they were sure that Williams had finished, the chief began to make his answer. Walking Bear had just said that he was glad to meet the white man who came in peace, when there was an interruption from the doorway of the tipi. A couple of younger men pushed their way in, blocking most of the bright sunlight. Murmurs of disapproval arose from the older men at the breach of courtesy. The taller of the two newcomers spoke rapidly and bitterly, pointing at Hyde, who sat very still and tense.

One of the two Indians was a tallish man, handsome in the Comanche way, and athletic, but his appearance was spoiled by a weak and twisted leg. Even at rest he stood awkwardly, the toes of his right foot turned in. In spite of the infirmity, he was well dressed with plenty of decorations on the long fringes of his leggings and moccasins and he wore an elaborate necklace of teeth and animal bones that clattered when he turned to stare at the two white men. The other Comanche had black paint smeared on his face and bare chest and had recently hacked off his left braid, leaving the other swinging plain and unadorned.

'Do Comanches attack a man who's eaten their salt?' Hyde asked Williams quietly.

'They're plumb strong on laws of hospitality,' Williams answered, never taking his eyes off the newcomers. He didn't need to look at Hyde to sense his partner's anxiety.

Walking Bear listened to the younger men before turning to his guests. He spoke carefully to Williams in guttural Spanish. Williams made a brief reply before turning to Hyde.

'The taller buck is Sloping Leg; he's Black Dog's brother. The other one is Turkey Feather; he says you killed his brother.'

'I was defending myself and the stage,' Hyde said indignantly. 'Black Dog and his men attacked us.' He glared at the Comanche brave.

'I know,' Williams said soothingly.

'Time for some more flattery.' He spoke to the Comanches again, telling them about the attack on the stagecoach which had brought him and Hyde to the area. He spoke admiringly of the courage of the warriors, while also playing up Hyde's skill as a gunman and his own part in holding off the attack. He said he was sorry for the deaths of Black Dog and many of his men, but added that they had died as men should. All his skill as a story-teller came into play, as he met the dark eyes of the Comanches and forced himself to speak like a brave about the whole terrifying encounter.

When he finished, the Comanches began to talk among themselves. The two white men sat silently in the tipi, surrounded by the copper-skinned Indians talking in their own strange language. Williams was developing cramp from sitting cross-legged for so long, but he didn't dare do more than shift slightly to try and ease the discomfort.

'I surely hope I get enough time to say 'I told you so',' Hyde remarked quietly.

The two younger Comanches were still angry. Sloping Leg seemed to be making a threatening gesture, demanding something from the older chief. Walking Bear answered back sharply. He made a dismissive gesture, his voice rumbling out in an unmistakable tone of command. The other men added their own disapproval, filling the tipi with a tense atmosphere that left the white men more nervous than ever.

Sloping Leg and his friend left reluctantly; the lame Comanche pausing to make a strange gesture and give them an evil look that needed no translation.

Walking Bear spoke to his men, letting each one give his opinion in turn. Each man spoke gravely until an agreement was reached. At last, Walking Bear spoke again in Spanish.

'I am sorry for the ill manners of the

young men, but they are both mourning for their brothers, and angry. We have told Sloping Leg and Turkey Feather that you are brave warriors and so were their brothers. It is no disgrace for a man to die bravely in battle and they should honour the memories of those who died. We will let you work at your mine while you do not attack us.'

'*Bueno*,' Williams answered with poorly concealed relief. He went on in Spanish, praising the chief and his council for their wisdom, saying that enough good men had died already.

Walking Bear nodded, enjoying the flattery. 'They have been told to let you alone,' he added in Spanish. 'But they are Comanche. The village will not make war upon you, but beware of these men. Sloping Leg has powerful medicine and will use Turkey Feather's grief for his brother.'

'*Yo comprendo*,' Williams answered. He translated the warning to Hyde.

'Do Comanche ever do what their leaders tell them?' Hyde drawled.

'Mostly,' Williams answered. 'Individuals do what they like iffen they reckon they can get away with it. The chief won't back Sloping Leg against us but he can't actually stop him holding a grudge.'

'Maybe we should hold that grudge first,' Hyde suggested. His next remark was interrupted by a whinny from a horse outside the tipi. 'That's Cob!' he exclaimed.

Williams scrambled hurriedly to his feet as Hyde lunged up and pushed his way out of the tipi. They found that Turkey Feather was holding the reins of Hyde's horse, clearly intending to lead it away.

'That's my horse,' Hyde growled. His horse was a good one, well trained and distinctive. It was a striking, rich liver chestnut with a flaxen mane and tail.

The older Comanches emerged from the tipi to see what was happening. A babble of voices broke out, demands and explanations in guttural Comanche.

'You let that horse be,' Hyde demanded, glaring at Turkey Feather and ignoring the others. He was the tallest man in the camp and to Williams, who had seen him in action, he looked just as dangerous as any of the half-naked Indians.

Turkey Feather snapped back a defiant answer that was translated into Spanish.

'He says he's taking your favourite horse and saddle as payment for his brother's death,' Williams translated for his partner.

As soon as he spoke, Turkey Feather took a step away, still holding the reins. Hyde drew both guns in a blur of motion but only the right one fired. The eagle feather in the Comanche's scalp-lock snapped in half, the broken section drifting to the ground. The horse shied away, pulling the Comanche off-balance until he got it under control again. Silence fell over the busy camp as everyone watched the confrontation. Turkey Feather stayed still, defying the white man as Hyde kept the guns aimed at him. Williams took a quick glance around at the other Indians. He wanted to back Hyde and have his hand on his own gun, but he didn't want to provoke any jumpy Comanches into a fight. Hyde changed aim with his left gun and fired again. Turkey Feather's one remaining braid jerked violently, almost severed by the single precise shot. The young Indian flinched momentarily before making an effort to regain his composure. Williams could hear laughter from some of those watching.

'Tell him that the next shot will take his goddamned hand off, unless he lets go the reins,' Hyde warned, never taking his gaze from his enemy.

Williams obligingly translated, adding that Hyde was the best shot he'd ever met. Some of the Comanches nodded, admiring the skill needed to hit the braid without touching the man. Walking Bear translated the Spanish into Comanche.

Turkey Feather swallowed, taking fast, shallow breaths as he tried to summon his fading courage. The ruined braid hung crookedly over his shoulder. Hyde slowly raised his right gun, sighting along the barrel. Turkey Feather stood still a moment longer, then dropped the reins. He hurried away, not meeting anyone's eyes as most of the other Comanches laughed. Hyde holstered his guns and whistled. The liver chestnut walked to him and nuzzled his jacket pocket.

Williams spoke in Spanish. 'There has been enough killing already. My friend did not wish to deprive the family of another brave.'

'Your friend is a better warrior than Turkey Feather,' Walking Bear answered calmly. 'Depart from this camp in peace.'

With a few last polite exchanges, Williams and Hyde mounted up and rode from the camp.

They rode in silence for some time. Williams was thinking over what had happened, aware that they had made enemies, even though the chief had been favourable. He mulled over the defensive possibilities of the canyon for a while before glancing at his partner. Much to his surprise, he saw that Hyde was relaxed, his grey eyes studying the landscape as they crossed the rough country. Williams grinned wryly. 'I learnt something today,' he remarked.

'What's that?' Hyde asked.

'Next time you get the blues, I'll fix up for someone to come by and make trouble so's you can face them down. Why, I might just send a horse to that Turkey Feather as thanks for cheering you up.'

Hyde laughed aloud for the first time in days. 'If there's a shortage of Indians, I'll make do with a mean miner. Why, I sure wouldn't mind shooting one of them.'

Williams shook his head. 'I need him a while yet to run the washing-pans and the furnace. You can't shoot him till I find a better one.'

Hyde shrugged. 'All right. Next time O'Malley gives me some lip, I'll hold my fire and think of that purty silver,' he promised.

3

Williams took great delight in telling the other three about the success of his visit to the Comanches. He told the story of Hyde forcing Turkey Feather to back down, emphasizing Hyde's short temper and his remarkable gun skills, all principally for O'Malley's benefit. The cantankerous miner made no obvious sign of taking the hint but his thoughts were on other things. Young Balzar gazed at Hyde with a wide-eyed admiration that made the Southerner faintly uneasy.

Balzar spent more time than ever in the corral, feeding the liver chestnut extra handfuls of oats, talking nonsense to it in Spanish, and grooming it until the horse's coat shone like a freshly shelled nut.

Hyde was mildly irritated by Balzar

but like the others, his thoughts were more concerned with O'Malley. The miner was smelting down the first load of amalgam to produce silver bullion. He watched over the furnace with all the nerves and pride of a father awaiting the birth of his first child. When it was finally done, Williams and the others gazed upon the block of silver with awe. Williams hefted it in one hand, his blue eyes shining as brightly as the new metal.

'I can't believe this is mine,' he said aloud. He looked down the canyon to the mine entrance and the crooked line of the flume. 'I never saw so much silver together in one place afore. I can't believe we really produced this metal from that dadblasted rock we hacked out of the ground.'

'Matter of findin' the right kind o' rock,' O'Malley said.

'Poppa sure earned his spurs there,' Williams said. He reluctantly passed the silver bullion to Hyde. 'I'm gonna go into town and wire Momma about this before I'm an hour older,' he said suddenly.

'Are you planning to take this to the bank?' Hyde asked, his hands closing around the precious metal.

Williams considered. 'I'd better, I reckon.'

'Seems a plumb shame to lock up something so purty,' O'Malley said in sentimental tones. He wiped his hands on the spotted neckerchief half-hidden under his matted whiskers.

Hyde handed back the silver, his fingers trailing over the shining metal.

'Sure and it'll be safer in the bank,' he drawled.

'It will,' Williams agreed reluctantly. He brightened up, smiling at the other men. 'While I'm in town, I'll draw some *dinero* and fetch you some pay,' he promised.

⋆ ⋆ ⋆

Williams did as he said, also bringing back two bottles of whiskey, which fuelled a celebration. Although he tried to keep his business at the bank quiet, word soon got around El Paso that a new silver-mine was running up in the Hueco Mountains. The news reached Casa de las Flores, a hacienda some fifteen miles from the mine.

Don Pedro de la Valle was out on the patio, eating with his family, when his *segundo*, Diaz, gave him the news.

'Some silver is already in the bank?' Don Pedro asked thoughtfully.

'*Sí, señor,*' Diaz answered.

Don Pedro leaned back carefully in his chair. Although of average height, he was a heavy man with ponderous jowls and broad shoulders. His curly hair was still thick, but now greying fast, which simply added to his natural dignity. All his movements were careful and deliberate.

'I had heard rumours of a mine being set up; someone was buying equipment in El Paso a few months ago.'

'I wonder how far away it is.' His son, Marco, spoke eagerly. 'If silver can be found in one place, there must be more nearby.'

'Oh, if there was silver here, it would have been found already,' his younger sister told him scornfully.

Both of Don Pedro's children were good looking and bright. Marco had reddish-tinged curly hair and a flashing smile that charmed almost every woman except his sister. Concepción had a sweet face framed by a fall of raven-black hair that was usually set off with a fresh flower from the carefully tended beds that gave the Casa de las Flores its Spanish name.

'That is very likely, Conchita.' Don Pedro used the family pet name for his daughter. 'My father had an American miner search our land for valuable metals and he found none.' Since his wife's death ten years earlier, he had petted and adored his little girl. As she grew into a woman, Don Pedro saw that she had a mind as quick as his own and came to treat her with greater respect than his impetuous son. 'This new mine cannot be on my land.' His dark eyes became hooded as he thought.

'Did you find out who owns it?' Marco asked Diaz. 'He might be willing to sell,' he suggested impulsively.

'If a man has the enterprise to find himself a silver mine in this wild country, he will not give it up easily,' Don Pedro told his son.

'I didn't check with the land registry, but I could do so,' Diaz offered.

'That will be a good idea,' Don Pedro said slowly. 'I think it is time we held a fiesta here. If this miner is nearby, I think it would be good to meet our neighbour.'

'You want to invite miners here?' Marco asked incredulously.

'Oh yes, let's,' Concepción said happily. 'And besides, *Padre* is going to invite the mine owner, not a common miner. You think too much of yourself,' she added, reaching around the table to prod her brother in his ribs. Marco jerked away, giving her a nasty look but she didn't care. She knew her father well enough to guess that he had some other reason other than sociability for holding a fiesta, but so long as she got to dance, she was happy.

Don Pedro smiled benevolently at his pretty daughter's playfulness. 'We will make it soon, Conchita,' he promised.

★ ★ ★

'That's sure some spread,' Williams exclaimed on his first sight of Casa de las Flores set in the valley below. 'You ever see the like of that before?'

The beautiful whitewashed Spanish hacienda stood within a high, broad wall built to keep out Comanches and Apaches. The main house was solid and well-proportioned, with balconies and porches to provide shade from the blazing Texas sun. Pots and tubs of flowers surrounded the house, adding a riot of colour to the simple white and brown architecture. Beyond the main house were the stables, a terrace, servants' quarters and all the other buildings necessary to run and maintain the ranch.

'A few times,' Hyde drawled briefly.

Williams forced a wry smile, regretting his tactlessness. Hyde had lived on a, no doubt, equally grand family plantation until forced to sell it after the War. Unable to think of a sensible comment, Williams wisely said nothing.

They rode down to Don Pedro's house together, Williams gawking unashamedly as they entered the gateway in the outer wall. Although it was only mid-afternoon, plenty of guests had already arrived and the whole place was alive with music and motion. Servants hurried about, orders were being given in Spanish and the smell of roasting meat came from a pit where whole sheep were being spit-roasted. Hyde heard feminine giggling from somewhere overhead as they rode past the house, and looked up. Two young women were leaning over the wooden railing of a first-floor balcony to watch the guests arriving. Williams also noticed and looked up as the two men rode past on their way to the stables.

'*Buenos tardes, señoritas,*' he called cheerfully.

One of the girls leaned right out to wave a lacy handkerchief at the two men below. There was a sudden crack as the balcony rail gave way, and the girl tumbled down with a shriek of fright. Williams didn't stop to think. He kneed his horse sideways, dropped his reins and caught the falling girl as she landed almost in his lap. The sudden weight pulled him sideways in his saddle but he kept his seat and righted himself. Then he found himself with a lapful of beautiful young woman. For once in his life, Pat Williams was lost for words. He simply stared at Concepción, not knowing who she was, but aware that she was one of the loveliest things he had ever set eyes on. Her dark eyes gazed right into his, and he could feel her heart beating under the yellow silk dress she wore.

'*Madre de Dios!*' she exclaimed. '*Que paso?*'

'I don't know,' Williams answered, too rattled to speak in Spanish even though he'd understood what she'd said.

Their mutual astonishment was interrupted by Don Pedro. '*Bravo, señor.* You have saved my daughter,' he said, hurrying over from the porch. In spite of his bulk, Don Pedro moved with a light grace.

'*De nada,*' Williams replied. He was so enraptured with Concepción's smile that it took a few moments for Don Pedro's words to sink in properly. 'Your daughter!' he exclaimed. His first thought was to dump her on the ground there and then, but he immediately realized that it would be an ungracious way to handle his host's daughter. He heard a soft chuckle from Hyde, who was being no help at all.

'I am Don Pedro de la Valle,' the Don

introduced himself. It was hardly necessary, as no one else would be so richly dressed and distinguished.

'I am Concepción Maria Flores de la Valle,' the girl added. She giggled as she spoke, quivering in Williams's arms in a most diverting way, but didn't show any inclination to get down.

He swallowed and turned his attention firmly to the man standing beside his horse. 'I am Patrick Cullen Williams and this is my partner . . . Mr Hyde.' Williams hesitated slightly over the introduction when he realized that he didn't know what Hyde's other names were.

'I am right honoured to meet you-all,' Hyde drawled, raising his hat politely to Concepción just as if they had met in a formal drawing-room.

She nodded politely to him and held out her arms towards her father. The girl slithered off Williams's lap with a delicious rustle of fine silk and lacy underskirts. As she settled the full skirts into place, she turned and smiled sweetly up at him. Williams suddenly noticed Hyde dismounting and did the same. A servant took his reins and led the horses away to the stables.

'Thank you so much, Señor Williams,' Concepción said, her faint accent charming the words. 'I look forward to talking to you again.' The top of her head barely reached past Williams's shoulder, even though he wasn't particularly tall. She tilted her head back to look up at him, a dimple in her cheek showing as she smiled sweetly. He smiled back but wiped the expression off fast when her father spoke to him.

'I owe you a great debt,' Don Pedro said seriously, clasping his hands together. 'Conchita could have been much hurt if you had not reacted so fast. You will always be a welcome guest at Casa de las Flores.'

'The pleasure was mine,' Williams said honestly.

Don Pedro smiled. 'You are a quick-thinking man and I believe lucky too. You own a silver-mine, do you not?'

Williams hesitated fractionally before answering. He still wasn't used to thinking of the mine as reality, after chasing it for four years, and he didn't want to boast about it in case the ore didn't last. But he knew enough about the Spanish *hacienderos* like Don Pedro to understand that they had more respect for men of position and wealth than for a salesman. Williams knew instantly that he wanted Concepción's father to respect him.

'I do,' he answered.

'There have long been rumours of a Spanish mine in this country, but no one ever found traces of it,' Don Pedro said. 'Now please, you are my guests here today. *Mi casa, su casa.*' He opened his hands to welcome both men.

'*Gracias*,' Williams replied gracefully. He glanced at Concepción and was startled to see her wink at him from behind her father's back.

At first Williams and Hyde stayed together. They were introduced to other guests, almost all Mexican, and were welcomed, especially when it came out that they had fought off Black Dog and put an end to his vicious raids. Williams naturally blossomed under the praise, although he was careful to point out that Hyde had contributed far more to the fighting. His outgoing nature was at home amongst a crowd and he was soon engaged in telling stories about the stage journey. The fact that Concepción always seemed to be within earshot, ready to smile at him, only encouraged him. In contrast, Hyde grew quieter than usual. His lack of Spanish embarrassed him, though many of the guests spoke English. He knew no one but Pat Williams and had never enjoyed the company of crowds.

Hyde increasingly felt like an outsider as he stood by and watched the festivities that went on through the day. The rounded arches of the colonnades, the splashing fountain in the centre of the patio and the low, red-tiled roof of the house were utterly unlike the elegant French and English style buildings he had known in South Carolina. The women's dresses were a blaze of colour and their black hair was covered with shawls or lace mantillas, instead of bonnets. The air smelt of chilli and garlic, both used liberally in the open-air cooking. There was wine, tequila, lemonade or something called chia to drink, or Hyde could take his pick from the strange fruits piled high in baskets: he recognized the plums, peaches and strawberries, but he had never seen chirimoya, chapote or granjeno berries before. The only thing that the Casa de las Flores had in common with his old home was the wealth on display: the servants, guests, quantities of food and fine horses were all a testament to a life of ease and grace.

Hyde took another glass of strong red wine and stood alone on the back porch, watching the steer roping contests that the *vaqueros* held amongst themselves. He couldn't help admiring their skills as they chased and roped the half-wild longhorns out on the range. His peace was interrupted by footsteps from behind.

'They are good riders, are they not?' Marco asked as Hyde turned towards him. He smiled brilliantly, as relaxed and gracious as the beautiful surroundings. For the fiesta he wore his favourite short jacket of dark green, embellished with silver embroidery. Under it was a red waistcoat and even his black trousers shone with silver trimmings.

Hyde nodded. 'I've seen some real fine horses here,' he drawled politely.

'I am Marco Felipe Tomas de la Valle,' the younger man introduced himself.

'Hyde.'

'I believe you are the partner of Señor Williams. Does that mean you have a share in the mine?' Marco asked, leaning gracefully against the low wall edging the patio.

Hyde paused a moment before shaking his head. 'I'm not a financial partner,' he admitted. 'But we work together. My job is to keep things safe.'

'*Yo creo*. I understand,' Marco corrected himself into English when he saw that Hyde didn't speak Spanish. He glanced at the matched guns the Southerner wore. 'You fought in the War?' he asked, a touch of envy in his voice.

'All four years,' Hyde answered. 'I made captain.'

There was real respect in Marco's face as he looked at the other man. 'I was old enough to join up in the last year but Father wouldn't let me. He said I was needed to protect folks here from the Comanche. I'm a real good shot,' he added with a touch of self mockery in his bright smile.

'There doesn't seem much point in fighting if there's nothing left to come back to when the fighting's done,' Hyde said, unable to quite conceal the bitterness in his voice.

'But you fought for your honour,' Marco said. 'Honour's very important both to us Spanish and to you

Yanquis,' he joked.

Hyde straightened, his grey eyes turning cold. 'You apologize now!' he barked.

Marco blinked, taken aback at the sudden demand. 'What the hell for?' he snapped.

'Don't try sliding out of it, you bastard!' Hyde growled.

Marco's quick temper flared in return. 'I don't understand you fool *Yanqui* owlheads . . . ' The rest of his sentence was abruptly cut off.

It was lucky for Marco that he didn't wear a gun to his family fiestas, because Hyde was furious enough to draw on him. Instead, Hyde lashed out with a vicious blow to Marco's face. The youngster's nose cracked under the impact and he staggered backwards with a cry of pain. Hyde didn't waste breath cursing or explaining, he merely closed in to continue his attack.

4

'I missed the Comanch' twice and so I just had to get a clear shot. Spragg had that team going hell for leather down the trail, no matter that there was a hundred-foot drop just to the right.' Williams leaned forward as he spoke, drawing his audience into his story. 'The Comanche behind us were hollering fit to wake the dead and the wagon was jouncing around. I was too busy hanging on to dodge any. The Comanche got me here, just in the ribs, with his club, right as I shot him.'

Williams was enjoying the fiesta. He had eaten well and was now sitting with Concepción, her friends and an elderly chaperon. He was telling them the story of how Black Dog had been defeated, and wasn't being too modest about his own part in it. Williams was a good story-teller and knew he was telling this one as well as he ever had. The sight of Concepción, gazing at him with her liquid, dark eyes, inspired him to his best efforts. If he impressed her enough, she might dance with him later. Williams wanted to feel that silk dress in his hands again. His brief experience earlier suggested that Concepción didn't wear the same amounts of rigid corseting that American women did, and he wanted to confirm his suspicion.

'Did he break your ribs?' Concepción asked eagerly as Williams paused.

'Not quite, but I still got some bruising.' Williams was gratified by the sympathetic noises she made. 'It almost knocked me clean off the wagon seat; I thought I was a goner for sure . . . ' The thrilling story was interrupted by a shout and yells from further along the patio.

Everyone looked round, trying to see what was happening. The chaperon woke from her doze with a start. The disturbance was round a corner, hidden from their position by a vine-covered pillar and urns of flowers. Williams couldn't make out the words but he recognized one of the voices.

'Hyde!' he exclaimed, leaping from his chair.

Other party-goers had heard the noise too and were moving to see what was happening. Williams ran to the noise, showing a fair turn of speed for a man of his build. He rounded the corner first and was appalled to find his partner, kneeling astride Marco de la Valle and pummelling the young man steadily.

'Jesus, Hyde!' Pat Williams exclaimed, running forward. 'What the blue blazes are you doing?' He grabbed Hyde under the arms and hauled him roughly to his feet. Hyde pulled himself free and whipped around. His face was alight with a deep, fierce anger that made Williams take a step back.

'He called me a damn Yankee!' Hyde pointed to the groaning man on the ground.

'A Yankee?' Williams repeated, half amazed and half annoyed.

A crowd had appeared already, most remaining at a respectful distance as they took in the scene. Marco sat up, holding a handkerchief to his bleeding nose. One eye was already swollen, his clothes were dusty and spotted with blood and his curly hair was in disarray. He glared at Hyde, all too aware of having been humiliated in front of family, staff and guests.

'What brought this about?' Don Pedro asked, his brows drawn down over his piercing eyes. He looked less like a placid ox and more like his true, iron-willed self for once.

'Your son called me a damned Yankee,' Hyde repeated angrily. 'I done gave him the chance to take it back, but he wouldn't apologize.'

Don Pedro turned his intimidating gaze on his son. 'Did you insult a guest?'

Marco shook his head then closed his eyes briefly at a wave of dizziness. 'I told him that *Yanquis* have as much honour as us Spanish.'

Hyde stiffened again at the word. Williams too felt a brief surge of anger at the insult before understanding dawned.

'He wasn't calling you a Yankee,' Williams exclaimed, taking Hyde's arm.

Hyde pulled himself free. 'You heard him just now.'

Williams shook his head. 'No, Marco there said *Yanqui*, not Yankee.' Williams exaggerated his pronunciation of the two words. '*Yanqui* is the general Spanish word for all Americans. He meant you as a white American, not a Mex.' He turned to Don Pedro and his son. 'Hyde thought you were calling him a blue-belly Yankee.'

To call anyone from the Southern states, whether they had been a soldier or not, a Yankee, was the deepest insult. Don Pedro had no real feelings about the Confederacy, being more closely tied to Mexico still, but he understood the depths of the perceived insult. He turned and bowed graciously to Hyde.

'I am sorry for this most unhappy misunderstanding. Marco was unforgivably careless in his choice of words to you, sir.'

Hyde took a deep breath, forcing himself to calm down. 'I was also at fault,' he said stiffly. He turned to Marco, who was still sitting on the floor and wiping at his bloodied nose. 'I apologize for hitting you. I misheard what you said to me.' If he was aware of the gaping crowd, he paid them no attention.

Marco glared up at him, his eyes bitter with fury, but a swift glance at his father warned him to answer properly. 'I accept your apology, Señor Hyde. Let us not speak of this again.' He was all too aware of being watched.

Hyde made a brief bow to him and faced Don Pedro. 'I hope I haven't spoiled the enjoyment of your fiesta. I'm plumb honoured to have been invited, but I shall take my leave now.' In spite of his obvious ill temper, he spoke with the gracious ease of a gentleman facing an equal.

Don Pedro smiled, impressed by the Southerner's self possession and manners. 'I am pleased to have met you,' he answered mildly, looking like a benevolent ox again. 'Please don't let this misunderstanding keep you away; I appreciate the chance to make the acquaintance of a gentleman. You will always be a welcome visitor at Casa de las Flores.'

Hyde's face lightened for a moment at being called a gentleman. He bowed again, more deeply, to the Don and to his daughter. '*Gracias*,' he drawled.

Williams watched this display with interest. He didn't really want to leave, but felt it was better to stay with his partner. 'I'll be going too,' he said. He complimented Don Pedro on his hospitality and said a more reluctant farewell to Concepción. She smiled back at him, looking lovelier than ever. Pat Williams grinned foolishly for a moment before pulling himself together and following Hyde to the stables.

Bright music started up out on the patio and the guests drifted away from the disturbance, chatting eagerly amongst themselves. Marco stood up slowly and brushed at the dust on his fine clothes.

'He made a mess of you, didn't he?' Concepción remarked, grinning.

'He took me by surprise,' Marco snapped. 'I'll pay him back good and proper.'

Don Pedro took hold of his children's shoulders. 'We will discuss that later,' he said firmly. 'But now, we have guests and we must be good hosts.' His glare was enough to make even Marco submit. Concepción made no objection either; she had no doubt that her father would be thinking things over. For now, she was content to eat, sing and dance and to think about the man who had rescued her.

Williams and Hyde rode away from the hacienda together. One glance was enough to show Williams that his partner was not in the mood to talk. He resisted the temptation to ask foolish questions and instead listened to the faint sounds of music coming from the hacienda. It reminded him of the dances he had hoped for with Concepción. Williams ignored his surly partner and drifted into happy day-dreams about the black-haired angel who had tumbled into his lap. Neither man noticed the *vaquero* who trailed them cautiously at a distance.

★ ★ ★

The last fiesta guests didn't leave until late the following morning so it was noon before Don Pedro and his two children could discuss the silver mine. Marco's face had stiffened up and he had to chew his tortillas and beans carefully, wincing now and again. His temper wasn't improved by the way Concepción kept looking at him and grinning.

'What are we going to do about that

silver mine?' he demanded truculently.

'Perez followed them back yesterday, so now we know where it is,' Don Pedro said, naming a half-breed *vaquero*. 'Did you gain any other information from Señor Williams?' he asked his daughter.

'Oh, yes,' Concepción answered brightly. 'Pat . . . I mean Mr Williams, told me about the other workers. There's two miners and an idiot who cooks and looks after the horses. And Mr Hyde, of course,' she added, with a sly look at her brother.

'He's a common ruffian,' Marco muttered, tearing a tortilla into small pieces.

'So five men altogether,' Don Pedro said. 'And Señor Hyde is a gentleman,' he told his son. 'His temper may be bad but you could learn from his manners.'

Marco looked up, his handsome face made bitter by anger, and saw the cold light in his father's eyes. He scowled for a moment, and dropped his gaze. Concepción said nothing, content to

71

wait and see what Don Pedro had in mind.

'It would be unbecoming for us to try and steal a silver-mine off a man who has found it for himself. And a man who is something of a hero for fighting off Black Dog. We should all be grateful to them for that,' Don Pedro said. The big man leaned back in his chair, clasped his hands together across his stomach and smiled benignly. 'On the other hand, it would be the most natural thing in the world for the Comanches to attack the miners. If this Williams and his men were to be driven off or hurt, then the mine might be sold off. That would be a gentlemanly way to acquire a mine; buying one that is no longer wanted.'

'Are you suggesting arming the Comanche?' Marco said doubtfully. Even his anger for Hyde didn't blind him to the dangers of letting Comanches loose with rifles.

Don Pedro shook his head. 'Real Comanches are too dangerous. We wouldn't be able to control who they turned the rifles on.'

'Williams hasn't done anything wrong,' Concepción put in. 'And he saved me when I fell yesterday.'

'Hyde made a fool out of me!' Marco snapped.

'You made a fool out of yourself,' Concepción told him saucily. 'Calling a Confederate soldier something that sounded like 'Yankee' indeed.'

Marco looked as though he wanted to throw something at his sister.

'Conchita's right.' Don Pedro leaned forward majestically. He waited until he had their attention before speaking again. 'We are not going to start killing or hurting anyone and we're not going to arm the Comanches. We're going to make life hard for Williams and the others.'

'He's not a quitter,' Concepción said with pride. 'It took him four years to find that map for his mine and he did it.'

Don Pedro ignored the remark.

'What trouble do Comanches cause, apart from scalping raids?'

'They steal horses,' Marco answered immediately.

Don Pedro nodded, smiling benevolently. 'We won't wait for them to find the mine for themselves. Tomorrow night, we will stage a Comanche raid of our own and take their horses. We may bankrupt Williams before the mine brings in much cash.' He smiled at his daughter. 'You will be able to wear jewellery made with silver from our own mine.'

Concepción smiled sweetly at her father. 'I would like that.'

★　★　★

Hyde woke with a start, his hand already on the butt of his gun. He lay still and listened, mentally cursing McKindrick's rich snores for muffling out other sounds. Even so, the second sudden bray from a burro was louder than the miner's snoring. Hyde started momentarily at the odd sound, then was about to roll over and go back to sleep when he realized that the burro had been braying from somewhere near by, not from the corral further up the canyon. He slid out from under his light blanket and padded silently to the door of the hut, taking both revolvers but not bothering to add any clothes to the trousers and cotton shirt he wore for sleeping.

Even the nights were hot so the door of the shack was left open day and night. Hyde stood in the shadows and listened, half aware of the crisp, fresh smell of the air. Now he was between McKindrick and the door, he could hear the soft thud of hoofs somewhere nearby. There was no moon but the brilliant stars gave just enough light to show the outlines of horses moving on the far side of the canyon.

'Goddamn it all to hell!' Hyde muttered. He turned and kicked the nearest sleeping figure: Williams. 'The horses're loose,' he growled. Hyde waited just long enough to see Williams move and wake up before leaving the hut at a run.

The ground underfoot was rough on his bare feet but Hyde ignored the stones he trod on as he ran towards the creek. The little group of horses was moving at a brisk trot past the mill on the far side of the water, heading for the entrance to the canyon where it opened on to the sierra. One of the burros trotted quickly at the back of the herd; the other had stopped a way back and brayed for its companion again. Hyde heard a voice from somewhere ahead and stopped moving. He peered at the shadowy figures moving past and realized that there were too many horses there. The corral held four horses and two burros, but he could see about six horses in the darkness. And at least one of them was ridden. Starlight glittered on something, a concho perhaps, and now Hyde could hear the soft creak of a saddle.

Hot anger fuelled his reckless

response. Hyde raised his right-hand gun and fired more from instinct than from conscious aim. Even through his anger he remembered to move immediately afterwards so the muzzle flash wouldn't betray his position in the dark. There was an indistinct human cry from among the horses as they leaped forward into a gallop. The little band raced towards the head of the canyon, kicking up dirt and stones as they went. Hyde broke into a run, holding his fire for fear of hitting one of the running horses. Cold water splashed his legs as he blundered into the creek, too intent on the horses to notice where he was going. He stopped, ankle-deep in the water and raised his gun again but couldn't make out a target worth firing at. The little knot of horses galloped away into the shadows of the night and there was nothing he could do to stop them. He swore aloud, then whipped round, raising his gun again at the sound of someone moving behind him.

'It's Pat Williams!' Williams stopped short of the creek and peered in the direction of the stampeding horses. 'You putting a scare into our mounts?'

'Someone just done stole them!' Hyde yelled back. He splashed out of the creek, the cuffs of his trousers dripping wet.

The other three men had left the shack and joined them. O'Malley wore his grubby undershirt and carried a polished Spencer rifle; his brindled coyote-dog slunk around his heels. McKindrick wore his kilt and a pair of moccasins, his magnificently hairy body on view to all. He had a shotgun in his hands and watched the darkness warily as he joined the others. Balzar was the last to arrive as he had stopped to put on his cowboy boots with the silver spurs he adored. The young man alone was unarmed.

'*Que paso?*' he called as he hurried towards them. His dark eyes were wide and frightened in his innocent face.

'You been sleepwalking or did you

always go shooting ha'nts at night?' O'Malley asked Hyde, staring pointedly at the other man's wet trousers.

'There's other things I'd sure rather be shooting iffen they make me mad,' Hyde snapped.

Williams interrupted before O'Malley could make Hyde's temper worse. 'You said someone stole the horses?' he asked.

'Some damned skunks took the lot!' Hyde answered. 'I heard them but no thanks to that coyote-dog; it doesn't have the sense God gave geese.'

O'Malley was translating the conversation into Spanish for Balzar. The Mexican let out an exclamation and set off for the corral at a run, anxious to see whether any of the horses he adored were still there. The dark burro brayed as he passed it but he took no notice.

'My Cicely's got sense enough not to get stole,' O'Malley said happily, going to catch the brown burro. It brayed once more, a strange and forlorn sound in the night. Williams shook his head, trying to think with his sleep-fogged mind. The burros both belonged to O'Malley but he'd paid good cash for three of the horses only a month back. Buying new stock wouldn't bankrupt him, but there wouldn't be much capital left until they produced more silver bullion. 'I'll get more horses,' he promised.

'They took Cob!' Hyde burst out, referring to his liver chestnut horse.

'Ye sound awfu' fond o' that there wee horse,' McKindrick remarked, resting his shotgun on his broad shoulder.

Hyde stopped short, uncomfortably aware of having revealed more of himself than he liked. Williams saw and understood the movement, and answered for him.

'Cob's a good horse; he didn't spook much when Black Dog bushwhacked the stage,' he informed McKindrick.

It was true enough but it wasn't everything. Cob had been born and raised on the plantation that had once been Hyde's home. He had ridden the horse through the last year of the Civil War and it was one of the very few things left to him from his old life.

'That's right,' was all Hyde said.

'We can look for tracks in the morning,' Williams said. 'We might as well get some sleep now.'

'That's right,' McKindrick agreed. 'There's no' much we can be doin' noo.' He turned and headed back to his bed.

Williams put his hand on Hyde's shoulder. 'I'm sorry about Cob.'

'Not as sorry as whoever took him will be if I ever catch up with them,' Hyde promised.

Williams didn't doubt him for a moment.

5

Hyde was the last to wake the next morning. When he opened his eyes, the others were all at breakfast outside. He dressed and wandered out to grab a tin mugful of coffee. Balzar poured it for him and gazed at Hyde with sad, tear-rimmed eyes.

'*Lo siento*, Señor Hyde,' he said, sniffling. '*Su caballo* . . . ' His voice cracked and he stopped to wipe his nose with the back of his hand.

Hyde hurriedly turned away and spotted Williams on the other side of the canyon. Williams was walking carefully, bending to examine the ground. Hyde crossed the narrow part of the bubbling creek to join him, stopping a short distance from where the other man was reading tracks.

'Found anything?' Hyde asked, trying to keep the hope from his voice.

Williams straightened up and looked over at him. 'Did you see any of the rustlers last night? Did you put lead in any of them?'

Hyde took a sip of his coffee while thinking, and almost spat it straight out again. Balzar's cooking had degenerated from passable to downright awful in his misery over the missing horses. Hyde glanced at Williams and saw the knowing grin on the other man's face. Ignoring the incident, Hyde said, 'It was so dark I didn't see anyone at first. Then I heard a saddle creak and I looked closer.'

'A saddle?' Williams asked, bending to look at the muddled tracks again. 'Ah.'

'What is it?' Hyde incautiously took another sip of coffee but barely noticed the awful taste this time, being more interested in what Williams had found.

Williams grinned at him. 'Comanches don't go much on using saddles, especially leather ones that make a noise during a raid. And they don't shoe their horses either. I knew there was something not right about these tracks; all the horses are shod.' He gestured at the marks in the dry soil.

'If it wasn't Comanches it was surely bandits then,' Hyde said. 'We can run them to ground and get our mounts back.'

'You planning to chase them on O'Malley's burro?' Williams asked. 'Bandits won't be travelling as fast as Comanches but all the same . . . '

'What are we going to do out here without horses?' Hyde demanded.

Williams walked over to join him by the creek. 'I've been thinking about that. There's no livery barn in Hueco, but if I walk to Casa de las Flores, Don Pedro's bound to lend me a horse. I can ride to El Paso and get more there. There's enough grub in camp to last you a few days.'

Hyde grimaced at the thought of nothing but beans, bacon and rice for a week. 'Have you enough cash money to buy more horses?' he asked.

'I can get by until we produce more silver,' Williams told him. He thought for a moment, then suddenly smiled. 'I know! Remember the Schmidts?'

Don and Mary Schmidt were a young married couple who had travelled out to El Paso on the same stage as Williams and Hyde.

'Sure I do.' Hyde followed his partner's thoughts. 'They inherited a stock ranch. I bet they'll let you have horses for a good price.'

'I'll pay them what's fair,' Williams said. 'But Don might let me make a down payment now and pay the rest in a couple of months. That'd be cheaper than getting a note at the bank.' He led the way back over the creek, the bounce back in his step.

Williams explained his intentions to the others then went back inside the shack to make ready for his long walk. O'Malley shrugged and went on eating his over-cooked breakfast, translating Williams's plans to Balzar between mouthfuls. McKindrick scratched the patch of hairy chest that showed through the opening in his collarless shirt. 'It's no the wee risk he'll be tekkin'. Would ye be plannin' te tek yersel' an' yer guns along wi' him?' he asked Hyde.

The Southerner hesitated while he worked out what the Scot had been saying, then shook his head. 'We can't afford to lose two men's digging time.' Hyde hated the work but he wasn't about to let Williams down, especially when things were getting difficult.

Williams reappeared from the shack wearing his low-heeled town boots, which were better for walking distances in, and carrying a canteen slung on a rawhide thong. His short-barrelled gun was in its holster but he had no other weapons.

'Do you want to take my rifle?' Hyde offered.

'No thanks.' Williams pulled the brim of his Derby hat a little lower. 'I don't want to carry too much extra weight, apart from what I can't set down,' he added, patting his waist. 'And there's less of this padding than there was.'

'You might run into the bandits that took the horses.'

'I'd rather take the risk than the weight,' Williams said. 'I aim to be back in four days. If I'm not back by then, you can start searching; if you don't see me inside of a week, I'm probably dead someplace.'

'You're too stubborn to die off like that,' Hyde told him, briefly showing his sharklike smile.

In spite of their light tone, both men knew that travelling on foot through this rough and empty country was a risk. Hyde was the more skilled gunman but Williams had grown up on the frontier and knew how to manage in this wilderness. Williams nodded and set off along the canyon. Hyde watched him for a moment before turning back to the cook-fire. His vague thoughts about hot water and shaving were pushed aside by a new consideration. If Pat Williams were to die the mine would be up for grabs. Hyde hesitated, the thoughts flashing through his mind. The mine would belong to Williams's family, which would be his mother, but she wouldn't want to come out here and run it herself. She would need a manager. And Williams probably hadn't written a proper will. There was nothing to stop anyone from claiming a share in the silver-mine, especially someone who was known to be William's partner. Hyde glanced at his work-scarred, calloused hands and remembered the riches so carelessly displayed at Don Pedro's hacienda. He shook his head suddenly and went about the business of shaving and then eating breakfast.

★   ★   ★

Pat Williams walked steadily, pacing himself for the long journey. The narrow brim of his smart Derby didn't give as much shade from the harsh sun as he would have liked. He'd meant to buy another hat last time he was in El

Paso, but in the excitement of wiring the news about the silver, he'd forgotten about it. This time, he promised himself, he'd get a Stetson, even if he had to live on rice and beans for a week to find the money. The sun rose steadily towards noon as he trudged on, now and again humming to himself. Even this wild, open country had a few trails which made the going easier. All the same, Williams didn't always stick to the hard dirt of the trails. He knew that a man afoot was an obvious target to any *bandidos* or Comanches around, so he tried to keep near cover when he could. Arroyo bottoms were often wooded and he kept himself in the welcome shade of the trees as often as possible. The higher mesas however were bare of all but tumbleweed, scrubby shrubs and cacti. Williams approached each crest in the trail cautiously, peering over to check that the way was clear rather than skylining himself where he could be seen from miles away. He watched the country with range-wise eyes, noting the movements of birds and animals.

The sun was high overhead when he came to the wide stretch of range that he knew was part of Don Pedro's hacienda. Williams couldn't see the whitewashed house yet, but he knew it was only a couple of miles away, on the far side of a long ridge. The thought was encouraging, even though his feet hurt and his face was dry with trail dust. He stopped for a breather, aware that his cotton shirt was sticking uncomfortably to his back. The canteen was almost dry by this time, the only water remaining was warm and stale. However, Williams could see a narrow arroyo not far away that was overgrown with juniper, creosote bush and even some small cottonwoods. The greenery suggested either a creek or a *tinaja*, a small clear pool of water. The thought of cold water was irresistibly tempting after his long walk in the blazing sun. It would also give him the chance to freshen up a little before arriving at

Concepción's home. With that thought in mind, Williams made for the arroyo.

The sides here were steep but he picked a spot where the ground sloped less steeply and scrambled down. He lost his balance part-way down and finished up sliding the last yard or two on his backside. In spite of the unintentional slide, Williams landed on his feet and regained his balance easily after one unsteady pace. His round face split into a grin as he dusted light soil from his pants, amused by his own escapades.

After a brief look around, he aimed for a thick patch of trees and lush grass that indicated a pool. His quick eyes noticed that the yellow plums were ripe; a sure sign that summer was finishing. A couple of fruit were lying on the ground with wasps humming over them. Williams bent down, flicked away a wasp with a fingernail and picked up the sweet fruit. The wasp merely moved to another plum, too eager for the juice to be angry. Williams ate the fruit with immense pleasure, spat the stone into some shrubs, and moved towards the pool to wash his sticky fingers.

He gave the ground at the edge of the water a brief glance for tracks but saw only cattle prints. There was nothing to indicate that pumas or bobcats were in the area. With that elementary check made, Williams crouched down by the edge of the water. He dipped his fingers in first, then filled his Derby with the cold water and poured it over his head. The chilly water trickled down his face and neck, cooling and refreshing him blissfully. Williams closed his eyes, forgetting about money, thieves and moody partners to revel in the sheer pleasure of cold water on a hot day.

The peace was abruptly disturbed by a tremendous crashing from the bushes right behind him and a bellow of anger. Williams opened his eyes as he leapt to his feet, turned and tried to draw his gun all at once. A red-and-white longhorn steer burst from a screen of juniper where it had been resting, and charged at him. The steer was a massive old beast, with one twisted horn and a short stump where the other had been broken off. One-horned steers were notoriously cranky and often turned solitary. They defended their own patch as viciously as any truly wild animal.

'Jesus!' Williams dodged frantically to his left as it charged him. The steer jabbed its one long horn at him, snagging his shirt in passing. The fabric tore as Williams twisted away. He fired without even thinking, pumping two shots into the steer. His gun was only a copy of the .36 Navy Colt and wasn't heavy enough to bring down a full grown steer, even from such short range.

It bellowed again, turning in a flurry of stones and mud at the edge of the water. Williams didn't stay to watch but ran at full pelt for the side of the arroyo, hoping to scramble to safety. It was a forlorn hope; the steer could spring as fast as a horse and caught up with him in a matter of moments. Williams jinked to his left, the side where it had a broken horn. The stump slammed into the back of his shoulder and knocked him clean off his feet. Williams came down rolling and gasping for breath as the steer thundered past but kept his hold on his gun. He continued rolling until he was sitting up and raised the gun to shoulder height, supporting it with both hands. It took a few moments longer but he wanted to be sure of his aim. A head shot would be quickest but he didn't think his gun packed enough punch to get through the steer's massive skull.

The steer turned on a dime, showing all the agility of a trained cowpony. As it charged, Williams fired two shots into its chest then twisted and rolled himself aside. He moved barely fast enough. The injured steer hooked at him, bellowing in pain and anger. Williams rolled on the loose dirt as the horn scraped across his back. His breath came in fast gasps. There were only two loads left in his revolver and the steer was madder than ever. Even in the middle of his frantic struggle, it occurred to Williams that after surviving two years of war and a full-on Comanche raid, getting trampled to death by a cow was an ignominious way to die. He squirmed on to his side and let off another fast shot as the steer turned for a fourth charge.

Streamers of slobber and blood hung from its mouth as it bellowed again. It staggered slightly, giving Williams some wild hope as the animal charged him once again, its head lowered and the lethal horn ready for attack. Williams got his feet underneath himself and waited, his heart pounding, as the steer thundered towards him. It covered the short distance in a flash, swinging its one good horn at the crouching man. As its head twisted, Williams fired up into its neck from barely four feet away. Then he dived towards the steer, trying to get under the horn as it swung towards him. He ducked under, close enough to smell the sweat and blood on its hide. The steer's shoulder hit him full on and Williams was brushed aside to land winded on his back. Sharp hoofs kicked dirt over him as the steer rushed past. Williams' chest heaved desperately as he tried to suck in air. He lay helplessly for a few moments, hearing the steer bellowing and moving somewhere nearby, but unable to lift his head and see it. Then he suddenly got his wind back and groaned, gasping irregularly and moaning with every spasm from his diaphragm.

Williams overcame the agony in his guts long enough to raise his head and see what the steer was doing. It was standing a few feet away, its head lowered. Gouts of blood fell from its nostrils and mouth. As Williams watched, it started turning, then staggered and fell to its knees. It tried to lunge up again but fell, this time rolling on to its side. The steer kicked a few times, trying to get to its feet and failing. It finally ceased to move apart from raucous, bubbling breaths that lasted only a minute longer. Williams let himself slump back and stayed that way until his heart had stopped pounding and his breathing was normal again.

'I done told you I didn't need a rifle,' he said to the sky.

He was just thinking about picking himself up when he heard rapid hoof-beats approaching along the arroyo. The shooting had attracted attention but he didn't know whose. Williams scrambled ungracefully to his feet, moaning as bruises and scrapes made themselves felt. He cast around frantically for his revolver, which had been knocked from his grasp when the steer had rammed him. There wouldn't be enough time to get it reloaded and put the caps on, but he could always pretend it was ready.

His distracted planning proved unnecessary. The new arrivals were Concepción and the *vaquero* who escorted her when she went riding. They reined in their horses, staring first at the bloodied steer and the torn-up ground, then at Williams. He felt a smile start on to his face the moment he recognized Concepción, then he collapsed untidily into a sitting position with a loud groan.

'What happened?' she called, scrambling down from her side-saddle to hurry over to him. Her horse moved away a few paces and began to graze, effectively tethered by the dangling reins.

Williams pressed his hand over his ribs where the steer's shoulder had rammed him. He was liberally coated in dirt that had stuck to his sweaty shirt and to the water that he'd poured over himself to cool down earlier. The shirt itself was untucked and torn in at least one place, his trousers had got torn and his hands and face were scraped too. Altogether, Pat Williams hadn't been in such a mess since his last battle in the Civil War, and he made the most of it. He gazed up at Concepción, and swallowed before speaking.

'I made a fool mistake,' he said,

pausing to repress a quick grimace of pain. 'Came to get some water and never saw sign of that steer.'

Concepción crouched in front of him, her face prettily anxious as she looked at him. Behind her, the *vaquero* was examining the dead steer and keeping a wary eye on Don Pedro's daughter and the gringo.

'Are you much hurt?' Concepción asked.

Williams was delighted to hear real concern in her voice but tried not to let it show. He shook his head, implying noble indifference to his dishevelled state. 'I'll be fit as a flea, soon enough,' he answered.

'Are you on your own?' Concepción asked next. 'Where's Señor Hyde?'

'Hyde? He's back at the mine.' Williams didn't want to talk about Hyde.

Concepción smiled. 'I do hope he's forgiven Marco for insulting him like that. I wouldn't like to cause him distress.'

'Hyde's fine,' Williams answered rather abruptly. He was on the point of manufacturing another groan of anguish when he saw the merry twinkle in Concepción's dark eyes. He burst into a wide grin, laughing at himself for getting tricked into acting jealous.

The *vaquero* walked over, leading his horse. 'I cannot see your horse.'

'I'm afoot.' Williams explained about the horses being stolen and his need to borrow a mount.

'Why, of course we will lend you one,' Concepción exclaimed, pleased at being able to help Williams. 'It will be a small way of paying back the favour we owe you. You need to take care, out in the wild territory. We are safe at Casa de las Flores but there are still so many bad men around.'

'You can ride double on my horse,' the *vaquero* offered.

Concepción nodded, not giving Williams the chance to decline. 'We will return to the house right away.'

'*Gracias*, Doña Concepción,' Williams said. 'And I could sure use a clean up,' he added, climbing to his feet with genuine stiffness.

Concepción impulsively took his arm to help him up. 'Please call me Conchita,' she said warmly, charmed by his smile.

They smiled at each other from close range, then Williams remembered his manners, and the watching *vaquero*, and moved away. Riding behind a saddle was never comfortable, but it was better than walking to the hacienda, and he would have Conchita's company. All in all, he was pretty satisfied. He was even willing to forgive the steer that had come so close to killing him.

6

Pat Williams hummed a cheery tune to himself as he rode across the range, hazing a small group of loose horses. The last couple of days had gone according to plan, and all was right with his world.

'That Miss Conchita, she surely be a mighty pretty l'il woman,' drawled a mellow voice nearby.

Williams felt his face colour slightly as he turned to the black man riding along with him. 'Now what makes you say that?' he asked.

Wilbur Jefferson grinned knowingly, showing uneven teeth. 'Why, nothin'. Ah jest knows me a pretty woman when ah sees one.' He was a sturdy man, with chocolate coloured skin, who wore new-looking range clothes. In spite of wearing low-heeled boots rather than riding boots, he rode his pinto gelding with the easy grace of a natural horseman.

Williams declined to answer Jefferson's remark.

The two of them had stopped at the Casa de las Flores to return the borrowed horse on their way to the mine with the new mounts that Williams had bought from the Schmidts. Wilbur Jefferson was a freed man who had travelled on the same eventful stagecoach journey to El Paso as the others and was now working happily for the young couple. He had offered to help Williams take the horses to the mine and had been interested to see the warm way Concepción had greeted Williams. That warmth was undoubtedly a good part of the reason behind Williams's cheerful mood, but he wasn't about to admit it out loud. Instead, he turned his attention away across the dry land. Only one other person was in view, a Mexican riding towards them on the same, half-marked, trail.

'Got company,' Pat Williams remarked casually, pretending an interest in the stranger. A few moments later, his interest sharpened and he sat straighter in his saddle. 'Now what do you reckon to that horse he's afork?'

The horse was a well-bred liver chestnut with a flaxen mane and tail and a snip of white between its nostrils. The colour was unusual although not too rare, like the horse's markings.

'It surely looks powerful like Mist' Hyde's hoss,' Jefferson drawled.

'It surely does,' Williams answered. He kept an eye on horse and rider as they approached.

The closer they got, the more sure Williams was that the liver chestnut was Cob, Hyde's stolen horse. He pushed the four loose horses off the trail and rode ahead, letting Jefferson haze them from behind. Williams swung wider than he needed to and got a look at the left flank of the liver chestnut just before it drew level. Like Hyde's, this horse lacked the branding which most range horses sported. Williams drew in his reins.

'*Hola, amigo*,' he called to the flashily dressed Mexican rider.

'*Hola. Que paso?*' came the answer. The Mexican halted his horse as Williams drew alongside. Dark, bright eyes watched the gringo with interest.

Williams smiled and nodded at the liver chestnut. 'That's a good horse,' he said in Spanish. 'Did you get it from somewhere round here?'

The Mexican rider frowned at the question, which was barely within the boundaries of range politeness. His right hand dropped towards the handle of the knife he wore.

'That's none of your business,' the Mexican said tersely. 'Now ride on.'

Williams knew he'd been rude but he didn't like being ordered around by a stranger, especially one who was probably a horse thief. Just as important, he saw a chance to do a favour for his partner. 'My friend has a horse like that,' he persisted. 'It was stolen three days back. Now, I'm sure that . . . ' His attempt to soften the remark was too late. Williams saw the Mexican *bandido* start to draw his knife and didn't wait to see what the other man intended to do.

Williams kicked his feet free of his stirrups and launched himself from his saddle. He grabbed the other man round the body and the two of them crashed to the ground together as the liver chestnut shied. The Mexican couldn't break his fall with his arms pinned and breath burst from him in a gasp as Williams landed on top of him.

'Drop the knife!' Williams yelled, forgetting to speak Spanish as he struggled to get himself together.

The Mexican wriggled furiously, trying to shake off the man sitting on his stomach. Williams got his right hand on the other man's wrist and pinned it to the ground. He glanced down, trying to see whether the Mexican still had his knife after the fall. As he lowered his head, the *bandido* spat in his eyes. Williams automatically reared back lifting his left arm to wipe his face. The

Mexican braced his feet against the ground and heaved his body upwards. Williams toppled forwards, thrown off balance, and saved himself by planting his free hand on his enemy's face. The Mexican promptly bit him hard.

Williams gave a yell of pain and anger, snatching his hand away. 'Dirty son of a bitch!' he exclaimed.

The Mexican wriggled and twisted out from underneath Williams's weight. They separated, rolling apart and scrambling to their feet. Sunlight glittered on the Mexican's knife blade as he swept it from its sheath. Williams didn't need Jefferson's warning shout to alert him to the danger. He leapt straight to the attack, showing the quick grace that had saved him from the charging steer. His left hand seized the Mexican's knife arm while his right hand closed on the man's jacket. Williams braced himself and swung the other man around hard, using all the muscle power in his sturdy frame. He let go at exactly the right moment and bounded after his attacker even as the Mexican staggered backwards, off balance from being swung around. Williams lashed up a kick, getting the other man in the belly.

The Mexican gave a choking cry of pain and dropped the knife, bending over as he clutched at his stomach. Williams kicked out with his other foot, aiming to finish the fight as quickly as possible. His boot caught the Mexican right on the chin, sending him over backwards. He followed up by dropping to his knees on the prone man, using his weight to drive the breath from the battered man's body.

'Happen that ain't Hyde's horse, I'll let you keep it,' Williams promised, somewhat breathlessly. 'But I don't apologize for cleaning your plough after you went and pulled a knife on me.' He stood up and backed off a couple of paces, keeping a wary eye on the *bandido*. The man had no fight left in him and curled up, moaning.

'This here's Mist' Hyde's hoss all

right,' Jefferson drawled. He had caught the liver chestnut's reins and was rubbing the horse behind its ears as he looked it over. The liver chestnut whickered softly at him and rubbed its head against his leg.

Williams bent and grabbed the *bandido*'s jacket, hauling the man roughly on to his back. 'Where at's my other horses?' he demanded.

The Mexican mumbled a protest, blood spilling from his mouth. He couldn't speak clearly although the pain and fear in his eyes were clear enough. Williams realized that his kick had probably fractured the other man's jaw, and he suddenly felt sick. He let go, pushing the *bandido* to the ground again and turned his back. Moving swiftly, he stripped the man's gear from the liver chestnut and dumped it on the ground. He was still sure that the Mexican had been part of the group that had stolen the horses, but he had had enough revenge. A broken jaw and a long walk with a heavy saddle would be sufficient punishment. Williams had already seen enough killing and death in his life. He led the liver chestnut to the other horses and mounted his own again.

'Let's be getting on,' he said to Jefferson. 'We've got good news for somebody anyway.'

* * *

Good news was the last thing on Hyde's mind as he swung his pickaxe at the mine face. The Two Moccasins Mine wasn't very large, especially by the standards of the silver-mines that had burgeoned around the Comstock Lode, but Hyde was still uncomfortable at being underground and out of sight of the mine entrance. The only light came from the lamp swinging from one of the box beams that supported the roof at intervals. O'Malley had improved the main level with pre-cut timber frames of the kind developed on the Comstock fields, but good lumber was scarce out here, so the newer, working portions of the mine were supported with old timbers from the disused tunnels.

Hyde swung the pickaxe viciously into the rock, channelling his dislike of the work into his motions until his energy ran out and he stopped for a breather. Fine dust hung in the air and stuck to the sweat on his face and his clothes. Hyde dropped the pickaxe on to loose rock and stretched upwards, trying to ease his shoulders and back, until he felt the hairs on the top of his head brush the ceiling. The other workers were all shorter than he was, and managed more easily in the confined conditions. Hyde not only had to watch his head as he moved around, he had found that he didn't have room to swing the pickaxe properly. He was as fit as any of the other men, but the labour took more out of him as he was forced to work in cramped, awkward stances.

Hyde flexed his hands and surveyed

the pile of loose rock around him. There was almost enough to make a full load for one of the wooden cars. He scraped some of the rock away to clear a new working space, took up the pickaxe again and went back to work. His ears and head ached to the bang of steel on rock, and his arms and shoulders were jarred with every blow, but he persisted. His body was damp with sweat and his mouth was dry and dusty. Hyde had promised to work the mine while Pat Williams was away and he wouldn't break his word of honour. But with every ache came the treacherous thought that if Williams never came back, he would have a chance to own the mine instead of working himself to death inside it. Hyde tried to batten down his feelings and work steadily, deliberately blanking his mind as he swung the pickaxe time after time.

It took a few moments to realize that someone was calling his name. Hyde stopped work and listened, wondering if he'd been imagining it. A few moments later he recognized Williams's voice, and gratefully downed tools to welcome him back. Hyde picked his way carefully along the mine levels, moving faster than he ever did on his way in. It only took a minute for him to see daylight at the entrance and he hurried out, blinking in the bright sunshine.

'Found you a good horse,' Williams drawled. 'Got you one as much like Cob as I could.'

Hyde squinted at the horse that Williams was holding, waiting for his eyes to adjust to the sunlight. Then he understood that he really was looking at his own horse and a bright smile spread across his face. He stepped forward, holding out a hand to his horse, which snorted a greeting to him. Hyde fussed his horse, letting it lick the salty sweat from his left hand as he patted it with his right. He made no attempt to conceal his pleasure from the other men, but just spoke softly to the horse.

Williams watched the rare display of emotion with pleasure. He'd picked up a couple of bruises in the fight but he thought they were a fair price for rewarding his friend's loyalty.

* * *

Don Pedro was waiting in his private room. This was where he ran the business of the hacienda, keeping the accounts and records; it was also his retreat from the busy life of his house. Thin shafts of sunlight came through the shuttered windows, spotlighting the Navajo rug on the floor and gilding the fine wood of his desk. Don Pedro was studying a hand-painted map of his property when the door opened and his son entered.

'How is poor Barrio?' he asked.

Marco strode sharply into the centre of the room and halted right in front of his father's desk. 'It was Williams,' he announced, his eyes flashing with annoyance. 'He all but broke Barrio's jaw.'

'Why?' Don Pedro asked, frowning.

Marco flung his arms wide in an impatient gesture. 'It's Diaz's fault. Barrio's good horse died from eating loco weed last week, so Diaz let him choose one of the horses from the mine as a replacement. He chose the one belonging to that damned Señor Hyde and Williams recognized it. I told Diaz to see the horses went to market over in New Mexico!' he exclaimed.

Don Pedro stared at his hot-tempered son until Marco regained some self-control. When the young man was paying proper attention, his father spoke.

'Did Williams learn where Barrio got the horse?' he asked.

Marco's temper had got the better of his ability to think straight. He hadn't thought beyond the simple fact of the *vaquero* getting injured and the horse being taken back. After thinking for a moment, he shook his head.

'He can't have done. Barrio can barely speak now, after Gene fixed him up. All he said was that the gringo accused him of stealing a horse and treated him like a *bandido*. They fought and Williams broke his jaw before he asked him any more questions.'

Don Pedro thought about that. Only a couple of his most trusted *vaqueros* knew about the raid on the mine. Barrio had known nothing about it and his indignation at being accused of stealing a horse that he thought belonged legitimately to his Don was genuine.

'Williams mentioned *bandidos* when he came to us for help,' he mused. 'From the way he spoke, I think he read the tracks himself. He is more resourceful than I had expected.'

'At least we cost him money, buying those new mounts,' Marco said. He began pacing the dimly lit room, his mind jumping impatiently to further action. 'Next time they send someone for supplies, we could jump him. If they can't get enough food, they'll either starve out there or come into El Paso.'

Don Pedro nodded. 'We may do that.'

'I'll send Perez out tomorrow,' Marco decided. He stopped pacing and ran his hand through his curly hair. 'Maybe I'll go with him. It might be Señor Hyde who travels on his own.'

Don Pedro's thoughtful gaze sharpened on his son. 'If you attack Señor Hyde he will probably kill you,' he said flatly. 'I have seen men like him before; he is very dangerous.' Marco attempted to interrupt but a glare from his father made him stay dutifully silent and listen. 'If you remember, Williams brought supplies back from El Paso,' Don Pedro went on. 'They will not need to leave the mine for a couple of weeks, and I won't have men wasting their time waiting around for them. We have the Fall roundup to start thinking about.'

'But this could get us a silver mine!' Marco insisted, leaning over the desk towards his father. 'Silver! It's so nearly on our land, it should be ours.'

Don Pedro rose majestically, dwarfing his son physically and mentally. 'We will take no action right now,' he announced. 'I will decide what is to be done next.'

'Yes, Father,' Marco answered, his eyes sullen. For all his spirit and hot temper, he knew better than to openly disobey his father. 'May I leave?'

Don Pedro nodded and moved over to the shuttered window as his son left. He was a patient man and was prepared to change his approach to getting control of the silver. The mutual attraction between Concepción and Pat Williams hadn't escaped his attention. Of course, Williams was hardly the first man to show an interest in his lovely, spirited daughter, but the way Concepción spoke about Williams was unusual. Don Pedro had noticed the way his daughter watched Williams when he'd been around, rarely taking her eyes from him. He hadn't intended for his daughter to marry a gringo but a gringo who owned a nearby silver-mine was another matter.

Don Pedro gazed through the slats in

the window shutter at the flowers outside. His daughter was as precious and delicate as any of the brilliant blooms at Casa de las Flores, but Don Pedro believed that Williams was an honourable man and generous. He was certainly quick-witted and even courageous; Don Pedro wanted to think well of the man who had rescued his daughter when she fell from the balcony. Most of all, he wanted Concepción to be happy.

He saw Marco striding past on his way to the stables, and shook his head slowly.

7

Once over his surprise at seeing Cob again, Hyde greeted Jefferson with almost as much warmth as he showed to the horse.

'It's surely good to see you, Jefferson,' he said, shaking the black man's hand. 'How are you doing with the Schmidts?'

'Ah's mighty fine, Mist' Hyde,' Jefferson answered, smiling widely. 'They done give me dis fine hawse, all to mahself.' He patted the neck of the pinto.

O'Malley had been listening to their exchange. 'You're being real polite there, Mister Hyde,' he mocked. 'I thought you high and mighty plantation folks called all the darkies 'boy'.'

Hyde turned to him but Jefferson spoke up first. 'Why ah'd rather be called 'boy' by a for-real gennleman than git called 'Mist' Jefferson' by some white trash what kain't even find a creek to wash in.'

It was hard to tell who was the most surprised at Jefferson's remark; Hyde or O'Malley. Pat Williams almost burst out laughing at the shock on both men's faces and at the simple accuracy of Jefferson's last statement. O'Malley washed himself now and again but rarely bothered washing his clothes or his half-matted, shaggy hair.

Williams spoke up before trouble could erupt. 'Come on, let's get these goods unpacked and Balzar can fix something to eat.'

As the stores were being unpacked, Williams told Hyde how he had got Cob back. Hyde listened to the story and laughed ruefully. 'And you done hired me for my gun skill then you knock some bandit sky west and crooked with your bare hands.'

'I knew you wanted Cob back. I got you some things in town,' Williams went on, removing a package from his saddle pack and handing it over. As Hyde unfolded the brown paper, Williams explained. 'I didn't think about you working down the mine when we came out here and I didn't know how hard it is on clothes. I figured I owed you some before yours get plumb worn out.'

The package contained a pair of stout leather gloves and some tan Levis. Hyde held the trousers up, inspecting the heavy cotton fabric. 'I never wore pants that were riveted together before,' he said, looking at the copper rivets that shone in the sun.

'Made specially for miners,' Williams explained.

They were working clothes, pure and simple, intended for heavy labouring. Hyde had never owned such clothes before in his life. Everything in his breeding and upbringing rebelled against wearing the Levis but plain common sense told him he must if he intended to stay at the mine.

'Thank you,' he said, hiding away his deeper feelings as he looked at his friend. 'I was getting worried I'd end up like O'Malley.'

Williams relaxed as his gift was accepted with good grace. Hyde noticed, and vowed to keep his feelings about mine-working to himself. It was the least he could do for the man who had returned Cob to him.

That evening was a merry one. The men sat around the cook-fire, swapping stories and playing cards. Jefferson wanted to know all about the silver mine and asked to be shown the mill and the furnace. Hyde showed him, explaining as best he could.

'You want to come work here?' Hyde asked as they walked back from the mill.

'Why no, suh,' Jefferson answered. 'Ah's free now an' ah kin work wherever ah wishes. I doan want ter work in de dark like some chain-gang man. Ah'll ride on my fine hawse and let de white gennleman work in de mine,' he added, grinning.

Hyde held out his calloused hands. 'I don't look so much of a gentleman now.'

'You's still a gennleman,' Jefferson said boldly. 'Dat O'Malley know it an' he sure resents dat. You don't take no notice of him, suh.'

Hyde smiled wryly, taking no offence. 'Who would have thought it? Me being lectured on being a gentleman by a man born a slave.'

'Din't yore mammy teach you gennleman manners?' Jefferson asked ingenuously.

'Why, yes, of course,' Hyde answered, slowing down as they came within earshot of the fire. He laughed at the irony, cheered up by Jefferson's common sense. It was good to know he had the black man's respect.

Jefferson returned to the Schmidts the next day and business went on as before at Two Moccasins Mine. O'Malley smelted down more silver bullion but Williams didn't take it straight to the bank. He wanted to work and produce as much silver as possible before he had to send anyone all the way to El Paso. They had enough supplies for a month, by which time the break from mining would be welcome.

Although he was keen to learn as much as possible about silver production himself, he arranged for McKindrick to teach Hyde first about sorting and crushing the ore. It was still long hours of work, but at least it didn't involve swinging a pickaxe or spending time in the dark mine. They often worked shifts together and Williams had noticed that Hyde could barely stand upright in some areas.

He also encouraged Hyde to ride out in the evenings on the pretext that Hyde could fetch back some game with his rifle. The hunts provided welcome fresh meat for the camp and kept Hyde and O'Malley apart. The old miner had been deeply annoyed when Jefferson, the former slave, took sides with the former slave-owner. Williams didn't entirely understand it himself but he could see that Hyde and Jefferson had once been on opposite sides of the same kind of life. That life had gone for both men, but it gave them a bond.

Hyde appreciated Williams' quiet tact. In return, he worked as hard as anyone else, trying to resign himself to the demanding labour and the need to leave daylight behind and walk into the confining walls of the mine. He didn't like the solid rock around him and he hated getting so sweaty and gritty. The leather gloves helped protect his hands and he became grateful for the tough denim Levis. Although he dressed more like a regular miner, he was still not experienced. The ringing of his pickaxe against the rock face almost muffled the faint sound of dirt running from the ceiling behind him. The slight noise meant nothing to him.

Hyde chipped away at the stone in front of him, grimly satisfied by the chunks of broken ore that piled up around his feet. It was Williams's turn to lead the burro and its carload of ore to the surface and the stamp mills but he would be back soon and with some cool, fresh water. They talked little when working but Hyde liked having someone with him when he worked underground.

He paused for a moment, shifting his grip on the hickory axe-handle. A little more dirt hissed down from the roof but Hyde couldn't see it in the yellow lantern light that pooled around him. The timbers behind him were old ones from a played-out area of the mine and some had warped with age.

Hyde was working again when the timber gave a faint, warning creak. He barely noticed the sound over the ringing of his pickaxe blade, but some instinct warned him of danger. Hyde stood up, almost banging his head against a low outcrop of country rock in the ceiling. He ducked away from it, swearing, and heard the sharp crack of a timber snapping. His first thought was to turn and dive back into the tunnel to escape but instead he stopped dead where he was.

A moment later, the roof of the tunnel gave way almost above him, right in the section he had been about to run through. Hyde flung himself backwards as rocks and dirt poured down from somewhere above him. He skidded on the fresh-dug ore and fell, cracking his head against the face he had just been digging.

The light was snuffed out and his world became a confusion of noise and fear. Dazed and frightened, Hyde curled up and stayed where he was. Dirt and stones rained over him, each impact making him shudder, never knowing which one might be big enough to kill him. The noise eventually faded until all he could hear in the pitch black was his own harsh breathing and the pounding of his heart. Slowly he sat up, straining his eyes into the darkness in the hope of picking out some faint light.

Debris slid off him to the floor as he moved. There was no light at all. Hyde could feel a rock wall behind him but had no idea how much, or how little, space was left around him. Shock numbed him for a long moment, but something of his usual calm sense returned and he began to think.

First of all, he took off the leather gloves and felt around himself until he put his hand on the jacket he'd taken off earlier. He pulled it out from some rocks and searched for the pockets. Working entirely by touch, Hyde got out a length of candle and a tin of matches. He managed to light the candle, nearly scorching his fingers in the process, and held it up.

The brave flame flickered slightly, casting fierce shadows on the walls around him. Hyde gasped once and fell silent, breathing shallowly. The tunnel back to the main mine shaft had fallen in altogether. His way out was filled with rocks, broken lumber and dirt piled together roof high, leaving him in a chamber about eight feet across. Hyde melted a little wax on to the floor and stuck the candle to it and then tackled the fall. He tugged away the nearest rock with his bare hands. It shifted slowly and dozens more sagged downwards, filling its place. He cringed back from the minor slide, watching in terror until it stopped. His fear calmed a little when he saw that no more was falling, but now he understood the danger he hadn't thought of before.

Hyde studied the rock fall more closely in the faint candle light. If he tried to shift any of it, he stood a good chance of increasing the fall or bringing it down in his direction. Even if he did succeed in clearing some rocks without disaster, he didn't have anywhere to put them. The mass that filled the tunnel now would soon start to fill the tiny chamber he was trapped in.

Hyde's heart bounced at the thought of being trapped. The sheer helplessness of his situation gnawed at his courage, bringing him close to screaming point. He felt the tension rising in his body and forced himself to start breathing slowly and deeply. As he calmed a little, his mind started working more rationally. Williams would be back soon; the others would dig him out. All he had to do was wait. Hyde wiped his gritty sleeve across his forehead. In the War, he'd often waited within earshot of battle, feeling the fear in the air as he and his men waited for their order to attack. This was going to be harder.

Pat Williams had been part-way back down the main level when he heard the rumbling further in. He was no more experienced in a mine than Hyde and it took a few moments for him to identify the sound.

'Great God!' Leaving the empty ore car, Williams sprinted recklessly along, turning left into the shaft where Hyde was working.

He stumbled on the uneven, poorly lit floor, but somehow stayed on his feet and kept running. Low burning lanterns hung from roof timbers at intervals, illuminating the rough walls and the tunnel ahead. The last lantern showed nothing but a dead end. Williams stopped, panting, and stared at the pile that blocked his way. Somewhere, beyond or under that lot, was Hyde.

Williams retraced his steps, unhooked the nearest lantern and carefully turned up the wick. He got as close as he could to the fall and held the lantern up to examine it. He couldn't make out whether there was a slight space at the top of the pile, a gap where the falling rubble had come from.

'Hyde! Hyde, can you hear me?' he bellowed. His voice echoed back off the tunnel walls around him. Williams held his breath as he listened for a reply.

'Yes!'

The cry was muffled but there. Williams let out his breath suddenly.

'Are you all right?' he called.

'I'm trapped!' There was a note of hysteria in the bitter answer.

Williams grimaced. 'I'll fetch the others,' he yelled. 'We'll get you out soon enough.'

The promise was more easily made than kept. Time passed as the men patiently cleared away rubble, propping up the weak places with timbers hastily torn from other mine sections. Williams found the progress frustratingly slow and he knew it had to be worse for the man on the wrong side of the fall. All the same, he made no effort to hurry O'Malley and McKindrick as they applied their knowledge to clearing a way out as safely as possible. At last, they had cleared a gap over the mound. Lantern light from their tunnel shone into the chamber beyond and they could see Hyde.

'Ye kin be climbing out noo. The rocks be safe enough,' McKindrick promised.

Hyde gazed warily at the narrow passage he had to crawl through. The fall was still chest high and he had to climb up it and wriggle through on his belly, with the repaired ceiling only a few inches above him. Williams had expected him to start moving at once, but the Southerner stayed where he was. He kept glancing at the roof of the gap and Williams suddenly understood that Hyde was as afraid of the makeshift tunnel as he was of the chamber he was in.

'I've sent Balzar to start fixing supper,' Williams said, apparently casually. 'There's enough time for you to wash up and get changed afore we eat.' He held out a hand across the rubble.

As he'd hoped, Hyde fixed his attention on the offered hand and started climbing. Williams reached across as far as he could and helped him through as soon as he came within reach. Hyde scrambled across the dirt and rocks on elbows and knees, sliding down the other side. Williams caught and steadied him, helping him regain his feet.

'Yer after being in a wee bit of a mess, laddie,' McKindrick said, beaming as he slapped Hyde on the back.

'That tunnel's a mess too,' O'Malley said disapprovingly. 'And you left your pickaxe behind in there. We'd be clearing this lot away faster iffen you'd used your head for something better than hanging your hat on it.'

Williams glanced anxiously at Hyde, but he luckily didn't seem to have heard O'Malley's remark. Taking his friend's arm, Williams walked them back along the shaft and out into sunshine again.

Hyde let out a long sigh and turned his face up towards the slanting evening sun. Williams started to smile in relief, then chuckled as he got a good look at Hyde in daylight.

'My,' he said. 'I've not seen anything like that since the time Billy Johnson and me got to wrassling and both fell in the cow wallow. Momma threw a conniption fit when I got home and she finally recognized me under the mud.'

Hyde was covered in grit and dust from head to foot. His dark hair was mussed and matted, there was a long scratch down his cheek, his shirt was out of his pants and he walked awkwardly because of the grit in his boots. He stared balefully at Williams, then glanced at his hands, seeing the black crescents under his short fingernails. One thumbnail had been torn raggedly, leaving a thin line of blood round the nail bed.

'A gentleman is still a gentleman, no matter what he looks like,' he remarked as his eyes began to gleam with amusement. 'And I sure haven't seen anything like this since me and Cousin Rafe overturned our boat on to a mudbank in the river. My mammy wouldn't let me back in the house until she'd sluiced me down under the yard pump.'

The image of Hyde as a boy, being rinsed under a pump by a black servant, was so stunning that Williams gave him a disbelieving look and simply burst into laughter. Hyde laughed too. 'You're no picture either,' he said, flashing his sharklike grin.

Williams nodded, still chuckling. He knew he was dirty and gritty too. 'Go get in the creek,' he advised. 'I'll fetch your kit.'

Hyde nodded. 'Thanks.' He meant the laughter as much as the rescue.

★   ★   ★

The next morning, O'Malley, McKindrick and Pat Williams set off to clear the rock fall and strengthen the damaged mine tunnel. Williams told Hyde to get on with sorting the ore that had already been brought out.

'Sure and we'd be getting the fall cleared faster if you weren't set on sparing the gentleman's dainty hands,' O'Malley remarked as they walked back along the main tunnel.

McKindrick was slightly ahead, pushing the squeaking ore car to remove the debris. No doubt he was listening, but he didn't turn his head.

Pat Williams glanced sideways at O'Malley, annoyed by the miner's carping. 'There's only enough room in the tunnel for three to work. Hyde might as well make himself useful sorting the ore.'

O'Malley grunted, hunching his shoulders under his dirty undershirt. 'Whyn't you hire yorself a for-real miner? I kin get you a man knows how to work for his living.'

'If we get trouble with *bandidos* or Comanches you'll be mighty grateful to have Hyde around,' Williams retorted.

'I've dug plenty of mines without needing no *pistolero* around,' O'Malley said. 'This place needs a miner more'n it needs a gunhand.'

Williams was acutely aware that O'Malley knew far more about mines and mining than he did but he didn't like to hear anyone insulting his friend.

'I own this damn mine and I'll hire who I like,' he answered. 'If I want a gunhand then it's my profit that's paying for it.' There was nothing amiable about his round face as he warned the old miner to keep his mouth shut.

O'Malley grunted, not bothering to look at Williams. 'It's yore money,' he agreed.

Williams cast a glance heavenwards for moral support. He didn't want to get O'Malley mad enough to quit but the miner had a point; Hyde was no miner. But Williams was sure he had been right in keeping Hyde out of the mine until the fall was cleared away. The fall had put a bad fright into him and he needed a break to recover his usual nerve. Shaking his head, Williams followed the two miners.

Hyde was working outside in the brilliant sunshine, sorting the crushed ore. He was getting better at it, learning to distinguish lumps of the non-productive country rock from the ore-bearing rock, but there was still plenty of pieces he couldn't identify. The waste rock he threw into a basket, to be dumped on the tailings pile later. The good and doubtful stuff went into a wooden box ready to be poured into the flume for water sorting. Without the stamp mill going, the mine was relatively quiet. He could hear Balzar, singing offkey as he groomed the horses in the corral further upstream. Rock wrens were singing more pleasantly from their hideouts in the canyon walls and the creek burbled as it ran nearby.

Hyde found the open air and the natural sounds refreshing. He paused in his work now and again, looking at the lush greenery of the canyon bottom or tilting his head back to look at the sky miles above. All the same, his eyes were drawn regularly to the dark hole in the canyon wall, and his face became drawn and thoughtful. He was scared of going underground again in a way that gnawed at the pit of his stomach.

This was different to any fear he had experienced in the Civil War. Every time he had gone into battle there had been a chance of getting maimed or wounded. He knew the sickly smell of gangrenous, maggot-infested wounds and had heard the screams of men having their limbs sawn off without anaesthetic. Hyde had lived with those fears but the thought of going back into the mine set him breathing faster as the panic rose in his guts.

He shook his head fiercely, hating his own fear. Forgetting the crushed rocks, Hyde took a few, slow steps towards the mine entrance. The sense of panic grew stronger, straining his nerves until he stopped dead. His hands brushed against the heavy cotton trousers where his guns normally hung.

'Goddamn it.' He spoke aloud without meaning to. 'I can't quit. I *won't* quit.' His brows drew down over his grey eyes as he stared at the mine. 'I swear I'll not run out.' With first one slow step and then another, he forced himself to approach the mine entrance and peer inside. The tunnel stretched away into darkness, lit only by gentle pools of yellow lamplight. Faint sounds echoed along the enclosing stone walls as the men inside cleared the rock fall. Hyde stayed where he was for a long moment, breathing stiffly and with his jaws clenched so tight that the muscles were rigid. Then he turned away and strode rapidly back to the stamp mill and the ore.

Hyde entirely failed to notice the movement above him on the rim of the canyon. As he bent over the crushed rocks, a Comanche drew back from the canyon edge, where he had been watching, and slipped away to report to his companions.

8

Marco de la Valle usually enjoyed riding but today he was discontented. His fine palomino horse lowered its head and pawed once at the ground as he stayed on the brow of the low hill, looking out over the rolling, arroyo-cut lands of the hacienda. Marco curbed the horse with a light touch on the reins as he continued scowling out at the distant groups of grazing cattle. Concepción was beside him, mounted side-saddle on her bay mare.

'What are you frowning about now?' she asked impatiently.

'We were granted this land nearly ninety years ago and nothing's changed since,' Marco told her. His dark eyes flashed as he spoke. 'Father still treats me as he was treated and as his father was treated.'

'Like a Don — or the son of one?'

Concepción suggested sarcastically. She tilted down the broad-brimmed hat she wore, careful to keep her skin from being burnt.

Marco snorted. 'He treats me like a boy. I'm twenty-one now and he still treats me like a child. He takes Diaz's advice before he takes mine and he won't give me any real responsibilities.' The horse tossed its head and he checked it impatiently, tugging harder than he usually would on the reins.

Concepción knew full well that her brother was nominally in charge of the day-to-day running of the hacienda. He worked with the *segundo*, Diaz, to give the men their orders and resolved disagreements. She was also aware that this was not what her brother was complaining about.

'You are his son. All children should obey their parents and honour them.' She reminded him of what they had been taught from birth.

'A woman's place is to obey, but I'm a man. I'm going to be Don some day,'

Marco said passionately. 'Father just won't listen to me, Conchita.'

'What are you particularly mad about now?' Concepción asked shrewdly.

Marco almost blurted out his annoyance at Don Pedro's inaction about the silver mine, but held his tongue in time. Conchita had already spoken her disapproval of any plan to injure Pat Williams and, besides, Marco felt that it was no kind of business for a lady to be involved in. His sister was still watching him, waiting for a reply, so he thought fast.

'There was that matter of Barrio being attacked by someone and having his horse stolen. He said it was a gringo and it may have been that Señor Hyde,' he added, throwing the blame on the man who had humiliated him at the fiesta.

Concepción burst into open laughter. 'Why should Señor Hyde choose to go around stealing horses?' she exclaimed. 'Did that beating he gave you knock the sense out of your brains?'

Marco scowled. 'He beat me because he didn't give me any warning. He fought like a *vaquero*, not like a gentleman.' Marco spat into the dirt.

Concepción tried to rein in her laughter, knowing how hot her brother's temper was. Her eyes still sparkled with suppressed merriment as she hid her smile.

Marco glared at his sister, infuriated at being mocked and silently blaming Hyde for it. 'I'm your brother; you shouldn't laugh at me,' he insisted.

'I'm sorry.' Concepción didn't sound it. She turned her face away, pretending to fiddle with her horse's mane as she tried to regain her self-control.

Marco wasn't fooled. 'I'll show you I'm better than father thinks,' he vowed rashly. 'I'll show you what I can do and what's more, I'll make Señor Hyde regret ever coming to Texas, on my oath as Marco de la Valle.' With that, he spurred his horse forward and galloped down the hill. Concepción picked up her reins and followed him, still half smiling at her brother's follies.

Marco had set off without any real plans, merely trying to leave his irritation behind him. He saw Perez, the half-Indian *vaquero* and rode towards him, a plan forming.

'Perez! Come here!' Marco hailed the other man imperiously.

Perez turned his horse and rode to meet his employer's son. Unlike the other *vaqueros*, he wore his straight hair shoulder length, usually tied back with a bandanna. His dark, leathery face was impossible to read as he obeyed the brusque command. Marco drew up alongside the *vaquero* before noticing Concepción nearby.

'Wait over near the cottonwood,' he told his sister. 'We have some business to talk.'

Concepción didn't have a great deal of respect for her older brother, but she was used to obeying the commands of men so she did as Marco told her. Besides, it wasn't fitting for a lady to know details of range work and cattle handling.

Marco saw her turn her horse away and rode his own closer to Perez in order to speak quietly.

'Have you been watching the mine?' he asked without preamble.

Perez nodded once. 'They have not left the canyon except for the tall one with two guns. He sometimes goes hunting; he is pretty good.'

'Hyde,' Marco said, his eyes glowing. 'Did he go hunting yesterday?'

Perez shook his head.

Marco made up his mind at once. 'Escort Concepción back to the house and tell her I may be late back.' Even as he spoke, he turned his palomino away and spurred the horse into a steady lope. He didn't bother looking back; he simply expected his orders to be obeyed.

Marco had been riding this range most of his life. Perez had described the canyon where the mine was and Marco knew how to find it without further help. He had no particular plan in mind beyond his impulsive wish to take some revenge on Hyde for humiliating him in front of guests and family. Marco travelled steadily and slowed as he approached the area of the mine, keeping close to cover. His precautions were wise because as he edged his horse through a stand of scrub oak, he caught a glimpse of movement in the clearing ahead. Marco dismounted and stalked through the trees, keeping low and using the cover as well as he could.

The clump of trees gave on to an open, grassy space in a wide valley. Hyde was on the far side of the clearing, about fifty yards away from Marco's position. The young man crouched down and watched. Hyde wasn't actively hunting game even though his Winchester was on the ground near his feet. Instead, he was practising with his handguns.

As Marco watched, Hyde drew both guns and started spinning them. The white-handled Colts spun backwards and forwards, pinwheeling around

Hyde's fingers as though they had a life of their own. Now and again he would slip one into its holster and draw it out again as fast. Marco and many of his *vaqueros* carried a gun, but none of them was particularly skilled with the weapons. He had never seen guns being handled in such a way and watched in amazement.

The display of gun skill went on for a good five minutes. Hyde was concentrating entirely on what he was doing and Marco realized he would never have a better chance to avenge his honour. He started to rise, intending to fetch the Sharps rifle booted on his saddle, then paused. It was a single-shot rifle; if he missed with that first shot, Hyde would probably kill him before he could reload. Marco had vowed that he'd prove himself better than Hyde, but his courage failed him. He dithered over the risk a few moments longer, then decided that shooting a man from ambush was dishonourable. The better way would be to ride out and challenge

Hyde to an open combat. Marco glanced out through the trees again, and knew he simply couldn't match the Southerner's gun skill.

Hyde finished his gun-handling practice and began shooting. He chose a solitary piñon pine as his target and fired at it, using both guns. He took a couple of quick, unaimed shots, then slid the guns into their holsters to practise his quick draw. Just at that moment, Marco's palomino came crashing from the trees, frightened by the shots. Hyde spun, drawing both guns faster than Marco had ever seen before, but he held his fire when he saw the unmounted horse. Marco felt a wash of fear at the thought of challenging someone so skilled. He didn't dare confront the other man but he had to go and claim his horse. Hyde had put one gun away and was approaching the palomino, which was cantering in a loose arc towards Hyde's mount. Marco moved a few paces away from his hiding-place and stood up, an excuse forming itself. He hurried from the trees, calling as he saw the other man.

'Can you catch my horse, *señor?*'

Hyde half turned, waved acknowledgement, and walked calmly to the palomino as it sniffed noses with the liver chestnut. By the time Marco reached him, Hyde had the palomino's reins and was holding them out for him.

'*Gracias*,' Marco said. 'I had just stopped in the trees to do what a man must. Your shots startled him.'

'I'm real sorry about that; I didn't know there was anyone hereabouts,' Hyde drawled casually.

Marco stroked the palomino's neck. 'I do not mind; it will save me some time. I was looking for you and Señor Williams because we invite you both to dine at Casa de las Flores tomorrow evening.'

'Why that's mighty kind of you,' Hyde answered unemotionally. 'I'll be sure and tell Williams when I get back.'

Marco forced a bright smile on to his face. 'You both left the fiesta in a hurry; you have not seen half the charms of our home. We want you to feel welcome.'

'That's a gentlemanly thing to say,' Hyde answered. 'I sure take it kindly that you don't hold my temper against me.'

'Of course not; I would react that way too if I thought I had been insulted like that.' The second part was true at least. Marco tossed his reins over his horse's neck and swung himself into the saddle without bothering with the stirrups. '*Hasta la vista.*' He saluted Hyde, keen to make his exit before he had to say more lies.

'*Vaya con Dios,*' answered Hyde, who heard the expression from Balzar every time he rode out to go hunting.

Marco rode briskly away, his handsome face troubled. He was pleased with himself for finding an excuse to be in the area, but his loss of nerve rankled. His father had warned him that Hyde was dangerous and Marco now knew that he'd been correct. He wanted to prove that he could do something his father couldn't. His displeasure settled on the man who had made him aware of his own failures. A black hatred filled him and Marco silently renewed his vow to prove himself the better man.

Pat Williams was washing his spare shirt in the creek when Hyde returned from his hunt. He paused from rubbing his shirt with soap as Hyde rode up to the shack. Balzar came running to take the liver chestnut, kissing the horse's muzzle as Hyde dismounted. Hyde handed the reins over and walked away, approaching Williams.

'Just like the old days,' Pat Williams remarked. 'Handing your horse over to the staff.' He nodded towards Balzar, who was unsaddling Cob.

Hyde showed his teeth briefly in a smile. 'I thought you paid the boy a wage,' he drawled. 'Slaves don't get wages.'

Williams knew better than to go on reminding Hyde of what he had lost. 'Couldn't you find any game?' he asked, absently swishing his shirt around in the creek.

'I found Marco de la Valle, and no, I didn't shoot him,' Hyde answered. 'We're invited to eat with them tomorrow evening.'

'Swell!' Williams exclaimed, his face lighting up into a smile. 'I never knew that a silver mine would get me to meeting quality folks,' he went on. 'You'd best teach me some company manners and kick me iffen I pick up the wrong spoon.'

'I don't reckon I'll go,' Hyde said. He was still standing over Williams, looking away from him as he spoke.

Williams fished his shirt from the creek. 'Why ever not?'

'Someone should stay at the mine.'

'Let O'Malley take charge for another evening. He can tell Balzar windies about digging gold in California.' Williams was impressed with Hyde's wish to do his duty and protect the mine when he could be meeting other quality folk and enjoying some civilized life for once. He stood up and flung his arm round the other man's shoulders.

'Come on, there'll be good food, and music, and wine and pretty women to look at. These *hacienderos* have as fine a life as you're going to find out here. You need to get away from these rocks and enjoy yourself.'

'All right.' Hyde moved away from Williams's reach.

'Good.' Williams bent to pick up his shirt, and began to whistle as he unravelled the tangled sleeves.

⋆　⋆　⋆

Hyde didn't know who had chosen the seating arrangements for the dinner at Casa de las Flores, but he thought it might have been Concepción. Don Pedro de la Valle sat at the head of the table; Concepción and Pat Williams sat on his right, which left Hyde and

Marco sitting together on the left. An elderly aunt sat opposite Don Pedro, the same chaperon who had been with Concepción at the fiesta. She said almost nothing all evening but slurped and chomped her way steadily through the offered dishes.

The dining-room was beautifully decorated with fresh flowers and long candles in elegant silver candlesticks. The table was swathed in a white damask cloth and set with silver cutlery. The hosts were dressed fittingly for such splendid surroundings. Concepción wore a full dress of ivory watered-silk with yards of gold satin ribbon binding the ruffles. Her brother was almost as richly dressed, resplendent in a snowy shirt of fine white linen and a dark red jacket, lavishly embroidered with silver and gold thread. Even the old aunt wore black silk and a mantilla of fine lace.

In contrast, Hyde was wearing the same clothes he had worn to the fiesta: a plain cotton shirt, his black jacket, stained with his own blood on the left arm, and his yellow neckerchief tied as a cravat. Even Williams was better dressed, as at least he had the brown townsuit he'd worn when working as a salesman. Of course, no one even hinted that Hyde wasn't properly dressed, but he felt the lack keenly. However, Hyde did his best to forget his discomfort and concentrate on enjoying the moment.

Opposite him, Pat Williams was having no difficulty in enjoying himself. Concepción was as lovely as he remembered, her skin warmed to honey colour by the soft candle-light and set off by her glossy black hair. She sat close enough for him to smell the faint, intoxicating scent of ambergris and now and again the ruffles of her sleeve brushed against his sleeve. Best of all, was the way she looked at him.

'Tell me, Señor Williams, what did you do before you found your silver?' she asked, tossing her hair back over her shoulder.

'I was a salesman,' Williams answered. 'Not a distinguished job but an honest living.'

'And what did you sell?'

Pat paused before answering, his blue eyes sparkling with mischief as he picked his words carefully. 'Clothes. Certain . . . delicate items of ladies' clothing.'

Concepción's eyes widened as she guessed that he meant underwear.

'No!' She giggled suddenly and covered her mouth.

Williams shrugged, enjoying himself. 'Ladies have to get them from somewhere and not everyone can, or wants to, make their own.'

She took a sip of wine before asking, in a voice barely above a whisper. 'Do you still have any?' She immediately moved back in her chair to restore a proper space between them.

Williams saw that her cheeks were flushed faintly red. 'A few samples,' he confessed. 'I quit the job rather sudden when I got the map for the mine.'

Concepción stared at him in something like wonder, obviously longing to ask what his samples looked like but unable to speak of anything so forward. Modesty won out and she picked up her knife and fork again. Williams grinned happily.

Hyde was finding it difficult to make polite small talk with Marco, so he was grateful when Don Pedro turned his attention their way.

'Marco tells me that you were an officer in the War Between the States,' the large man remarked with benevolent curiosity. 'A captain, I believe.'

'That's correct,' Hyde answered, with a touch of pride. 'I volunteered with Hampton's Legion and got elected a second lieutenant right off.'

'I'm surprised that a man of your calibre didn't reach a higher rank.'

Hyde smiled suddenly. 'I nearly made major in the winter of '64 but I got bad pneumonia instead. They needed to give the rank to someone who was in the camp, not in hospital.'

Marco spoke up. 'Did you spend much time behind the lines in hospital?'

Hyde heard the insult in the question but a quick glance at the handsome youth showed him the plain jealousy that prompted it. Hyde couldn't resist the chance to needle Marco a little.

'I took a ball across my thigh in Virginia. It took a month before I was fit enough for the rough riding we did. It was a real man's work.'

Marco's face darkened. 'I was needed here. Someone had to stay and defend women and children from the Comanches and *bandidos*,' he insisted, a little too firmly.

Hyde nodded. 'Why, for sure. I've fought Comanche and I've done fought Yankees and the Comanche might be savages but they're sure devils in a fight.' He paused to take a mouthful of chicken. It wasn't too hard to guess that the Don's son had led a sheltered life at the hacienda. If Marco had any exploits to boast about, he would be praising them up, but instead he merely glowered in silence.

Hyde didn't normally care to talk about himself but tonight he did. 'I guess you-all heard Williams tell about Black Dog and his bucks attacking the stage we were on,' Hyde drawled, looking at Marco with a mocking light in his grey eyes.

Marco nodded, his face sullen.

'Did he tell you-all how they came to steal our horses in the night?' Hyde went on. 'That fool newspaperman ran clean out of the station and got himself trapped in the open. I done gave him covering fire so he could get back safe and that's how I got a bullet across this arm.' He indicated the bloodstain, faint against the dark material of his jacket, on his upper left arm. 'It left me another scar but it's an honourable one.'

'Well said, Señor Hyde,' Don Pedro exclaimed genially. 'Your family must be proud of you.'

Hyde straightened a little. 'I believe that they are,' he answered in reserved tones.

'What family do you have?' Marco asked, keen to change the subject from warfare and glory.

'My brother Jed was killed in the War, and Father died soon after, but my mother is living, and I have a married sister,' Hyde answered.

'You have a sister too,' Marco commented, glancing across the table at Concepción, who was laughing at a story Williams was telling her. 'Is she blessed with children?'

'No. Felicity was married in the first months of the war and her husband was killed at the First Battle of Bull Run.' Hyde tried to keep his voice neutral as he spoke, but he knew that bitterness showed.

'I'm sorry to hear that,' Marco said politely. 'It's a shame for a lady to suffer such a loss and without even the consolation of children. She must be lonely, but no doubt your mother provides her with sufficient companionship.'

'Felicity lives with her husband's

family,' Hyde answered, not looking at Marco. 'My mother lives with her cousins.'

'Your Southern families have the same traditions as ours,' Marco said, watching Hyde like a hawk watching its prey. 'That an unprotected woman will be taken in and sheltered for as long as she needs it.'

'It's a gallant tradition,' Hyde answered. He sent money to his mother when he could but the blunt fact was that his mother and sister lived on the charity of other relatives. From having two grand homes of their own and dozens of slaves to tend to their slightest wish, Hyde's closest family made do with rooms in other people's houses. That knowledge ate at Hyde's pride more deeply than the loss of wealth or any amount of manual labour. Everything around him in the gracious dining-room, the china, fine glasses, silver candlesticks, all this was what he wanted to restore to his family.

Hyde knew that Marco was watching

him, a dark gleam of satisfaction in the younger man's eyes. The bitter frustration swelled up inside him, threatening to overspill into anger. Hyde picked up his wineglass, trying to appear calm. Glancing across the table, he saw Concepción lean close to Williams. The candlelight flashed off her garnet earrings, just like the ones his mother had once had. Those earrings had been sold during the war to raise money for food. Hyde's mother had no jewellery of her own left except for the jet mourning-brooch with a lock of his father's hair woven into it. His hand tightened suddenly on the stem of the wineglass, snapping the crystal. Red wine and sparkling shards of glass exploded across the table.

Exclamations of shock filled the air around him as Hyde sat with his head high and still, and blood oozing from his hand.

9

The shattered wineglass was mopped up hurriedly by the servants, as Hyde apologized and Don Pedro and his family offered condolences for the misfortune. The shallow cuts on his hand were soon attended to as he sat aloofly still. Williams ceased to devote so much of his attention to Concepción and used his ready wit to smooth over the embarrassment. He got the conversation flowing again and kept the company entertained for the rest of the evening.

Don Pedro insisted that his guests stay overnight, pointing out that the next day was Sunday and a day of rest. Williams agreed and Hyde made no objection. The next morning, Williams attended Mass for the first time in months, sitting by the Don and his family in the small chapel on the hacienda. Hyde stayed alone in the grand house.

Unknown to the rest of his family, Marco had ridden out first thing in the morning. The night before, he had sent Perez out to arrange a meeting. When Marco arrived at the rendezvous he'd asked for, he met Perez and three Comanches. The Indians were squatting on the ground, their horses tethered to stakes a short distance away.

Although Perez was wearing boots, trousers and a shirt, he looked just as wild as his companions. Marco dismounted, acutely aware of their silent attention.

'This is Sloping Leg, Turkey Feather and Spotted Horse,' Perez said in his slow Spanish, indicating each Comanche in turn.

Marco saw the twisted foot that marred Sloping Leg's looks and felt happier about coming face to face with the Comanches.

'Give this to them,' he said, handing out a packet of coffee he'd taken from the kitchen earlier.

Perez passed the packet to Sloping Leg, who sniffed it appreciatively before speaking.

'He's telling them he will divide it when they return to the village,' Perez translated. 'Sloping Leg is a generous warrior,' he added as his own opinion. 'He has eagle medicine and it is good.'

Marco was unimpressed by Comanche superstitions. 'Hyde and Williams will be riding back to the mine this morning soon after Mass. You know which track they'll be taking?'

Perez nodded. Marco looked at the three Comanches for a moment. Spotted Horse was gazing enviously at the palomino; Marco tightened his hold on the reins without knowing he was doing it.

'I want Hyde dead,' he said. 'The tall one who wears two guns. I don't care what happens to the other one; hurt him or kill him. Tell the Indians they can take whatever they want; the horses, guns, money.'

Perez translated this, and held a brief conversation with Turkey Feather. The young brave had cut off the braid that Hyde had shot at, leaving his hair even shorter than Perez's. His dark eyes glittered as he spoke harshly, looking at Marco.

'What's he saying?' Marco asked uneasily.

Perez's face was inscrutable as he answered. 'He wanted to know why you won't fight him yourself, if he is your enemy.'

All three Comanches were staring at Marco, who felt his colour rise under their critical gaze.

'My father has offered them hospitality; I can't attack our guests,' he explained, his voice high with fear and anger. 'Father would be furious.'

Perez translated. The Comanches understood hospitality, but as Walking Bear had told Williams, the younger men had no compunction about disobeying the elders if they could make a name for themselves. The palomino lowered its head to graze but Marco jerked on the reins. He waited impatiently as the Indians talked.

'Are they going to do it?' Marco interrupted, his quick temper rising.

Perez answered, 'Sloping Leg and Turkey Feather both wish to kill those two men. They will kill the white men for their own reasons, not for yours.'

'I've told them where to find Hyde and Williams,' Marco snapped.

'They have been watching the mine for days,' Perez said imperturbably. 'Sloping Leg has made his medicine; he says today will be a good day. The others have listened and they will fight today.'

Marco was used to being obeyed immediately by servants and *vaqueros*. The Comanches' near indifference to him was maddening but their silent, almost mocking gaze, helped him keep the lid on his temper. Much as he wanted to yell at them, Marco tried his best to appear equally calm.

'Are there more than just these three?'

Perez nodded. 'Other young men will follow Sloping Leg.'

'Good.' Marco swung astride his horse and gathered up the reins. 'Come straight back to me when you're done,' he ordered Perez.

The half-Indian man nodded silently and turned away. Marco hauled his horse around and left at a gallop.

★   ★   ★

It was mid-morning by the time Williams and Hyde left the hacienda.

'Conchita told me she plays the guitar,' Williams said cheerfully as the two men rode along. Happiness showed in every inch of his good-natured face. 'She's promised to play for me sometime soon, maybe at the next fiesta, and I'm sure looking forward to it.'

'That's swell,' Hyde answered, glancing once at his friend and turning away.

'I bet she sings well,' Williams went on blithely. 'She's got such a lovely speaking voice.' He fell silent for a moment, lost in pleasant thoughts. 'I'm kind of surprised that they asked us to eat with them,' he went on. 'Those *haciienderos* are plumb proud. Conchita told me her family were granted that land by the government way back in 1782! But her pa didn't seem to mind me talking to her so much. Letting me spark with his daughter!' He grinned at his friend, colouring slightly as he admitted his attentions.

'You own a silver mine,' Hyde said. It wasn't the kindest way of putting it, but he didn't feel kindly disposed.

'True,' Williams admitted, his face falling a little. 'But I don't have an old name or a good family like yours. Don Pedro doesn't know much about you but anyone can tell you're quality folk.'

'You don't want to be a gentleman,' Hyde answered. 'A gentleman's a mighty useless critter without . . . his servants.' He had been about to say 'money' but covered it up. The subject was too bitter.

Williams must have finally sensed something of his mood because he fell silent, leaving Hyde to brood in peace.

As he rode along, Hyde tried to turn his thoughts to better things but they kept coming back to injustices old and new. The wage that Williams paid him was the first steady money he had earned in months, certainly the first wage that paid enough cash for him to send something to his mother. Earning that money meant going back into the narrow, dark mine and the fear that frayed his nerves all the time he was down there. And Williams didn't only own the silver mine, he had the luck to be falling in love with a beautiful girl from a wealthy family. Hyde wasn't interested in Concepción but Williams was on his way up in the world. Jealousy occupied Hyde's thoughts, his envy turning to resentment of Williams's good luck.

With both men preoccupied in their

thoughts, neither stood a chance of seeing the ambush. Half a dozen Comanches came bursting out from cover that looked hardly big enough to hide a jackrabbit. Their war screams startled both men and horses, causing Williams's mount to shy sideways in a stiff-legged leap. Hyde instinctively leaned forward as Cob reared up. He stayed in his saddle but couldn't take a hand from his reins to draw a gun. The Comanche were only a few feet away, armed with hatchets, knives and war-clubs as they charged in, screaming. Hyde turned his horse's head towards them.

'Goddamn you!' he yelled, a rare, dark anger taking over. He spurred the liver chestnut towards the nearest man, not even thinking to draw a weapon. His horse took off in a leap, bearing down on the stocky Comanche, who twisted aside like an eel. Hyde got a glimpse of the man swinging his club and felt a numbing blow on his left knee as they passed one another. The pain brought back his usual common sense and he had a Colt in his hand almost without thinking.

Three of the Comanche were closing in on him; about the same number were rushing towards Williams, who was having trouble with his frightened horse. Hyde noticed briefly that there was something odd about one of the three near him but he had no time to think about it. His Colt lined on the nearest man and he fired. The Comanche staggered back, blood pouring from the wound in his shoulder.

A war scream gave Hyde a moment's notice of the next attack. He spun Cob, the horse turning on its haunches, as he reached across himself to fire to his left. The awkward shot went wide. Hyde saw light shining on a knife and swung himself half out of the saddle, hanging on to the horn. Something scraped his leg as the knife missed and rammed into the tough saddle leather. Hyde swung himself back, hanging on hard as the horse circled. Upright again, he saw his attacker was Turkey Feather, the man who had challenged him and tried to take Cob away in the Comanche village. Hyde lashed out with a kick and hit him hard in the chest. Turkey Feather staggered back a few paces, his painted face grim with pain.

A familiar yell made Hyde pause, looking across for his friend. Pat Williams was surrounded by three Comanches and in trouble. One of them had hold of him by the waist and was dragging him from the saddle. If they unhorsed him, he stood little chance of fighting off all three. Hyde had a brief chance to help and started to raise his gun, knowing he could take down one of the Comanches at least. Then he deliberately turned his back on Williams's danger.

Turkey Feather launched himself back into the attack, howling with fury. The injured brave grabbed for the liver chestnut's bridle at the same time. Hyde fired a wild shot at Turkey Feather and jabbed his spurs into his horse's sides. Cob bucked forward, the horse's chest ramming aside the injured brave and throwing him to the ground. Hyde stayed in his saddle but missed the chance to fire at Turkey Feather. He heard a gunshot nearby; the light note of Williams's short-barrelled revolver. The third Indian leaped in at Hyde, slashing with a long knife. He held it differently from the other Indians but Hyde didn't have time to notice the difference. He got off a single, fast shot that missed and tried to twist away from the knife. He felt a blow against his side and something tugging at his jacket. Hyde gave a yell of anger and swung his horse around. The frightened animal's quarters barged against the Comanche, pushing him away.

Hyde turned to look for Turkey Feather. He got a glimpse of Williams on the ground, fighting hand to hand with a Comanche. Another had seized his horse and was mounting, helping the injured one up behind him. There was no time to see more. Turkey

Feather jumped at him and grabbed his clothing.

'Let go, damn you,' Hyde cursed as the Indian's weight pulled him sideways. Turkey Feather was on his left, difficult to aim at with his gun. Hyde clubbed him with it instead, slamming the metal down on to the Comanche's bare head. Turkey Feather grunted but hung on, trying to drag Hyde down. Hyde gritted his teeth and hung on, starting to feel the pain of the knife-wound in his side. His seat slid in the saddle and his breath was coming fast as he fought to stay atop his horse. Every muscle in back and legs strained against the heavy drag. The other Indians were moving, recovering themselves; he needed to get out of this mess.

Hyde slipped his gun back into its holster and dropped his shoulders. He wriggled his right arm out of his jacket and twisted, letting Turkey Feather's weight tear it loose. As it came off, the Comanche staggered backwards and

Hyde lurched the other way, clinging to his saddle horn. Turkey Feather gave a scream of frustration and threw the jacket to the ground. It delayed him just long enough for Hyde to draw and shoot the wounded Comanche who was trying to catch Cob again. This shot was clean, smashing the man's face to a pulp as the bullet tore through his head. There was no time for Hyde to congratulate himself. He turned the other way, wincing at a spasm of pain from his side. He was vaguely aware of dampness on his shirt.

Thundering hooves were heading towards them. The Comanche on Williams's horse was shouting something. Turkey Feather replied with a wild cry. Hyde fired a quick shot and saw the Comanche stagger and clutch at his side. He took another shot but the hammer clicked on to an empty chamber. The determined resistance had broken the Comanches' nerve. Sloping Leg, their medicine leader, was injured, blood seeping from a wound in his side. One of the white men was still mounted and armed; one of the Comanches was dead and two more injured. The other Comanche who had been attacking also started to run, making for the arroyo where they had hidden their horses.

'That's it!' Hyde yelled. 'Run, you bastards!'

Turkey Feather saw his companions leaving, and found himself alone against the white man who had proved his courage back in the village. He didn't know that Hyde had run out of shots, but he remembered how well Hyde had used the gun in the village. Turkey Feather's courage left him and he started running.

Hyde spared a glance for Williams and saw him still pinned down by the same Indian. They were fighting for possession of a war club, Williams hanging on to the Indian's arm grimly as they struggled. Once more, Hyde turned his back on his friend. Swapping guns, he fired two more shots at the fleeing Indians. One of them scraped across the horse's rump, making it squeal as it ran under its double burden.

Only when they were a safe distance away did Hyde turn to help Williams. He was just in time to see his companion finally roll the Comanche off him. Williams grabbed for his fallen gun and shot the Comanche in the stomach at point-blank range. The Comanche screamed, tumbling backwards in a fountain of blood. Williams sat up and shot him again, this time aiming for the head.

Then it was all over. Williams climbed slowly to his feet, his face tired and his clothes spattered with blood. The sight reminded Hyde of his own troubles. He swung down off his horse, giving the liver chestnut a brief pat on the neck. After that he got more cartridges and caps from his saddle-bag and reloaded his guns. Only then did he pull his grey shirt loose from his trousers and use it to mop at the long cut just above his right hip.

'You much hurt?' Williams asked anxiously. He had walked over and was looking at the wound. He had a bruise on one cheekbone and grass in his hair.

'More messy than deep, I reckon,' Hyde answered succinctly.

'They sure got the jump on us,' Williams said bitterly. 'And they got my horse. That's another one!' He sighed. 'Still, we made honest Indians of two of them, whoever they were.'

'I saw Turkey Feather,' Hyde said. He tore his shirt-tail off and wadded it up to press over his injury. 'And I reckon that Sloping Leg was there.'

Williams's grim expression lifted a little. 'I do believe you're right. I noticed one of them moved funny.' He took off his cotton bandanna and used it to fix the pad efficiently over Hyde's knife wound.

Hyde stood still, letting his companion help him out and listening to Williams speak. 'I'm sure glad that was Turkey Feather and not just any buck from Walking Bear's village. I know he can't forbid the youngsters to jump us but I'm glad to know it was those renegades. I'd hate to think he didn't keep his word to us.' Williams sighed. 'You want to get on to the mine or go back to the hacienda? They could fix you up a sight better there.'

'Let's go to the mine. We can ride double.'

'All right.' As Hyde remounted, Williams picked up his torn jacket and handed it up to him. Hyde slipped it on then helped Williams up behind him.

He felt oddly numb inside. The Comanches hadn't killed Pat Williams and he was no closer to owning the silver mine. That mine represented wealth, a chance to look after his mother and sister in the way he wanted. Hyde had been raised in the tradition that looking after kin was a man's highest duty. He gave no thought to the status that wealth brought; poverty had never affected his family's belief in themselves. But the silks and silver of

Casa de las Flores were what his family deserved. For a brief moment, Hyde had seen a chance to take them and it had been snatched away by Williams's survival. To be so close and then lose increased his frustration, and his envy began hardening into resentment

About an hour later they stopped to stretch their legs and let Cob take a rest from his double burden. Hyde unsaddled his horse to ease its back and let the liver chestnut loose to graze for a few minutes on the dry grass.

'I shan't bother getting another mount,' Williams remarked, wandering over to the thin shade of some bushes. 'We've got the other two I got from the Schmidts and we're not likely to need more than three at once.'

'Likely not,' Hyde answered him automatically. He watched Williams intently, calculations running through his mind. He was faster on the draw than Williams. He could kill the other man before Williams even knew what was happening. After that, he could pack Williams's body back to where the Comanches had ambushed them and let the Indians take the blame. Get hold of the land deed, he knew where Williams kept that, and keep hold of the mine.

Pat Williams was walking slowly, stretching his legs after being perched behind the saddle. Hyde's right hand dropped slowly, his fingers finding the smooth ivory grips of his gun. Williams wasn't even watching. Hyde stood still a long moment, then his hand lifted again. Shooting didn't seem right.

Williams spoke. 'I'm going to inspect the timber.' He disappeared from sight amongst the bushes.

Hyde scowled briefly, annoyed with himself. Glancing around for inspiration, his eyes lighted on the heavy saddle lying on its side. He moved swiftly to the dry scrub and snapped off a short length of spiny twig, pressing it lightly into the underside of the saddle blanket.

'Sorry about this, boy,' he said quietly

to his horse as he lifted the saddle and settled it carefully on to the liver chestnut's back. The horse snorted a little and rippled its skin, but the spines weren't pressing in hard enough to hurt. When Williams reappeared from the bushes, Hyde was fastening the girth up. He stood back and offered the reins to his companion.

'You take the comfortable seat this time,' he said.

Williams started to smile at the considerate offer. 'You sure? Cob isn't the easiest ride, is he? And he's your horse.'

'You got him back for me,' Hyde said.

Williams took the reins and swung himself astride, landing easily in the saddle. His weight pressed the sharp spines in the saddle blanket hard into the horse's back The first Williams knew about it was when the horse flung its head up with a snort.

'Easy, boy,' Williams said, leaning forward to pat Cob's neck.

Cob responded by rearing, balancing high on his hind legs. Williams grabbed a handful of the horse's flaxen mane as he hung on. 'Whoa!' he called.

Cob plunged forward, landing on stiff legs in a way that jarred Williams's teeth together. The horse got its head down and started to buck, frantic to get rid of the painful thing that seemed to be digging claws into its back. It jumped high, coming down with an extra twist of its hindquarters that rammed the cantle of the saddle hard against Williams's back. It was a dangerous action, one that could break a man's spine if it hit wrong. Williams gritted his teeth and hung on, trying to stay in control but anxious not to further upset the horse. He tried to tighten the reins so the horse couldn't get its head down to buck but Cob plunged in a whirling leap that almost hurled Williams sideways from the saddle.

Hyde had retreated to a safe distance, watching anxiously. He hated to see his horse's pain and fear; Cob's eyes were rimmed with white in a way he'd never seen before. Hyde wanted to call out, to soothe his horse and stop the frantic bucking, but there was nothing he could do. The horse leaped in another twisting buck, quite different from the straightforward bucks it often gave in a morning when full of high spirits. Hyde could see Williams getting jarred as the saddle crashed into his lower spine. All the same, he pulled up on the reins, tightening them. Cob crowhopped and jumped straight in the air, fighting to get his head down again. Williams had a good hold of him now but the horse was still driven by panic.

Cob jumped forward on stiff legs, throwing Williams off balance, then he reared. This time Cob went almost vertical in its efforts to shake off the thing that terrified him. Williams was loose in the saddle from the last buck. He instinctively held tight on to the reins as he leaned forward, struggling not to slide off.

'Let go!' Hyde yelled, as he saw the horse start to wobble.

Williams tried to grab hold of the horse's flaxen mane. Now Cob was off balance too, fighting to remain upright while Williams's weight was pulling him over. The horse took a short step and then toppled backwards. Williams panicked for a moment, hanging on to the saddle for too long before kicking his feet free of the wooden stirrups in an effort to get clear. Then Cob came down on his back, with Pat Williams underneath him. The horse kicked frantically for a moment then managed to roll over, its weight crushing against Williams, and scrambled to its feet. Hyde ran to catch his frightened, blowing horse. Williams lay where he had fallen, his eyes closed. Hyde glanced at him and turned away, sick and frightened.

10

Hyde stroked the horse's sweaty neck, automatically soothing the distressed animal while trying to calm his own nerves. A gasping moan from behind brought him whirling round.

'Pat?' Hyde ran to kneel by his companion. 'Pat? Can you hear me?'

Williams opened his eyes and pressed a hand gently against his chest. 'I think your Goddamned horse just tried to break every rib in my chest,' he said faintly. 'He came plumb close but he don't get the prize.'

Hyde drew in an unsteady breath, grinning with the sudden sensation of relief that swept through him. 'God, I'm sorry,' he said impulsively. 'I thought he'd killed you.'

Williams shook his head slowly. Colour was coming back to his face now and he shifted position carefully as the first shock wore off. He grimaced a bit but there was none of the sharp agony of a broken bone. 'I may just be the luckiest man alive,' he remarked. 'Half a ton of horse just rolled on me and there's nothing worse than bruises to show for it.' He took a slow, deep breath and let it out again gently. His ribs ached but that was all. 'All the same, I reckon I'll just lie flat a while.'

'Good idea,' Hyde drawled. 'I'll see what upset Cob so.'

Hyde took the saddle off and gently removed the embedded spines from his horse's skin. He showed the crushed vegetation to Williams. 'I guess I must have put the saddle too close to those bushes. I should have checked it better when I saddled up. I'm real sorry,' he added, not acting the last part.

'No wonder Cob went wild,' Williams remarked, sitting up now. 'I know he doesn't take to being ridden by anyone but you, but I didn't reckon he was that set against me.'

Hyde studied Williams's face but

there was no trace of suspicion there. It never occurred to Williams that Hyde would hurt his own horse. Well, there was punishment enough for his sin; Cob had a sore place on his back and couldn't be ridden just now. Both men would have to walk back to the mine.

★   ★   ★

Later that same evening, Marco was waiting outside the stables. He stepped forward as a man rode in, his face lighting up expectantly.

'How did it go, Perez?' he demanded in Spanish. Marco seized the man's bridle, halting the horse.

Perez shook his head. 'They are alive.'

'Both of them? I told you particularly that I wanted Hyde dead.' Marco half raised a hand, longing to strike his *vaquero*, but thought better of it.

'We tried. I cut him but it wasn't bad.' Perez's face was impossible to read as he gazed down at the impetuous young man.

Marco didn't bother asking whether any of the Comanches had been hurt. 'Still alive,' he repeated. 'Now he just looks braver than ever, Goddamn you all. Hyde's got the luck of the devil!'

'He fights well,' Perez said simply.

'He's lucky!' Marco insisted. 'No one can fight that well all the time; not even cavalry officer, Captain Hyde.'

Perez didn't bother trying to argue. He merely waited to see if there would be any more instructions.

Marco brooded for a few moments before he realized the other man was waiting for him to speak again. 'You can go,' he ordered. 'I'll think of something else. No one's luck can last forever.' He turned away abruptly and strode back to the house.

Perez shook his head, dismounted, and led the horse to the stables.

★   ★   ★

Hyde couldn't get to sleep that night. He tried to tell himself that it was the nagging pain from the knife-cut in his side. The long walk back, leading his horse, had strained the knife-wound, which continued to ooze blood. Williams had largely shaken off the effects of his bad fall and now suffered nothing worse than a sore chest and some messy bruises.

Hyde had been weak and tired by the time they got to the mine. Williams had renewed the padding over the wound and had ordered him to lie down and let it heal over properly. While Hyde had been resting, grateful for the chance to be alone, Williams had told the others about the attack by the Comanches. He praised Hyde's courage and gun skill to the other men, causing Balzar to gaze at the Southerner more wide-eyed than ever with admiration.

As he turned over on his bedroll, Hyde thought about Williams again. He told himself that he hadn't tried to kill

Williams, but his conscience knew that he might as well have done. He had turned his back on him in the fight. Williams could well have been crushed to death under the horse when it fell on him. How badly did he want this mine? Was he willing to sell his honour for it?

'Mother and Felicity are starving,' Hyde whispered to himself. His fists were clenched so tight that his short nails dug into the palms. 'They're living on charity.'

They weren't the only ones. Hyde knew full well that Williams had taken the risks he had to find the mine because he wanted to support his own mother and sisters in the way they deserved. If he died, they would have no other support. But they were strangers and Hyde had a duty to his own kin. Looking after kin was the highest honour and duty of all; it was a code that Hyde had been taught from his earliest childhood.

He sat up for a moment, fiercely rearranging the jacket that he used for a pillow. It was no more comfortable when he had done. Thoughts of money, silver and family went round and around in his mind. Should he do his duty to his family or should he betray his friend? The silver would buy so much. Killing Williams would be dishonourable. He didn't want to kill Williams. Hyde thought of Williams lying under the struggling horse as it rolled on top of him. Even the memory brought a surge of panic to him, and a rush of shame. Hyde knew that if Pat Williams had died then, he would have lost his honour for ever.

The solution came to him suddenly. Leave Williams and the mine alone but steal the silver bullion from the shack. Pat had a mine full of it; he wouldn't miss those three or four ingots in the long run. It would surely be worth enough to rent a small place for his mother and sister. At least it would give them an income at last. Stealing was far less dishonourable than killing. Hyde stretched out, his tall body relaxing.

With something settled at last, he quickly fell into a deep, exhausted sleep, and barely moved until he was called for breakfast.

'You'd best get on with the sorting today,' Williams told him, watching his friend anxiously. He didn't like the strained look in Hyde's eyes. 'It'll pull the wound less than swinging a pickaxe.'

'All right,' Hyde answered. He scooped up another spoonful of beans and molasses, eating without tasting it.

Williams dropped a hand on Hyde's shoulder as he passed. 'Set down and rest anytime you need to. You look plumb tired.'

Hyde almost flinched from the kindness and told himself that Williams was a fool. All the same, when he'd eaten and shaved, he spent two hours sorting crushed ore and sending it down the flume. After dumping a batch of waste on the tailings pile, he straightened up stiffly and walked slowly downstream.

Balzar was at the corral, no doubt fussing over the horses again. Williams and McKindrick were underground and O'Malley was in the mill building, preparing another batch for pan processing. Hyde entered the relative coolness of the wooden bunkhouse and knelt down by the box where the silver was stored. There wasn't so much as a padlock to protect it. As he looked at it, O'Malley's coyote-dog wandered in and started sniffing at him.

'Get out of here, you mangey cur-dog,' Hyde ordered, dealing it a sharp smack on the muzzle. The coyote-dog yelped once and retreated outside.

Hyde ran his hands over the rough wooden box before suddenly lifting the lid. The silver gleamed dully in the poor light inside the windowless bunkhouse. Hyde touched the top bar, then lifted it, trying to gauge its weight. The bars could be distributed evenly between his saddle-bags and the bedroll. He could tell Balzar that he was going hunting, saddle up at the corral and pick up his things on the way out of the canyon. If he left the bedroll, they might not miss the saddle-bags at once. He could be a hundred miles away before they started looking for him. He could even get across the border into Mexico and swap the silver for gold there.

'What're you doin' there, Mr Hyde?' said O'Malley from behind him.

Hyde almost started but kept his self-control. He replaced the block of silver and closed the lid of the box before standing and turning.

O'Malley was just inside the door of the shack, his eyes suspicious. 'Well?' he demanded. 'What's a fine gennleman doin' lookin' at another man's property?'

'I was reckoning it was time Williams took his silver to the bank,' Hyde drawled, thinking fast. 'I wanted to check that there was enough to be worth while.'

'Was you plannin' on saving him the trouble by haulin' that purty silver off someplace by yoreself?' O'Malley demanded.

'Pat Williams is my partner!' Hyde snapped, feeling a rush of guilt at the words.

'Williams sure reckons so,' O'Malley answered coldly. 'I ain't so sure. An' even if I was, I reckon he could do a whole heap better'n you. Why, he might even find hisself a partner that ain't scairt to go into the mine.'

Guilt flared into anger. 'I'm not scared of the mine!' Hyde yelled, knowing the other man was right.

O'Malley laughed rudely, scratching his whiskers. 'I seen the way you look when you goes in. You're powerful scairt o' that mine and I reckons you figgered you pay yoreself some silver and go take yoreself where you don't need to get yore gennleman's hands blistered no more.'

Hyde lost control for a split-second. It was just long enough for him to draw his gun and fire it at the taunting figure of the old miner. At the very last moment, almost before O'Malley had realized what was happening, Hyde switched the aim of his gun. The shot tore a hole in the shoulder of O'Malley's faded undershirt without touching the man, and crashed through the wall of the bunkhouse behind him. Hyde froze, unnerved by what he had done.

O'Malley had no idea that the miss had been deliberate. He let out a roar of rage and charged across the narrow space between them. He got one powerful hand on Hyde's wrist and twisted it as they fell to the ground together. The miner landed on top, almost driving the breath from Hyde.

'I'll carve you up good, you low-down skunk,' O'Malley promised. He slammed his elbow across Hyde's face and twisted his arm hard, forcing him to drop the gun. Hyde grunted at the blow, tasting blood in his mouth. He fought back savagely, wanting nothing more than blind revenge. He rammed his free hand into the pit of O'Malley's

stomach and brought his legs up
sharply, throwing the miner off balance.
He wriggled round on the packed-dirt
floor, getting out from under O'Malley's
weight. O'Malley had fought in some of
the wildest mining towns in the west
and knew a few tricks. Keeping hold of
Hyde's gun hand, he bent it back,
forcing a cry of pain from the other
man. O'Malley sat up, smiling with
unholy glee as Hyde writhed to get his
arm into a less painful position.

'You sure don't look such a fine
gennleman now,' O'Malley sneered,
gripping tighter. 'Why, even yore own
Mammy wouldn't know you now.'

Hyde used the firm hold on his wrist
as support for a wild move. Still lying
mostly on his back, he brought his legs
up fast, twisted, and kicked out hard.
Both boots crashed into O'Malley's
chest, sending him over and breaking
his hold. Hyde's right wrist was
throbbing but he barely noticed as he
scrambled to get his feet underneath
himself. O'Malley didn't try to rise at

once, instead regaining his balance. As Hyde stood, O'Malley knocked his feet out from under him and brought him down again.

Hyde instinctively put out his hand to break his fall and cried out with pain at the impact. He curled up momentarily, holding his injured wrist and arm close against his body as his senses swam. Behind him, O'Malley lunged to his feet and closed in to kick the fallen man. The blow from O'Malley's heavy boot hit the knife wound on Hyde's hip. It was already bleeding again but the fresh pain almost blacked him out. Hyde moaned, lacking breath to make a louder noise. Another kick landed on his back, thudding against his spine.

'What the hell are you doing?'

Hyde heard someone running and the sound of a scuffle behind him. It was Williams's voice, remonstrating with O'Malley. Hyde summoned the energy to roll over and see what was happening.

'Yore fine damned gennleman was

thievin' yore silver. I heard my Tara bark an' came to take a look-see. I done caught him takin' the silver,' O'Malley was yelling.

'Hyde helped me get the silver,' Williams said fiercely. His blue eyes were as cold as Hyde had ever seen them as he faced the old miner. 'Why should Hyde start to stealing it from me?'

'You reckon it was me fired that shot?' O'Malley gestured at the splintered hole in the lumber wall. 'He's the shootist!'

'And I changed my aim,' Hyde put in. He struggled to a sitting position, still breathing raggedly as he fought the pain. 'I drew and then I changed my aim.'

'You missed. You plain lost yore nerve an' missed!' O'Malley insisted.

Hyde made himself look at Williams. 'You've seen me shoot,' he said simply.

Williams turned on the miner. 'That's so. I've seen Hyde shoot and he couldn't miss you in a shack this size unless he wanted to. And I never saw him lose his nerve.'

O'Malley started to speak but Williams didn't give him the chance.

'Get outside now. You can get your kit and your burro and leave this mine today,' he ordered, his voice rising. He waited until O'Malley had left, then hurried over to his friend.

'You're bleeding again,' he said, seeing the patch of blood soaking into Hyde's increasingly ragged grey shirt. He pulled the shirt loose and used a handkerchief to mop blood away from the knife cut. 'I reckon that wants stitches. Are you hurt anywhere else?'

Hyde carefully worked the fingers of his right hand, more concerned about his gun hand than the blood in his mouth. 'He didn't break anything,' Hyde said aloud. 'But it needs rest and maybe strapping.' He tried turning the hand and grimaced swiftly at the stab of pain that shot up his arm.

'I'll see that old buzzard leaves afore I'm an hour older,' Pat Williams promised, looking his friend in the eyes. 'McKindrick knows about smelting and processing; he can take charge. I've heard O'Malley spin some windies but telling me that you were stealing the silver! I owe you my life.' He started to stand.

'Pat!' Hyde caught Williams's sleeve. The trust was almost too much for him to bear. 'I was looking at the silver. I wanted to know how much there was. I thought it was surely time you took it to the bank.' The lie came out before he could stop himself.

'Whatever O'Malley thought, there was no call for him to stand and kick you when you were down,' Williams answered hotly. 'I told him already to quit ragging on you and this time he's gone too far. Now you set and rest in here,' he went on more kindly. 'An' I'll fetch some water and get you cleaned up some.'

Hyde just nodded and let him go.

* * *

Concepción was in the shade on the patio, practising the guitar, when her father arrived and sat down. She glanced up but he nodded towards the instrument and smiled, so she carried on picking out the tune for a few minutes longer. She was trying out the fingering of a new phrase, getting it slowly at first and then repeating each few bars faster until the tune came. After playing both phrases right through twice, she sat up and regarded her worn fingertips ruefully.

'I do want to learn this tune but my fingers are getting so sore,' she said.

'It is lovely. Playing a little more each day will help,' Don Pedro said.

Concepción slid the guitar to the ground, propping it carefully against the low wall.

'I heard you telling Señor Williams that you played,' Don Pedro said, taking a peach from the bowl of fruit on the wooden table. 'Do you intend to play for him when he next visits?'

'Oh, yes,' Concepción answered

impulsively. A moment later she remembered that such eagerness was unladylike, and dropped her gaze modestly. 'That is, I believe that music would be entertaining for your guests.'

Don Pedro's eyes gleamed. 'You would like me to invite Señor Williams to Casa de las Flores again? You may answer honestly, my child.' He turned the peach over and over, enjoying the soft suede of its skin.

Concepción continued to study her hands but her father saw the faint flush of colour on her cheeks. 'I would like that,' she said simply.

'Conchita, *mi hija.*' Don Pedro leaned a little closer to his lovely daughter. 'You are seventeen now and we should think about finding you a good husband. I will not always be here to look after you.'

'Marco will take care of me,' Concepción said quietly.

Don Pedro nodded. 'I am sure what he will do what he thinks is best. But Marco is . . . rash sometimes.' He sighed sorrowfully. 'He is not the reliable kind of man I would wish for your guardian. He does not think in the long term.'

'Did you have anyone in mind?' Concepción ventured to ask.

'I want you to be happy,' Don Pedro answered. 'I would like you to marry a man who wishes to make you happy; a man with courage and what the *Americanos* call gumption. And of course, he must be wealthy enough for a Don's daughter.' He paused before adding the last part. 'If you wish, I am willing for Pat Williams to court you.'

Concepción didn't speak for a moment but her answer was in the glow of her eyes. 'I would like that, *Padre*.'

'I was pleased that he attended Mass with us before he left. He is a good Catholic, so there will be no problem of faith,' Don Pedro went on. 'That is important.'

'He told me he was named for the saint who brought Christianity to Ireland, because his parents were from

209

Ireland,' Concepción said, happiness clear in her voice as she spoke of him.

Don Pedro smiled. 'I shall invite him back soon,' he promised, beginning to peel the skin from the peach. He laid strips of peach skin neatly on the table.

In normal circumstances, a couple would be expected to court politely for two years or more before an engagement was announced. Don Pedro had no intention of recklessly sacrificing his daughter's future for the sake of a silver mine, but so long as Williams seemed honourable and capable, Don Pedro saw no reason to let things drag on for so long that the gringo changed his mind. Six months should be long enough to know how much the mine was producing and to find out more about Pat Williams. He had no doubt that his lovely daughter could keep a man entranced for that long.

Engrossed in thoughts of the future, neither of them had noticed Marco approaching. He had stopped on overhearing the gist of the conversation, and listened in silence to the plans being made. A look of thunder crossed his face and he backed away again silently before he was noticed.

11

Marco retreated hurriedly before his father saw him, his mind whirling with what he had overheard. Conchita marrying a gringo! Why, his sister was the beauty of one of the oldest and most honourable families in Texas. She was a Doña, after all. Pat Williams was a jumped-up Texan of no background or family, not particularly handsome or well dressed. Merely owning a silver mine didn't make him fit to marry someone like Conchita. Marco's face hardened as he remembered his father's other comments.

'How dare he say I wouldn't take good care of my sister?' Marco whispered to himself. And as for not thinking long term, why, he had been trying so hard to get hold of the silver mine that would increase the family's wealth and ensure their status for years to come.

'I'll show you all,' he promised, thinking hard. 'I'll show you I know how to get things done.' He turned and strode towards the stables. Enough time had been wasted. He needed to deal with both Williams and Hyde now. With Williams dead, the mine would be free for taking, and there would be no chance of Conchita marrying someone so unsuitable. And as for Hyde. Marco felt a surge of envy and self-loathing every time he thought of the confident gunman who told so many tales of *macho* deeds.

'Saddle my horse now,' he snapped at the stable boy. 'I want it ready by the time I get back.'

Marco broke into a run as he headed for his room and the money he kept there. He needed to find Perez. The Comanches had to kill Hyde and Williams as soon as possible, no matter what it took to get them on the warpath. Marco smiled grimly to himself as he imagined what the Comanches would do to the men he hated. After that, the silver mine would be his, and Comanches would take all the blame. Marco's smile broadened.

★   ★   ★

One of the men Marco hated was trying to conceal gnawing unhappiness. It wasn't the ache he'd known after the deaths of his father and younger brother or even like the helpless misery of being forced to sell his family home. Hyde had gone through those things with a clear conscience. Now he had lied to Williams and had put his life at risk. He didn't care about getting O'Malley fired because of the lies; the absence of the filthy old man and his sly remarks was a relief.

There was nothing else to be cheerful about. McKindrick had crudely stitched up the knife wound and strapped Hyde's wrist with a strip of linen, but it still jarred him with every incautious movement. Hyde fed chunks of ore slowly into the stamp mill and watched numbly as it thunderously pounded the rock into small pieces. He suddenly remembered showing Jefferson around and explaining the mill workings to him. He knew immediately what the former slave would think of a man who tried to kill his partner. Jefferson had called him a gentleman but no one could be a gentleman if he betrayed his honour.

The great steel-shod stamp went steadily, untiringly up and down. Hyde watched it, barely aware of what he was doing as the shaming thoughts went round in his head. He certainly didn't notice Pat Williams approaching until the other man spoke.

'Whyn't you go take a rest?' Williams said kindly. 'You look powerful tired.'

The kindness stabbed at Hyde's conscience. 'Leave me alone!' He stepped away, an angry light in his eyes.

Williams reached towards him but stopped himself. 'I don't mind you taking a rest,' he said, watching Hyde warily. His partner was usually neat and as clean as possible but Hyde clearly hadn't shaved that morning and was still wearing the same dusty, blood-stained grey shirt he'd had on the day before. 'There's no point wearing yourself down so much you can't work at all.'

Hyde glared at him, longing wildly to be free of the problems that plagued him. Everything seemed to centre around Williams; the mine, the silver, the lie, his guilty conscience. Hyde was aware of the two heavy guns in their holsters, hanging just where he needed them. He could be rid of Pat Williams in a mere second. Without knowing what he was doing, Hyde started to flex his fingers. Only a stab of pain from his wrist shocked him into reality.

'No!' he exclaimed, not knowing what he meant. Hyde faced Williams a moment longer, then did what he'd never done before and tried to run away.

He brushed straight past Williams, who grabbed his sleeve and hung on.

'Wait a minute. What the hell's going on here?' Williams demanded. He seized Hyde's other arm and forced the other man to face him. 'What's wrong with you?'

'Nothing!'

'Nothing? You've been acting plumb crazy in the head these last days.'

Hyde stared wildly at him. 'I'm going. You don't want me around.' He tore himself free of Williams's grip and turned to run.

'Well then go, you bastard!' Williams's voice rang with anger and hurt. 'Run out on me after I done took your side and paid you all I promised.'

Hyde stopped. 'I'm sorry, Pat,' he said. 'I . . . '

Williams gestured. 'Go on then. Don't let me stop you iffen you want to quit.'

The bitterness in his voice and face almost made Hyde gasp. He suddenly realized that he had probably lost the only real friend he had found since the Civil War had turned his life upside down.

'Pat, I didn't mean to. I didn't want to hurt you,' he pleaded, not sure what he wanted to say. How could he tell the truth without hurting Williams's feelings any worse?

Williams's face softened at Hyde's bewildered pleadings. He took a long breath before speaking, his generous nature to the fore as always. 'I don't really want to stay out here with no one but a Scots dirt-digger and a half-loco Mexican kid for company. But iffen you can't handle the mine work, there's . . . ' He shrugged.

'I hate going into that damned mine worse than I ever let on,' Hyde admitted suddenly. He stopped again, trying to think clearly. 'It's not labouring I mind; I got to get cash money somehow. Mother . . . '

His confused thoughts were interrupted by wild whoops and cries as five mounted Comanches came riding hell for leather along the canyon. Dust filled the air behind them as they bore down on the two men, each Indian urging his pony on in the race to count coup first. Each brave had taken a share of the tequila that Marco had supplied and they were riding to kill or be killed. They wanted revenge, for the braves killed in the last ambush, and those killed attacking the stage weeks before, and they wanted to regain their own honour. Sloping Leg, Turkey Feather and the other braves who had fled from the ambush two days before, all wanted to show themselves as worthy warriors. Perez rode amongst them, both to obey the orders of his Don's son, and to regain his own place as a warrior after fleeing the failed ambush.

'Hell Almighty!' exclaimed Williams, grabbing for his gun. His hand touched his trousers as he belatedly remembered that he took the gun off when working down the mine.

Hyde was fully armed. As soon as he saw the racing bunch of Comanches, he drew and raised the twin Colts without even thinking and fired both together. The recoil from the heavy guns jarred his injured wrist so badly that he gave a cry of pain and dropped the right hand Colt. The Comanches whooped again as they closed in at a gallop, their mustangs jostling one another as they ran. Williams dived for the fallen gun, scooping it up and firing all in the same motion. His own revolver was lighter and had a short barrel; he knew his shot had gone wide. Hyde just had time for one more shot before the Comanches were on them. He stayed still and aimed carefully, sending a warrior tumbling backwards off his horse. Then Hyde and Williams separated as the horses reached them.

A warrior with short-cropped hair jumped from his galloping horse on to Hyde. It was Turkey Feather, screaming promises of revenge. Hyde had shot at him in their last fight, giving the Comanche a broken rib and a deep graze across the side of his chest.

Turkey Feather landed just short of Hyde, kept his balance with skill and used his momentum to fling himself at the white man even as another warrior attempted to ride them down. Hyde was diving away from the horse and firing at its rider as Turkey Feather crashed into him.

The two tangled and went down almost under the hoofs of the horse. It whinnied shrilly and half-reared as its injured rider hauled on the hackamore reins. Hyde hit the ground hard, losing his hat and getting a jolt of pain from the stitched knife wound on his hip.

The tequila and his own war-fury kept Turkey Feather from feeling the pain from his already cracked rib. He saw Hyde's involuntary wince and screamed his war-cry as he reared up on to his knees, bringing his knife up for a killing blow. The frightened horse half-reared again, catching Turkey Feather in the back with one hoof. The blow pitched him sideways, tearing open a flap of skin. As the Indian

221

writhed in pain, Hyde rolled the other way, still clinging to his Colt.

Williams was little better off. He let off another shot as he ducked and twisted away from the wheeling horses. A grey horse screamed shrilly, blood pouring from its chest to smear the medicine designs painted there. Its rider jumped down, leaving the dying animal to stagger away and fall in a thrashing heap. Williams didn't waste time feeling sorry for the horse. He snapped off another shot at the Comanche, missing again because of the unfamiliar gun. The Comanche leaped in with his feather-decorated club, swinging it in a vicious blow as he closed in. Williams threw up his arm to defend himself, managing to catch the shaft of the club against his left forearm. The force numbed his arm but he pushed the club aside and with his other hand, brought the muzzle of the revolver up against the Comanche's chest and fired.

He was close enough to feel the

shock as the lead tore clean through the other man's torso and ripped him apart. There was a reek of scorched meat mingling with the acrid smell of burnt gunpowder in the air. The muzzle flash had charred the Comanche's chest, blackening the bare tawny skin. He collapsed against Williams, a look of blank shock on his face. Williams instinctively moved to catch the falling man and found himself tangled up just as Sloping Leg limped in to kill the man who had broken his medicine in their last fight.

Hyde kept rolling and got to his knees. He was faced by two men, Turkey Feather and an uninjured warrior who kept his shoulder-length hair tied back from his face with a dark blue bandanna. This warrior had also dismounted and dashed in with a knife. Hyde fired once at him, grazing Perez's leg without doing serious injury. A quick move got him to his feet as both Indians came at him. Hyde dodged a knife slash from Perez and tried to duck under Turkey Feather's blow. Turkey Feather's knife tore across his shoulder, slicing open Hyde's grey shirt and cutting a deep groove over his shoulder. Hyde ducked in closer, getting his shoulder against Turkey Feather's bare chest, and tried to push him off balance. He was taller than the Comanche, though not as heavy, but the fight with O'Malley the day before was taking its toll. His muscles ached and every sharp move tugged the stitches in the knife wound on his hip. He was breathing heavily and could feel the warmth of blood oozing from old and new wounds.

Turkey Feather resisted the shove and twisted his arm around, trying to get his knife into Hyde's left side. Hyde guessed what he was doing and jabbed a short punch into the Comanche's ribs. He couldn't reach the gunshot wound over the broken rib but his blow still sent a wave of pain through Turkey Feather. The Comanche gasped, instinctively holding his breath for a moment to try and calm the stabbing pain. Hyde got in two more quick jabs, jarring his injured wrist with each blow. Turkey Feather broke his hold and jerked away, pressing his left hand flat against his chest. The gun-wound was bleeding sluggishly, blood oozing from under the broken scab.

Turkey Feather's retreat gave Hyde just enough time to dodge a slashing knife attack from the other brave, Perez. Hyde was openly gasping for breath as he moved, feeling a slight greyness that warned him he couldn't keep up the fight for much longer. He kept his back turned to Turkey Feather for just long enough to get a single, clear shot at the second Comanche. This one went true, hitting right in the face. Perez toppled backwards, dead before he hit the ground. Then Hyde was turning, stepping sideways to avoid a slicing blow that almost tore the left sleeve from his shirt. He had one shot left and he had to make it count.

Williams saw Sloping Leg advancing

and recognized him at once. Sloping Leg attacked furiously in spite of the shallow bullet-wound in his side from Williams's shot at him in the failed ambush. Williams twisted to face him, using the dying man in his arms as a shield. The Comanche's long knife plunged deep into his companion's back, killing him outright. The impact staggered Williams backwards as the body was pressed against him. Sloping Leg saw and followed up, screaming his war cry as he pressed home his attack.

Williams tried to drop the weight that was hampering him. The dead Comanche slithered to the ground, pushing Williams even further off-balance. He had almost recovered when the heel of his boot slid on a stone and he fell. The impact jarred the revolver from his hand. Williams barely had time to get his breath, let alone grab for the gun, before Sloping Leg was on him.

Hyde tried to get a shot at Turkey Feather but the Comanche was moving too fast in spite of his damaged rib.

Hyde backed off a pace, moving awkwardly, and saw Williams fall. There was barely time to think. Hyde chose to ignore Turkey Feather and used his last shot on Sloping Leg as the Indian dived on Williams. Turkey Feather was rushing in, his knife raised. Hyde caught a glimpse of Sloping Leg twisting as the shot hit him, then turned to Turkey Feather.

The Comanche brought his knife across in a sideways chop, aiming to slash his enemy's throat. Hyde jerked his head back as the knife brushed against his neck, tugging at the yellow bandanna he wore and cutting the skin beneath. The cold touch sent a jolt of fear through his stomach. Hyde moved to block the return blow, expecting Turkey Feather to bring the knife back in a low slice against his ribs. Instead, the Comanche swiftly reversed his last move, slamming the metal-bound knife hilt against the side of Hyde's head.

Hyde felt the heavy blow, felt another as he hit the ground untidily even though he hadn't felt himself falling. His vision greyed out as he lay on the verge of unconsciousness, suddenly too weak to move. Even Turkey Feather's whoop of triumph sounded only faintly through the dim fogginess before he went limp.

12

Pat Williams was flat on his back as Sloping Leg leaped in to the attack. He saw the Comanche twist suddenly as Hyde's bullet took him in the side. Sloping Leg landed clumsily on his twisted leg, falling forwards off balance beside the white man. Williams sucked in a deep breath and brought his foot up in a wild kick. It caught the Comanche hard and knocked him sideways. Williams flung himself over and snatched up the gun he'd dropped when falling. Still on the ground, he fired the last shot into Sloping Leg's body. The Comanche collapsed, moaning and wailing as blood bubbled from his mouth and the terrible wounds in his chest.

As Williams scrambled to hands and knees, he heard Turkey Feather's triumphant war-whoop. Just a few yards away, the last Comanche was standing over Hyde, about to bring his knife down in a killing blow.

'No!' Williams yelled, lunging upright. As he started to sprint, he flung the empty gun at the Comanche.

It struck Turkey Feather in the face as he was bringing the knife down. The Comanche jerked backwards, halting the stroke as he looked up to see Williams charging empty-handed. He dropped into a crouch, holding the knife ready to stab as Williams came in.

Williams didn't slow down. He grabbed for the knife arm as he barrelled straight into the Comanche, the two of them rolling over together. Turkey Feather hit the ground on his back and screamed as the end of his broken rib was driven into his lung. Williams went right over him, rolled, and came up on hands and feet. Turkey Feather was gasping for breath, rolling on to his belly as he left smears of blood on the ground.

More blood trickled from his mouth

as he struggled to rise. Williams plunged a step forward and kicked as hard as he could. The toe of his boot caught Turkey Feather under the chin and jerked his head backwards hard. Turkey Feather was lifted half-way to his knees by the impact, then flopped down carelessly, his head at an odd angle and his eyes still open.

Williams caught his balance and paused, fighting for breath as he warily watched the Comanche. No one around him was moving but he heard footsteps behind him and spun. It was McKindrick, carrying his shotgun.

'I heard the shootin' and came oot to see whit was happenin',' the Scot explained. 'Looks tae me like ye snapped yon gallus Indian's neck.' He nodded at Turkey Feather.

'Sure. Yes,' Williams replied, his shoulders sagging as the adrenalin started to wear off.

'I'll see these fellers are no playin' deid while ye see tae yer friend,' McKindrick suggested, moving to the nearest Comanche.

Williams nodded and went to look at Hyde. His heart jumped when he saw blood on the yellow bandanna but a quick look showed him nothing more than a shallow cut beneath it. Hyde moaned faintly as Williams cut open the remains of the grey shirt to examine the knife-wound on Hyde's shoulder. He opened his eyes and blinked as Williams was mopping up blood with one of the cleaner patches of the shirt.

'Just lie still a bit,' Williams said, pressing a hand against Hyde's chest as the other man struggled to prop himself up. 'There's no danger.'

Hyde subsided readily, his face pale under its tan and the dirt. It took a few moments before his grey eyes focused clearly on Williams, leaning over him.

Williams smiled with relief. 'Thanks for the save; I reckon Sloping Leg might have finished me iffen you hadn't got that last shot in.'

'I don't rightly remember,' Hyde admitted, reaching up to feel cautiously at the side of his head. 'I guess you must have finished them off.'

'Well, between us, we accounted for five Comanches. I reckon we make a pretty good team.' It was a typically generous comment from a man who didn't know how much he was owed.

'Thanks, Pat,' Hyde said. He grinned self-consciously at realizing he had used his friend's first name. 'My name's Robson. Robson Edmund Hyde.'

'Pleased to meet you, Mr Hyde,' Williams answered, smiling back. 'Let's get you into some shade then you can rest up a bit whiles McKindrick and I clear up this mess some.'

'Balzar's probably hiding in the corral,' Hyde reminded him, taking Williams's hand to be helped to his feet. 'He can help some.'

Williams drew Hyde's arm round his shoulder and was helping him towards the bunkhouse when Hyde halted him.

'Look at that.' Hyde indicated one of the dead horses. 'Look at the brand.'

It was an elaborate brand, typically

Mexican in style. Both men recognized it as the brand of the Casa de las Flores.

'Must have been stolen from Don Pedro,' Williams said. 'I reckon he must lose stock to the Comanches pretty regular.'

'It's still shod,' Hyde said, detaching himself from his friend's support and carefully kneeling beside the dead horse. He dragged one of its legs round so he could see the hoof more clearly. 'This was shod not a week back,' he said.

Williams looked at the unworn shoe and firm clenches himself. 'We don't know when it was stolen,' he said uneasily. 'And why should Don Pedro have anything to do with the Comanches? We know Sloping Leg and Turkey Feather hated us. Look at the way they threatened us in the Comanche village.'

Hyde got slowly to his feet. 'I'm going to take a closer look at the Comanche anyhow,' he said.

Looking at the Comanches again without the urgency of trying to stay alive, they soon saw that the one wearing a blue headband was different from the others. His face was less broad and his shoulder-length hair had a waviness never seen in a true Comanche.

'A half-breed,' Hyde remarked. He leaned closer and sniffed the body. 'Smells a little of some spirit.'

'Aye,' McKindrick agreed. 'They've taken a wee touch of tequila, I'd be saying.'

Williams spoke slowly. 'When I told Concepción about fighting off Black Dog, she told me that one of their *vaqueros* is a half-breed. A man called Perez. She said she didn't like him much but Marco got on with him all right. She said she sometimes wondered whether he went on war-raids with the Comanche, because there was something wild about him.'

McKindrick pulled the plain moccasin off one of the dead half-breed's feet.

'He's worn boots; ye can see the marks. He's no' spent all his time running wild.'

'He held his knife differently from the other Comanches,' Hyde remembered. He looked at Williams and was surprised at the look of misery he saw.

'I thought it was too good to be true,' Williams said quietly. 'I knew really that a Don's daughter wouldn't be paying me attention just because she liked me some. I hoped . . . I guess she just wanted to know about the silver.'

'She'd be a fool to pass up a good man like you,' Hyde said.

Williams managed a rueful smile and changed the subject. 'We'd better let them know their raid failed.' Life came back to his face and his blue eyes hardened. 'Let's go find Don Pedro and show him what happened to his man. I've fought white men and Comanches for this mine. I'm not letting any Mexican take it from me either.'

'I'm with you,' Hyde promised.

It was late afternoon when they rode

up to the white-washed walls of Casa de las Flores. Williams was leading a horse with a blanket-wrapped body strapped across the saddle. The big wooden doors in the outer wall stood hospitably open as they rode straight in. Servants ran to fetch the family as Williams led the way to the front of the house and reined in his horse by the porch.

Don Pedro appeared a few moments later, smiling genially at his visitors as he greeted them. Concepción hurried through the door after him in a rustle of cotton and lace from her flounced dress. Her eyes went straight to Pat Williams, who sat quietly on his horse, watching Don Pedro.

Williams didn't return the polite greetings. 'We done brought one of your men back,' he said. 'I believe his name was Perez.'

Don Pedro lost his smile. He gestured for one of his servants to examine the wrapped body. The man took a quick look at the head of the body and nodded. Marco arrived on the porch too, wearing his fancy Colt in its elaborately tooled holster. Don Pedro ignored his son, watching his visitors instead.

'Please come inside and we will talk,' Don Pedro said.

Williams dismounted and for the first time flicked a swift glance at Concepción. She was watching him, puzzled and confused. Hyde dismounted more slowly and walked carefully up the steps to the house. Both men had cleaned up and changed after the fight. The worst effects of the stunning blow had worn off but Hyde was sore and tired. Even so, he had refused to stay behind and now he shadowed Williams as they entered the grand house.

Don Pedro led them into his office. 'Perhaps you should leave,' he told Concepción.

She wanted to protest but was too used to obeying her father. All the same, she made sure that the panelled door didn't quite close and she stayed just outside, listening.

'Your idea didn't work,' Williams said heavily to Don Pedro. 'Getting Sloping Leg and his friends likkered up so's they come boiling after us for revenge. They got the drop on us but we plumb finished the lot.'

Don Pedro stared impassively at Williams. 'I don't know what you mean. I'd flog any of my men who gave drink or weapons to the Comanches.' He spoke with deep authority and majesty, like a judge passing sentence.

'Then why was Perez dressed like a Comanche and riding with them?' Williams asked. His voice rose, bitterness in every word. 'He was riding one of your horses; it's back at the mine.'

'You killed Perez,' Marco interrupted, stepping forward. He pointed accusingly at the two gringos. 'One of you killed Perez and you're trying to cover it.'

'If we killed Perez, why would we bring his body here?' Williams retorted, his round face cold and unfriendly. 'If we buried him out on the range you'd never know what had happened to him.'

Marco took little notice of him, his attention focused on Hyde. He had noticed the careful way Hyde moved, the slight stiffness in his right leg and the lines of strain around his eyes. Marco's plan to use the Comanches hadn't succeeded in the way he had intended, but he saw a chance to finish the job. His heart began to beat faster as he saw his best chance for getting revenge on the man who had beaten and scared him.

'I bet you attacked him like you attacked me,' Marco said, pointing at Hyde.

The tall Southerner straightened a little, a dangerous light coming into his grey eyes. 'I mistook what you said. I apologized for my actions,' he answered.

'You insulted me,' Marco said hotly. 'You jumped on me like a common *vaquero*. You have no honour.' His hand was already moving towards his gun as he uttered the insult.

Hyde drew as fast as he could but his swift reflexes were dulled by pain and tiredness. Two shots crashed in the shuttered, sun-warmed room. Hyde's belated shot missed, gouging a long splinter of wood from the desk; Marco's shot was better. Williams saw Hyde knocked backwards and heard his cry of pain. He was reaching for his own short gun but Marco's was already pointing at him. Williams froze, feeling bitterly helpless. He couldn't see Hyde but could hear the ragged half-moans of pain.

'See that, *Padre?*' Marco cried triumphantly. He glanced at his father, wild with joy. 'I shot him. I'm as good as he is.'

Cold anger burned in the Don's face. 'You fool!' he said icily. 'I didn't want this.'

'I know what you were planning,' Marco answered. 'I overheard you talking to Conchita yesterday.' He turned his attention back to Williams.

'Father was going to marry Conchita to you to get at the silver. You're not fit to marry her maid!'

'He's a better man than you,' Don Pedro said, turning his bulk towards his son.

'No!' Marco yelled. 'I'm Don Marco. See, *Padre*; your plans failed but mine worked and now we'll have the mine. It'll be my silver and he'll never stop us!'

Marco began to lift his gun to shoulder height, drawing back the hammer as he aimed at Williams's head.

Reckless with excitement and triumph, Marco made a simple mistake that an experienced gunman like Hyde would never have made. He forgot to watch the man he had just shot. Hyde was half lying against the office wall, his right arm broken and bleeding, but he had his left Colt still in his other hand. While Marco talked, Hyde gathered the remains of his strength. By sheer effort of will, he held the gun steady long enough for one, aimed, shot as Marco turned his gun on Williams. Hyde's bullet tore through

Marco's head, spinning him round to slide bonelessly to the floor.

Startled as he was by the shot, Williams had the presence of mind to draw his own gun and hold it steadily on Don Pedro.

'Don't shoot him!' Concepción screamed from the doorway.

Don Pedro stayed where he was, a few feet from his son's body, and watched Pat Williams.

'You heard what Marco said. He was the one who used the Comanches.'

People were running through the house, drawn by the gunshots. Williams glanced at Hyde, who was leaning back with his eyes closed, then at the shuttered window. He might be able to get away on his own, but he couldn't take his friend, or leave him behind to face the angry Mexicans. The Don's men were more likely to shoot than to ask questions when they saw Marco's body.

'Let me speak to them,' Don Pedro asked, his air of self-possession undisturbed by Williams's steady aim. 'I do not wish you more harm.'

'All right,' Williams agreed, lowering his gun. 'I trust you.'

Don Pedro moved to the door swiftly in spite of his massive bulk. There he issued orders in rapid Spanish, calming the fears of his household.

Once he had made the decision, Williams turned to Hyde. His friend had collapsed into a crumpled heap against the wall, white and unconscious but with his gun still in his limp fingers. Williams carefully rolled him on to his back, handling the damaged arm gingerly.

'Help me, please,' he begged Concepción. 'He's my friend.'

Concepción saw the deep anxiety in Pat Williams' eyes and walked forward to help him tend the man who had just killed her brother.

★   ★   ★

Williams felt a definite stab of jealousy as he entered Hyde's room at the hacienda to find Concepción seated by his friend's bed and helping him drink coffee.

'How are you today?' Williams asked, perching on the end of the bed where he could see both of them easily.

Hyde had been lucky. One of the old women who worked on the hacienda was a skilled bone-setter. She had set his broken arm, sewn up the torn flesh and bandaged it firmly with a poultice that smelt noticeably of garlic. Both Hyde and Williams found the smell off-putting but so far there was no sign of the dreaded gangrene that had killed and maimed so many with similar wounds in the Civil War. Two days after the confrontation with Marco, there was colour in Hyde's face again and he was clearly on the road to recovery.

'Why, I don't feel so weak as yesterday, but this just hurts the more,' Hyde answered, indicating his right arm where it lay over the covers.

'Do you want to finish this?' Concepción asked, holding up the coffee-cup. She was wearing black mourning for her brother but the dull look of the last two days had left her pretty face.

'I do, *gracias*,' Hyde drawled.

Concepción rose gracefully. 'I will come back soon,' she promised as she left. Her smile included both men equally.

'How are you making out at the mine?' Hyde asked.

'Balzar's helping some with the digging at the moment,' Williams said. 'I'm going in to El Paso this afternoon to deposit the silver in the bank. McKindrick reckons there'll be enough to hire a couple more men on,' he finished happily.

'That's good,' Hyde said, meaning it. He had made up his mind that he would never confess the full truth to Williams. It would clear his own conscience but it would hurt his friend too deeply. Instead, he would carry the memory as his own punishment and keep doing his best to protect Pat Williams.

'I wanted to let you know before I go into town and see a lawyer,' Williams continued, his good-natured face alive with mischief. 'I figured you should know what's happening, you being a partner in the Two Moccasins Mine an' all.'

Hyde's grey eyes widened. 'Partner!'

'Yes.' Williams held his face still, then burst into a grin. 'We make a good team, remember? Besides, I could use a good manager and someone with book-learning. I was a good salesman, but I never could keep the sales accounts straight. I had to go home to Momma every month and let her sort it out for me,' he confessed frankly. 'If you can run a plantation and a couple hundred slaves, you can sure make a better job of running a silver mine and five men than I can, Captain Robson Hyde.'

Hyde held out his left hand. 'It's a deal. And thank you, Pat.'

Williams shook the offered hand. 'And for your first job, you can give me some advice. Don Pedro just done told me I can go on and court Conchita. I was thinking to bringing her something from town. Maybe gloves?'

Hyde shook his head. 'Never give a lady jewellery, perfume or something to wear; that would be improper. It should be candy, flowers or some small book, say. Mammy was always powerful strict about that kind of thing.'

'I never had a mammy to teach me fancy manners,' Williams said. 'I done told you we worked well together. You helped me get the silver mine and I reckon you can help me win Conchita too. But you don't get any partner's rights in her,' he added firmly.

Hyde laughed aloud. 'All right. I give you my word of honour on that.'

Williams grinned too. 'There's nothing stronger than a gentleman's word of honour.'

Hyde nodded; he still had his honour and he would never risk it again.

We do hope that you have enjoyed reading this large print book.

Did you know that all of our titles are available for purchase?

We publish a wide range of high quality large print books including:
Romances, Mysteries, Classics
General Fiction
Non Fiction and Westerns

Special interest titles available in large print are:
The Little Oxford Dictionary
Music Book, Song Book
Hymn Book, Service Book

Also available from us courtesy of Oxford University Press:
Young Readers' Dictionary
(large print edition)
Young Readers' Thesaurus
(large print edition)

For further information or a free brochure, please contact us at:
Ulverscroft Large Print Books Ltd.,
The Green, Bradgate Road, Anstey,
Leicester, LE7 7FU, England.
Tel: (00 44) **0116 236 4325**
Fax: (00 44) **0116 234 0205**

Matt Matthews had carved his ranch out of the wild Wyoming frontier. But he had his troubles. The big blow of '86 was catastrophic, with dead beeves littering the plains, and the oncoming winter presaged worse. On top of this, a gang of desperadoes had moved into the Snake River valley, killing, raping and rustling. All Matt can do is to take on the killers single-handed. But will he escape the hail of lead?